Songs of Gods,

The Epic Tradition of the Ainu

Songs of Humans

Donald L. Philippi

with a Foreword by
Gary Snyder

NORTH POINT PRESS
SAN FRANCISCO
1982

Contents

PART II SONGS OF HUMANS

Foreword

There are two basic modes of learning: "direct experience" and "hearsay." Nowadays most that we know comes through hearsay—through books, teachers, and television—keyed to only a minimal ground of direct contact with the world. (The "world" is perceived as a rolling outdoor space with weather above, obstructions underfoot, and plants, people, animals, buildings, and machines occupying various niches.)

Hearsay is the great organizer of this apparent chaos via myth, science, or philosophy. Not too long ago there were no writing systems and the world-view/myth/frameworks came to young listeners as long stories chanted in the evening. These old stories are the foundation stones of what the Occident calls classics, and indeed all literature.

In a completely pre-literate society the oral tradition is not memorized, but *remembered*. Thus, every telling is fresh and new, as the teller's mind's eye re-views the imagery of origins or journeys or loves or hunts. Themes and formulae are repeated as part of an ever-changing tapestry composed of both the familiar and the novel. Direct experience, generation by generation, feeds back into the tale told. Part of that direct experience is the group context itself, a circle of listeners who murmur the burden back or voice approval, or snore. Meaning flashes from mind to mind, and young eyes sparkle.

All later, civilized educations are by degrees removed from this primacy of together-hearing. An urban cosmopolitanism is gained, with the loss of a keen sense of human/natural systems integration. In the Ainu tales it is gods and animals who speak in the first person as well as human beings, and the several worlds of sense-experience and imagination are knit together.

The many motifs of oral literature found world-wide, which at least prove that humanity enjoys the same themes over and over, are not heard as part of some comparative study demonstrating the brotherhood of man, but as out of the minds, hills, and rivers of the place—maybe through the mouth of a bear or salmon. A people and a place become one.

Such were the Ainu, on one level a remnant population of a few bands, isolated for centuries from the "centers of world civilization." But it's all here: the planet-wide themes; the great adventures of love, sorcery, and battle ("The Epic of Kotan Utunnai"); and the almost uniquely Ainu telling of tales direct from non-human entities, a mode of "inter-species communication."

On another level the Ainu are at the center of an archaic internationalism. Their big island was a meeting place of circum-polar hunting culture pathways with Pacific seacoast cultures. In the practices they lived by are some of the purest teachings according to those old ways that survive: the sacramental food-chain mutual sharing consciousness that was likely the basic religious view of the whole northern hemisphere paleolithic. This view clearly has relevance, after a lapse of many millennia, to us again: the planet Earth:: Gaia must now be seen as *one system*.

The people of pre-civilized times or places knew their specific watershed ecosystems and mastered those details with beautiful and empirical precision. Natural systems, even in small areas, are of the utmost complexity, and to be understood must be grasped in their wholeness. This means, so to speak, leaving the trail and walking up hill and down, through the brush. The trail is what village people use as a straight line between garden plot and garden plot. Hence, "linear." The forest, for hunting and gathering people, must be grasped, visualized, in its simultaneity: "Where do you suppose the deer are moving today?" Hence, "field." The Ainu term *iworu*, "field of force," is a term that can mean simply biome, or territory, but has spirit-world implications as well.

So an Ainu group would live along a river in a house facing east, fire at the center. Upstream was a forest, swamp, and mountain wilderness, penetrated by the trails of the hunters. (The arctic brown bear of Hokkaido is as large as a grizzly.) Downstream was the coast and the ocean, full of herring and salmon, cod and crab; and before the Japanese came, rich in seals, sealions, and whales. When men returned from hunting and fishing, and women from gathering plants for food, fiber, medicine, poison, and dyes, they sat by the fire. Men would carve intricate bas-relief designs on knife-sheath and quiver. Women wove, sewed, and embroidered the graceful linear swooping designs that are instantly recognizable as Ainu. An elder perhaps told these stories. The life of mountains and rivers flowed from their group experience, through speech and hands, into a fabric of artifacts and tales that was a total expression of their world, and themselves. As the Ainu saw it, from the inner mountains upstream, and from the sea depths downstream, game came as visitors. Master of the one realm is Bear, master of the other is Killer Whale. The deer or salmon would leave behind their flesh bodies in exchange for being entertained with songs, stories, and wine by the humans. Humans are good musicians as the whole world knows. Returning to their sea or mountain home with gifts, the animal or fish spirits would hold another party in the spirit realm, and many would agree it was good to visit the human world, and more would soon go. Thus, cycles in and out of a real landscape, and cycles in and out of life-and-death, attended by that highest of pastimes— singing and feasting (in or out of mask) with food and friends.

Paradoxically, only now, in the last years of the twentieth century, can this view be understood for its real worth. Millennia of rapacious states spilling out of their boundaries to plunder the resources and people within reach created a false image of limitless space and wealth on the planet, available for whoever had the weapons, organization, and willingness to kill without saying thanks. Through no wisdom of its own, but out of necessity, industrial civilization in particular is forced to realize that there are limits, and that there is a life support system composed of millions of sub-systems all working or playing together with amazing grace.

Through Donald Philippi's translations, the Ainu suggest to us with great clarity that this life support system is not just a mutual food factory, it is mysteriously *beautiful*. It is what we are. We now see the Ainu not as a fading remnant, but as elders and teachers whose playful sense of their own bio-region points a way to see and live on our planet as a whole.

Gary Snyder

Preface

Such a large amount of folklore material in the Ainu language has been col-
lected that it is extremely difficult to make a selection of the representative
pieces. In this volume I have included mainly materials from the Saru Ainu
of Hidaka. They are the most numerous group of Ainu, and their culture may
have preserved many of the more archaic features. The number of selections
taken from the repertory of Hiraga Etenoa may seem to be disproportionate.
I have done this because of the very high artistry of the materials obtained
from this reciter, who was, in my opinion, the best Ainu epic reciter whose
repertory has ever been recorded in writing.

All of the selections in this volume have been translated directly from the
Ainu originals in the extensive materials collected by pioneers in the study
of Ainu epics. I did not use any source materials which did not give the texts
in the original language because I believe that a true translation can be made
only by a translator who knows the original language and translates directly
from it. For most of the mythic epics (*kamui yukar*) I used *Ainu jojishi: Shin'yō,
seiden no kenkyū* by my teacher Kubodera Itsuhiko. It is the authoritative
collection of epics of this genre and is the fruit of many years of patient re-
search. The texts of two of the longer epics (selections 31 and 32) are from the
typewritten manuscripts copied by Dr. Kubodera from his field notes. These
two longer epics have never been translated before, either into Japanese or
into English. One selection was obtained from the field notes kindly lent to
me by Kindaichi Kyōsuke, and another was taken from one of his published
works; three were taken from Chiri Yukie's publication; and one from John
Batchelor, collected in the 1880s.

As mentioned earlier, most of the texts come from the Saru area of Hidaka
(informants Hiraga Etenoa, Hirame Karepia, Nabesawa Wakarpa, Nabesa-
wa Taukno, and Hiraga Tumonte). Three texts (selections 7, 8, 12) are from
Chiri Yukie, and two are from Chikabumi in Ishikari Province (informant
Shikata Shimukani, selections 26 and 29). The final selection in the volume,

"The Epic of Kotan Utunnai," was collected by Batchelor. He does not name the reciter, but it appears certain from the diction that the reciter was a native of the Saru area.

All of the selections in this volume are in verse as they were sung by their reciters. In translating them into a sort of English free verse, I tried to preserve the sequence of perceptions, the general style, and the turns of speech of the original. Unfortunately, the word order in English is often exactly the opposite of that in Ainu, and it was not always possible to retain the same sequences in the translations. In most cases the number of lines in the translation is approximately the same as the number in the Ainu original. This will give the reader an idea of the way in which the Ainu epic reciter arranges the text into verses. It will also be possible to estimate the length of time required to sing each epic, since there were often pauses between verses, and the mythic epics in particular were sung with burdens (*sakehe*) repeated after every verse.

The selections are grouped into two parts. In part I, the speakers who appear in the songs and narrate their adventures are all gods of various kinds. There being so many of these god songs, I subdivided the first part into three sections. The first section, "The World of Gods," contains songs narrating experiences of gods who live apart from humans in their own god-worlds. There is very little or no human involvement. The second section, "The World of Gods and Humans," contains selections which narrate different types of experiences shared by both gods and humans. The third section, "The Culture Hero and His Work," is devoted to songs about the Ainu culture hero. In part II, all the speakers who narrate the action are human (i.e., Ainu) men and women.

The names of the reciters, the dates of recording, the sources where the texts were obtained, and explanatory notes are given in the introductory sections preceding each of the selections. The introduction provides the history and culture of the Ainu and gives a brief outline of the Ainu epic tradition. A bibliography has been appended for those who wish to read further.

I lived in Japan from 1957 to 1970, and my interest in the Ainu folklore began there when I was working on a translation of the *Kojiki*, Japan's earliest book. My studies of early Japanese oral literature—the tales, the songs, the prayers, the ritual formulas—led me to the works of Kindaichi Kyōsuke, who connected the oral beginnings of Japanese literature with the literature of the preliterate peoples of northern Asia, in particular, the Ainu. Kindaichi was convinced that the origins of oral literature could be found in the archaic north Asian practice of shamanism, and he pointed to the Ainu epics with their ubiquitous use of the first-person diction as clear evidence of this idea. I read all of Kindaichi's published writings, and Kindaichi allowed me to use his original field notes, which were collected during the early decades of this century and were of priceless value in my study of the Ainu language and epic literature. In 1967, Kindaichi introduced me to his disciple Kubodera Itsuhiko, who had won his doctorate at my alma mater, Kokugakuin University, in 1960, with the above-mentioned book on the Ainu mythic epics as his dissertation. I was given access to Dr. Kubodera's extensive collection of original texts of various genres of Ainu folklore, most of which had never been translated or published. I did extensive work on the vocabulary and grammar of the epics for a 14-month period in 1967 and 1968, and I continued my work in this field after returning to the United States in December 1970. I spent many useful hours working closely with both Kindaichi and Kubodera, and I hope that their teachings have been reflected not too inadequately in the present volume. My entire program of research, and the present volume as well, would have been unthinkable and impossible without their assistance and encouragement. I owe everything to them.

I wish to thank the Institute of Japanese Culture and Classics and the Library of Kokugakuin University for allowing me to use their facilities to study the Ainu-language manuscripts deposited in their custody by Dr. Kubodera. I am grateful to Dr. Kubodera's surviving family for their continuing good will and interest in my work, and to Kindaichi Haruhiko for permission to translate songs recorded by his father. I owe much to Yamada Hidezō, another disciple of Dr. Kindaichi, who has devoted many years to the study of the Ainu language and the toponymy in particular. Mr. Yamada's encouragement has been very helpful to me. I also thank Minowa Shigeo, former director of University of Tokyo Press, for his enthusiastic encouragement, without which I might well have faltered in view of the immensity of my task. Special thanks are due to Urushibara Hideko of Tokyo, who helped me greatly at an early stage of my work by patiently listening to me read the first translations.

A number of Americans have been very helpful to me. David Guss of San Francisco has shown a great interest in the Ainu epics. He read masses of my manuscript materials and gave me valuable advice concerning the selection of the songs for inclusion in this volume. We had many animated discussions about styles of translation. Although I alone must take responsibility for the translations, I hope that they will not disappoint him.

Peter and Judy Berg of San Francisco kindly read and listened to some of my translations and gave me much-needed encouragement in my work. They introduced me to the poet Gary Snyder, who read the manuscript and kindly supplied this volume with a foreword. I imposed heavily on the time and patience of Irving Rosenthal, Ellen Cooney, and other friends, who read translations and gave me helpful suggestions.

Part of the research concerning the Ainu epic folklore was accomplished with a fellowship from the Translation Center at Columbia University.

My deepest gratitude of all is to the Ainu epic reciters whose immense knowledge of their people's traditions was made available to me indirectly through the texts recorded in writing.

This is the first of a series of volumes I intend to publish concerning the Ainu epic folklore. I am currently preparing the texts and English translations of some 220 mythic epics of the Hokkaido Ainu and am working on an Ainu-English dictionary of the vocabulary used in the folklore of the Ainu of Hokkaido (Saru, Horobetsu, and Chikabumi) and Sakhalin. There are many other excellent examples of epic songs and prose tales that deserve to be made public in English translation. I hope that readers of this volume will look forward with anticipation to the publication of these other projected works on the Ainu folklore.

Introduction

This is a collection of English translations of thirty-three epic songs of the Hokkaido Ainu. Except for one selection, all of them were collected during the first three decades of the twentieth century. Most of them were obtained from female Ainu reciters by two Japanese scholars, Kindaichi Kyōsuke and Kubodera Itsuhiko.[1]

The reader may be surprised to find that all of the songs without exception use first-person forms of diction. They are, so to speak, monologues or self-revelatory utterances in which a personage describes his or her experiences and adventures from the subjective point of view. The speakers who tell their stories in these songs may be either gods (*kamui*) or humans (*ainu*). These are the two main orders of beings recognized by the Ainu (the word *ainu* means "human being"), and this is why I have chosen the title "Songs of Gods, Songs of Humans." The title describes the contents of the book exactly: the book contains, literally, songs sung by gods and songs sung by humans. The audiences intended for the songs may also be beings in either of the two categories. The songs of the gods may be intended to be heard by gods as well as by humans, and the songs of the humans may be sung to audiences consisting of gods or of humans. The archaic epic is a form of inter-species communication in which gods or humans speak of their experiences to members of their own or other species. The mythic epics (*kamui yukar*) are especially important as vehicles of mutual communication between the two orders of being, and I have included a large number of them in this volume.

In order for the humans to survive successfully in this world, which they share with the other non-human species (the *kamui*), the humans must elaborate techniques of communicating with them. This is done in a number of ways.

First, the humans address the other species directly by praying to them. Praying is a specialty of the Ainu men. When they are at home by the fireside, the men drop droplets of wine into the fire in the hearth while intoning prayers to the Fire Goddess (*kamui huchi*), who is the deity most closely concerned

---

[1]Twenty-seven of the songs were collected in the province of Hidaka along the Saru river; three are from Horobetsu in Iburi; two are from Chikabumi in Ishikari; and one (selection 33) is from an unknown reciter but is probably from Hidaka.

with the affairs of the humans. She acts as an intermediary and will relay the prayer to the proper deity. When the men are hunting in the mountains, they pray to the gods who appear to them in the disguise of birds or animals. Here are two hunters' prayers taught to Kindaichi in 1915 by Utomriuk, the chieftain of the village of Shumunkot in the Saru region.[2] The first is a prayer by a hunter to a bird after it had been shot down.

Tekkup e-ush kusu	Winged creature that you are,
rik peka	you travel
kotan enka peka	high in the skies,
e-apkash kusu	high over the land.
rikun kanto	Thus your spirit
oro un	is now about to
e-yai-ramat-ka	return to
hoshipi kusu ne na.	the Upper Heavens.
Pirkano	You have been treated
ainu otta	magnificently
a-e-tomte na.	by the humans.
Kamui huchi	The Fire Goddess
e-e-kashpaotte na.	commands it of you.
Rikun kanto un	You will now ascend
e-rikin kusu ne na.	to the Upper Heavens.
Eramuan 'an.	Hear this and obey!

The second is a prayer by a hunter after shooting deer.

A-kor moshir	Let your spirits
moshit tapkashi	return
echi-ko-yai-ramat-ka	atop the summit
oshipi	of our native country.
ashir kamui ne	May you
echi-oka yakne	abide there
pirka na.	as newborn gods.
Tapan inau	Take these *inau*,
pirka inau	these lovely *inau*,
echi-kor wa	and may you
echi-yai-kamui-	enhance with them

---

[2]The texts of the prayers are from Dr. Kindaichi's field notes for 1915, copied with his permission.

nere kane	your glory
yak pirka na.	as deities!

A second means of communication with the non-human is through shamanism, which is called *tusu* or sometimes *nupur*. Among the Hokkaido Ainu, almost all the shamans are women. In shamanic seances, the shamaness goes into a trance and becomes possessed by a god or gods speaking through her mouth. The prophecies will usually assume the form of recitatives in the first-person form of diction, as if the god were merely borrowing the mouth of the shamaness.[3]

A third technique of inter-species communication is the epic folklore, particularly the mythic epics. Although the epic reciter does not go into a trance, the gods borrow the reciter's lips in the same way as those of a shaman. Through the mouth of the reciter, the gods describe their worlds and tell, in their own words, about their lives and adventures.

In this volume the reader will find a large selection of these songs in which the gods themselves appear as speakers, describe the landscape of their world, and narrate their experiences in the self-revelatory style of the Ainu epic tradition. The reader will also become acquainted with human beings, the Ainu men and women, who speak about their experiences in the traditional Ainu world of many centuries ago.

The Ainu, Past and Present

The Ainu are the ethnic group forming the native population of the island of Hokkaido, the large island (78, 513 square kilometers) located between the main Japanese island of Honshū and the island of Sakhalin, which belongs to the Soviet Union.[4] The Ainu population in 1822 totaled 24,339 (21,768 in Hokkaido, 2,571 in Sakhalin), but by 1854 there was a sharp decrease in the Ainu population of Hokkaido. At that time, the total Ainu population was found to be 18,805 (16,136 in Hokkaido, 2,669 in Sakhalin). This decline in the population of the Hokkaido Ainu between 1822 and 1854 is attributed chiefly to the effects of contagious diseases (smallpox, measles, and cholera, as well as venereal diseases and tuberculosis) resulting from contact with the Japanese.[5]

During the 1920s, at the time of the final collapse of the Ainu culture, the

[3]Actual songs performed by shamanesses have been recorded in writing and are in the first-person form of diction. However, the shamaness's song given below in "The Epic of Kotan Utunnai" is in the third-person form. See below, pp. 389–90.

[4]In addition to the Ainu population of Hokkaido, 1,600 Ainu also lived in Sakhalin as of 1922, and there were 97 Ainu living on the Kurile Islands as of 1884. Sakhalin and the Kuriles no longer have Ainu populations, and the descendants of the Sakhalin and Kurile Ainu now live in Hokkaido. In the following discussion, the word *ainu* will refer to the native Ainu population of Hokkaido unless otherwise specified.

[5]Kodama Sakuzaemon writing in *Ainu minzoku shi*, vol. 1, p. 6.

number of Hokkaido Ainu was somewhere between 15,000 and 16,000. The census of 1940 listed 3,676 households with a population of 16,170.[6] Today the Ainu population is said to be approximately 16,000 but it is now difficult to establish who is an Ainu since the ethnological boundaries between the Japanese and Ainu populations have been obscured by massive intermarriage and acculturation.[7]

Like many other peoples, the Ainu are known to the world by a word in their language which means simply "human being." The word *ainu* is used chiefly to distinguish human beings from other non-human species, the *kamui*. The word *ainu* has a number of honorific uses; in eulogistic expressions it is synonymous with the word *nishpa*, "chieftain." It can also mean "father" (*a-kor ainu* is a common way of saying "my father"). The word is also used to distinguish the Ainu from the Japanese, who are called *shisam*.

The terms *ainu kotan* and *ainu moshir* are used in the Ainu epic texts to refer to the world of the humans, the "human homeland" as distinguished from the world of the gods (*kamui kotan* or *kamui moshir*). However, these are not, strictly speaking, geographical terms. The Ainu have a word for their homeland which is strictly geographical. They call it *yaun moshir*, which means "the country on land," "the mainland." The inhabitants of the "mainland" are called *yaunkur*, "people of the land," "mainlanders." This is the ethnonym applied by the Ainu to themselves in their epic literature. The name of the hero of the epics is Poiyaunpe, which means literally "little mainlander" or "young mainlander." *Yaunkur* is used in contradistinction to *repunkur*, "people of the sea," the enemy people whose domains are to the north of the Ainu.

The homeland of the Ainu, their *yaun moshir*, was until quite recently one of the parts of the world where the population had adapted most successfully to the environment by means of a hunting, fishing, and gathering economy. Hunting and fishing were the main sources of livelihood for the Ainu. The mountains had abundant supplies of deer, which were hunted by the men in the fields and hills during spring and autumn. Bear were also hunted during these seasons. Fishing in the rivers was practiced throughout the year except between January and March; the most important varieties of fish were the cherry salmon (*ichaniu*), caught from June to September, and the dog salmon (*kamui chep, shipe, chuk-chep*), caught from August to December. Various types

---

[6]Ibid.
[7]Kodama states that pureblooded Ainu are today less than 1 percent of the total.

of edible wild plants, notably the bulbs of a type of lily (*turep*), were gathered by the women, mainly in the summer. Women cultivated small plots of domestic plants, mainly Deccan grass (*piyapa*) and foxtail millet (*munchiro*). A beerlike beverage was brewed from the former, and the latter was made into millet dumplings at festivals. Some beans and a type of turnip (*atane*) were cultivated. The agricultural techniques were extremely primitive, and fertilizers were not used at all. Plant cultivation was of little importance in the economy, and venison and salmon were the main articles of food.[8]

The Ainu settlements were located along rivers near salmon-spawning grounds. The areas for food-gathering, called the *iwor*, were the rivers and the wooded mountain ranges. The *iwor* were regarded as the property of the local populations, and Ainu from other areas were not allowed to hunt or fish in them. The salmon-spawning grounds were called *pet iwor*, "river fishing beds," and the wooded mountain ranges upstream along the rivers were called *kimun iwor*, "mountain hunting grounds," where the local Ainu men would hunt deer and bear in the spring and autumn. The women would collect edible plants during the summer months in the woods or in the unwooded fields on the river banks and river terraces.

The Ainu had domesticated dogs, which played an important role in their hunting activities. Horses were introduced by the Japanese in fairly recent times. No other domesticated animals were known. Metal working was not practiced by the Ainu themselves, but supplies of metal implements were obtained by trade with the Japanese.

According to Watanabe, the techniques and skills employed by the Ainu in their food-gathering activities were extremely successful and enabled them to adapt themselves well to their habitat. They were able to lay up stores for the winter, when economic activities stopped for about two months and were able to accumulate a surplus. As a result, the Ainu lived in permanent settlements while continuing to rely on a gathering economy. They never adopted nomadic ways of life.[9]

According to Ohnuki-Tierney, most Ainu enjoyed a surplus fairly regularly, and trade was a means by which they disposed of their surplus goods, receiving luxury items in return. Bear ceremonialism was a "sensitive barometer" indicating the amount of surplus in each area. "The Ainu," according

[8]The best study on Ainu economic activities is Hitoshi Watanabe, *The Ainu Ecosystem*. See especially pp. 69–78.
[9]Ibid., p. 42.

to Ohnuki-Tierney, "were not foragers forced to survive in an undesirable environment, but had adapted superbly to their environment. The environment was fairly rich and the Ainu mode of life enabled them to produce surplus. Surplus gave the basis for elaborate bear ceremonialism and trade with other peoples as well as the basis for well developed modes of aesthetic expression as part of a rich and complex cognitive world."[10]

Generally speaking, Ainu settlements were small, consisting of perhaps one to ten households. The most densely populated area of Hokkaido was the Saru river area of Hidaka, where one settlement might house as many as thirty-one households.[11] Each settlement was autonomous and economically self-sufficient. "Ainu technology did not require the cooperation of a unit larger than the local group. In fact the family was often self-sufficient in this respect although members of a few families sometimes joined together for certain activities. Social intercourse beyond the local group seems to have been rare, although there had been a degree of intermarriage. The principal occasions for Ainus to meet members of other local groups were at the bear ceremony in winter."[12]

Thus, the Ainu were living a way of life rooted in the remote past, and Hokkaido remained untouched by the main currents of Asian history. The technologies of animal husbandry (domestication of horses and cattle, reindeer breeding), rice cultivation, and the working of iron and bronze, which had played such important roles in the history of the peoples of Asia, were unknown to the Ainu. The Ainu never developed any system of writing or any concept of a political state. Even though there were cultural ties with the Japanese dating back to great antiquity, actual contacts with the Japanese were peripheral during the early centuries. There were no contacts with the Chinese. As nomadism was not practiced, the Ainu of one river valley lived in comparative isolation from the Ainu of other river valleys. Naturally, this isolation resulted in considerable local diversity in culture.

This state of affairs was made possible by the relative abundance of the natural resources, the relatively small Ainu population, and the remoteness of the Ainu homeland from neighboring states. The Ainu remained free from foreign interference in their life until the imposition of Japanese influence after 1669. On the other hand, the Ainu came in time to depend on trade

[10]Ohnuki-Tierney, Emiko, "Another look at the Ainu," pp. 193–94.
[11]Watanabe, *Ainu Ecosystem*, p. 97.
[12]Ibid., p. 12.

with the Japanese for their imported goods. They received from the Japanese metal implements, lacquerware (Japanese lacquer bowls were considered treasures by Ainu families), cotton and silken garments, rice, malt for brewing alcoholic beverages, and Japanese rice wine (*sake*). In exchange they provided the Japanese with animal furs and skins, dried fish, bear's gall (prized in East Asia as a medicine), live hawks for use by Japanese hunters, and imported Chinese goods obtained by them at second hand from the tribes of the Amur basin, adjacent to Sakhalin. The Ainu dependence on trade, which is clearly reflected in the epic texts, eventually had disastrous effects on the Ainu, and the geographical isolation of the population and their inability to unite on an island-wide basis for self-defense made them vulnerable to economic and political subjugation by the Japanese.

At any rate, the Ainu have an extremely long history of undisturbed occupation of their homeland, and there have never been any accounts either written or oral, of any migrations on their part. It is almost certain that the Ainu culture as we know it was developed in the present homeland, Hokkaido. For this reason, the question of the ultimate origins of the Ainu can only be answered in terms of vague speculations.

Racially, the Ainu appear to be unrelated to the surrounding Mongoloid populations. There was a time when scholars pointed to possible Caucasoid, or even "Austronesian," affinities of the Ainu. The more plausible explanation is that the Ainu are a Paleoasiatic people who always lived in Asia and who are not related to any other race of mankind (a "Rasseninsel"). If this is true, the Ainu would be "a surviving remnant of the ancient population of this part of Asia prior to the great expansion of the modern Mongoloid populations."[13]

The Ainu language is basically different from the Japanese and other surrounding languages and cannot be genetically connected with any other language groups in the world. In view of the historical relations known to have existed over many centuries between the Ainu and the Japanese, it is surprising that there is so little resemblance between the two languages. The only similarities are those in phonology and sentence structure; the Japanese loan words in Ainu are fewer than one might expect.

Kindaichi pointed toward possible northern affinities for the Ainu lan-

[13]Chard, Chester S. "A New Look at the Ainu Problem," p. 98. The Caucasoid theory was argued by George Montandon; the "Austronesian" theory by Sternberg and Levin; the Paleoasiatic theory by L. von Schrenck.

guage. According to him, incorporation or polysynthesis[14] is one of the characteristic elements of Ainu grammar. He argued that the language may be connected with the Paleoasiatic and American Indian languages, among which there are languages with a strong polysynthetic tendency. Particularly in the archaic diction of the Ainu epics one finds lengthy verbs incorporating a number of different semantic elements.[15]

There are a number of identifiable cultural influences which might well have played formative roles in the Ainu culture. One of these would be pre-agricultural Japan, the Japan of the Jōmon period, which lasted in Hokkaido until about the beginning of the Christian era. The culture which existed in Hokkaido during the Jōmon period—and therefore, presumably, the culture of the ancestors of the present-day Ainu—is practically the same as that which was found all over the Japanese archipelago during that period. However, with the introduction of metals and rice cultivation from the Asian continent into the southern part of the archipelago, the entire mode of life underwent a radical change there, and the Japanese culture such as we know it was formed. The new culture imported from the continent gradually spread northward but did not take firm hold in Hokkaido. Thus, the ancestors of the Ainu remained relatively untouched by these continental cultural influences; and their culture developed in a different direction, managing to retain many archaic features which disappeared elsewhere in the archipelago. The early Japanese loan words in the Ainu language indicate close cultural ties between the emerging Japanese state and the Ainu at an early period.

Another important formative element in the Ainu culture must have been that coming from northeast Asia. Kindaichi, pointing to the prevalence of shamanism among the Ainu and to the polysynthetic elements in the Ainu language, holds that in early times the influence of northern Asiatic culture must have been much stronger, deeper, and more permanent than that of Japanese culture.[16] Izumi Seiichi connects the economy, the general pattern of living, the religion, and the sociopolitical organization of the Ainu with those of the hunting peoples of northern Asia.[17] The "Okhotsk people," who lived in close proximity with the Ainu for many centuries, had many affinities with the cultures of the Amur and Maritime regions, and the Ainu must have been influenced by them to a great degree.[18]

---

[14]Incorporating or polysynthetic languages are those which have very long and morphologically complex word forms. They contain many bound morphemes which would be translated by separate words in languages of other types. R. H. Robins, *General Linguistics*, p. 334.

[15]Kindaichi Kyōsuke, *Ainu-go kenkyū*, pp. 318–25. Examples of this are given below on pp. 36–37.

[16]Kindaichi Kyōsuke, *Ainu no kenkyū*, p. 349.

[17]Izumi Seiichi, ed., *Ainu no sekai*, p. 9.

[18]See below, pp. 40–44.

In establishing the history of a preliterate people, the following types of materials must be considered: (1) archeological materials; (2) historical documents of other peoples describing the people in question; and (3) the oral traditions of the people in question. In research on the Ainu, the first two types of materials have been utilized, but only limited attention has been paid to the third. This is unfortunate, since the Ainu epic folklore presents a clear picture of the traditional Ainu society before the Ainu were subjugated by the Japanese. That is, the social conditions and the cultural milieu which are reflected in the epics must be those which ceased to exist in the latter part of the seventeenth century.

Difficulties in understanding the Ainu epics arise because the conditions reflected in them are different from those of the Ainu population studied during the nineteenth and twentieth centuries. The Ainu who came into contact with Japanese and Western scholars during the past hundred years were no longer able to furnish satisfactory explanations of a number of puzzling aspects of the epics referring to earlier periods. As a result, the evidence presented by the oral tradition has often been ignored or regarded as the product of the native imagination. For example, no one took at all seriously the plain accounts in the epics of the existence of the *repunkur*, the Okhotsk people, since nothing was known about the Okhotsk culture until the 1930s. However, the evidence found in the epics coincides superbly with the archeological evidence. This indicates the need for a more careful sifting of the folklore evidence.

The following is a hypothesis of the cultural history of the Ainu based on impressions derived from a study of the Ainu folklore. Although it contains many conjectural elements, it can serve as a working hypothesis. There are at least four different cultural periods that, it seems to me, can be distinguished on the basis of the folklore evidence.

(1) Proto-Ainu Period. The folklore refers vaguely to a dimly remembered period of "barbarism" during which the humans were ignorant of the hunting and fishing rituals. The people do not know how to make *inau*, whittled sticks that play an important role as ritual artifacts. When they kill game animals, they merely skin them. They do not clean the meat off the bones, but carry the whole carcass home. When they are hungry, they hack off a

section of the carcass and cook it. It is possible that the fishing practices of this period involved the use of walnut poison in the rivers, which is mentioned with disapproval in some of the more archaic mythic epics (see selection 21). No doubt these accounts are based on racial memories of the period before the formation of the Ainu ethos, when the predecessors of the Ainu lived in Hokkaido along with representatives of other ethnic groups and had a culture which differed little from that of the rest of Japan during the Jōmon period.

(2) Early Ainu Period. This is the period when the Ainu ethos formed itself in Hokkaido. It is probable that neighboring groups were assimilated and a single language adopted. It appears to be a period of cultural electicism, with much borrowing from adjacent peoples. This period may have started around the sixth or seventh century and probably lasted until about the tenth century. During these centuries the Ainu gradually gave up making pottery and began to use imported iron and lacquered products.

The more archaic mythic epics, in which the basic concepts of the religious ideology are stated, appear to reflect this period (see selections 7 and 8). Performance of the hunting and fishing rituals is necessary to placate the God of the Game and the God of the Fish, who are archaic "masters of the animals." The Owl God, called Kotan-kor-kamui, probably figured prominently during this period as the protector and advocate of the human race (selection 8). The culture hero appears only peripherally in these myths as a supplicant on behalf of humanity. During this period, there is concern about famine, and humans must make constant efforts to placate supernatural forces which control the food supply.

The two adjacent peoples which influenced the early Ainu were the Japanese and the people of the Okhotsk culture. The *Nihon shoki* describes a military campaign led by a general Abe no Hirafu in Hokkaido in the years 658–60. The southwest part of Hokkaido was undoubtedly under the influence of the Abe family who ruled the northern provinces of Honshū during many of these centuries. Small burial mounds of the Late Tumulus type are found in southwestern Hokkaido from Sapporo, Esashi, and Chitose as far east as Tomakomai on the Pacific coast, and the Japanese artifacts found in the mounds are dated to the Nara and Heian periods (A.D. 710–1185). It was no doubt during this period that a considerable stratum of Old Japanese loan words found its way into the Ainu language. These loan words reflect the phonology of Old Japanese and include names of various artifacts as well as certain religious concepts. Many of these loan words are of great cultural importance, for example: *kane*, metal; *sake*, wine; *kamui*, god; *pito*, spirit (the original Japanese word means "human being"); *onkami*, worship; *nomi*, worship; and *inotu*, life-spirit (the Japanese word means "life"). It is curious that the Japanese word for "god" should have been adopted by the Ainu.

It was during this same period that the Okhotsk culture flourished on the Okhotsk Sea coast of northern Hokkaido. It was probably the people of this culture who introduced into Hokkaido some of the Paleoasiatic elements in the Ainu culture. The wars fought against the Okhotsk people during this period were later commemorated in the *yukar* heroic epics as the wars between the *yaunkur* and the *repunkur*. The epics make no mention of any wars against the Japanese. Is it possible that the Ainu formed an alliance with their Japanese neighbors in order to struggle against the Okhotsk culture? It is clear that there was an Ainu population living also in the northernmost parts of Honshū.

(3) Middle Ainu Period. This period was the time of the greatest flourishing of the Ainu culture, extending perhaps from the tenth until the sixteenth century. The Okhotsk people on the northern coasts of Hokkaido were defeated, and their remnants were probably absorbed into the Ainu population. The Ainu were forged into a single homogeneous cultural entity, and the period must have been a progressive one characterized by optimistic cultural progress, ethnic self-confidence, and considerable social stratification.

During this period, the epics, in particular the heroic epics (*yukar*), must have developed; the subject matter of the epics was the wars which had occurred between the *yaunkur* and the *repunkur* during the preceding period. The two great heroic figures of the Ainu folklore tradition were worked out: the culture hero (the god of the *oina*, the "sacred tradition") and the *yukar* hero Poiyaunpe. The culture hero is now regarded as the head of the human race, and the supernatural forces are more and more subjected to his (i.e., human) control. "Masters of the animals" recede from cultic practice and are replaced by the more favorably disposed deities such as Hashinau Kamui (the goddess of the hunt) and the Fire Goddess.

The word *kotan* at this time meant a "domain" ruled by a definite chiefly family. One can easily imagine that the Ainu were moving away from the primitive tribal system and in the direction of a patriarchal system. However, a unified political organization was never attained, and the middle period seems to have been punctuated by many internecine wars. The social conditions must have been unstable, and it was necessary for the population to concentrate itself at easily defensible places. Warfare must have been cultivated by the upper chiefly stratum, which formed a sort of military elite. The vigor and martial spirit of this upper stratum are clearly reflected in the heroic epics.

The society depicted in the Ainu epics is clearly the society which existed during this period. The Ainu population was organized in socially stratified regional bands, called *utar*, headed by a family of hereditary chiefs. The *utar* was a fictitious kinship group and also had a military organization. The ruling families, calling themselves *utarpa* ("head of the *utar*") or *nishpa* ("chieftain"), were clearly a military elite. The well-born men devoted themselves to warfare and spent all their spare time engaged in leisurely carving. The well-born women devoted their time to embroidery and practiced shamanism (*tusu*). The ruling family lived in a stronghold (*chashi*) surrounded by a stockade (also called *chashi*) on an easily defensible cliff or mountain overlooking the surrounding terrain. Inside their strongholds they had numerous servants or slaves (*usshiu*) who hunted for them and did their household work. Occasionally the ruler would have a large boat built for him and would go trading with the Japanese (see selection 19). The local rulers accumulated large stores of Japanese products in their strongholds; these were their treasures.

The common people, called *usekur* or *wenkur*, lived in settlements outside the stockade of the stronghold and would withdraw inside the fortified area in case of attack. The social differences, the differences of dress, and even the differences of physical appearance between the well-born members of the population and the low-ranking individuals are constantly mentioned in the epics. It is quite clear that the bulk of the population was subordinated to local ruling families who lived in strongholds.

Most of the mythic epics (with the exception of a few archaic ones and some recognizably dating from the following period), all of the heroic epics (both the *yukar* and the *hau*), and most of the women's epics appear to be rooted in this historical period. It should be possible to establish clear-cut concepts about the social life and customs of this period on the basis of a thorough-going study of all the available epic texts.

During this period, Japanese continued to live in the southern parts of Hokkaido, and there was considerable friction during the first half of the fifteenth century. A great war against the Japanese was led by a chieftain called Koshamain in the years 1456–57. Other anti-Japanese uprisings occurred in 1471, 1501, 1515, 1525, 1529, 1531, and 1536. According to Takakura, the Ainu were more powerful than the Japanese, and the latter were on the defensive. They resorted to such tactics as feigning peace and then striking by surprise.[19] Distrust of Japanese treachery is frequently mentioned in the texts (see selection 28).

(4) Late Ainu Period. The period from the seventeenth until the twentieth century is one of decline and loss of independence. The process began as early as the fifteenth century, and the downfall of the Ainu became inevitable after the defeat in the war of 1669.

During the sixteenth century, the Matsumae clan, which had established itself in the southernmost tip of the island (Hokkaido was in those days called Ezo), did not exercise direct political power over the Ainu.[20] The trade with the Ainu became extremely lucrative for the Matsumae, and Japanese traders began to penetrate more and more deeply into the interior of the island. The Ainu became increasingly dissatisfied with the conditions, and a general rebellion, led by Shakushain, a chief of Shibuchari, broke out in 1668. It was finally suppressed, after much bloodshed, during the years 1670–72, and the whole territory of Hokkaido came under the rule of the Matsumae.[21]

As the Japanese gradually extended their direct political domination over the Ainu population, the native social organization underwent great changes. The Ainu ruling stratum was defeated in battle by the Japanese, and the for-

[19]Takakura Shin'ichirō, *The Ainu of Northern Japan*, p. 12.
[20]Ibid., p. 27.
[21]Ibid., p. 27–29.

mer military elite ceased to exist. The breakdown of the old social organization was accompanied by social mobility. Considerations of wealth (measured in terms of Japanese imported goods) came to overshadow hereditary social status, and those who had formerly been *wenkur* could now acquire wealth and prestige, perhaps by siding with the Japanese. This type of social upheaval is clearly reflected in selection 12. The need for military organization of the populace and for elaborate hilltop fortifications disappeared, and internecine fighting among the Ainu ceased to occur.

The dynamic optimism of the previous period was replaced by a sense of resignation to fate and a backward-looking conservatism. In religious life, the old cultic observances came to be petrified, and there was a process of semantic depletion in which the original insights into the nature of reality were more and more forgotten. The ethnic heroes, the culture hero and the *yukar* hero, are said to have departed in indignation, leaving their people behind (see selection 25). There is a forlorn atmosphere and a sense of distrust, hatred, and fear of the Japanese, who are regarded as conquerors. The period was one of dissolution and degeneration of the native culture.

However, the people's conservatism during this period no doubt caused them to cling even more tenaciously to their rich folklore traditions, which were not only handed down but enriched and developed. New themes were elaborated in the epics, and the prose tales (*uwepeker*) attained a high level of development. The tales were enriched by the introduction of Japanese themes (in the *shisam uwepeker*), and some of these themes even found their way into the epic songs.

The final Ainu rebellion occurred in 1789, but it was only a local revolt in the Menash area (on the Shiretoko peninsula in Nemuro province) and on the island of Kunashiri in the Kuriles and was easily suppressed.[22]

At the time of the Meiji Restoration in 1868, the Ainu population of Hokkaido was about 15,000 to 16,000. This was the proper population-land ratio that had to be maintained to make a hunting–fishing–gathering economy viable. During the Meiji era (1868–1911) the Japanese began large-scale efforts to settle Hokkaido with Japanese agricultural immigrants. Hokkaido came to be regarded as Japan's "new frontier," and the rapid influx of large numbers of Japanese colonists soon destroyed the very conditions on which

[22]Ibid., p. 34–47.

the traditional Ainu culture had been based. The abundant herds of deer were killed off. Japanese farmers cleared the forests and burned the underbrush to open up fields. Permanent fishnets were set up along the coasts and at the river estuaries, and the Japanese began deep-sea fishing using dragnets.

The effect on the Ainu was appalling. General demoralization resulted among the entire Ainu population, who found their traditional land preserves usurped and their time-honored way of life impossible. They were decimated by diseases, and alcoholism took a high toll among the menfolk. Unscrupulous Japanese *sake* merchants and speculators used devious means to obtain possession of Ainu land and property. With the once-proud hunter reduced to a migrant laborer, the women were left at home in the villages to raise the children and defend the native culture as well as they could. The Ainu people described by Chamberlain, Hitchcock, and Batchelor at the end of the nineteenth century were a pitiful, doomed people living in the most abject conditions of poverty, disease, and degradation.

The Japanese government, which had allowed all of this to happen, finally took a few half-hearted measures to introduce the Ainu to agriculture. The children were put into Japanese schools, and the Ainu were encouraged to adopt the Japanese language and customs. Nothing was done to foster the native language. During the 1920s and 1930s there were still many Ainu who had been alive during the last half of the nineteenth century, when the traditional life was maintained, and the Ainu language was still spoken in many homes. There were during the 1920s and 1930s many excellent folklore reciters. However, even then it was being predicted that the Ainu language would die out completely within a few decades. By the 1940s the native culture was virtually at its last gasp. The native straw huts had been replaced by wooden farmhouses heated with wood-burning stoves. The people had begun to take up agriculture and horse-breeding. The children no longer spoke Ainu. Only a few elderly women still had tattooed faces, and only a few elderly men still wore long, white beards. But even these elderly persons were usually bilingual, and all of them could understand Japanese to some extent.

Today the total population of Hokkaido numbers some 5,255,000, and the small community of persons of Ainu ancestry, who may number 18,000 or more, has been submerged in this vast sea of Japanese. Racial mixing and acculturation have gone so far that it is sometimes difficult to distinguish between the Japanese majority and the Ainu minority in many areas of Hokkaido. The Japanese educational system has never made provision for teaching the Ainu language in the school curriculum, and the Ainu language has gradually gone out of use, even in the home, during the past several decades. A survey made in 1955 revealed that there were probably less than twenty fluent speakers of the Ainu language in all Hokkaido.[23]

It has only been during the 1970s that the question of a rebirth of Ainu ethnic consciousness has begun to be raised publicly in Japan. Japanese authors have written a number of books about Ainu history, pointing to the similarities between the position of the Ainu in Japanese society and that of the native Americans in the United States.[24] Koshamain and Shakushain have been depicted as heroes in the Ainu struggle of resistance against Japanese conquest. Ōta Ryū, a Japanese writer, has argued strongly that the Ainu should reject assimilationism and press for a national revival, aiming eventually at the establishment of an independent Ainu republic.[25] Efforts are being made to revive the Ainu language.[26] Many of the Ainu themselves have begun to play an active role in preserving the native arts and folklore traditions. For example, Kayano Shigeru, an Ainu who was born in 1926 in Niputani village in the Saru area, has begun to publish his own recollections and translations of the folklore of his native area.[27] Kayano is also director of an Ainu culture museum in his native village. Although the movement for a revival of the Ainu culture is still in its infancy, it appears certain that it will gain considerable support among the persons of Ainu ancestry in Japan and among many Japanese.

History of the Study of Ainu Language and Folklore

The first European ever to visit Hokkaido and observe the Ainu was an Italian Jesuit missionary, Girolamo de Angelis, who came to Japan in 1602 and remained there illegally until 1623, when he was burned alive in Edo. In 1618 he visited Matsumae for the first time, and his second visit was in 1621. He met some Ainu there and wrote reports about them to his superiors. In his reports he gives a short vocabulary of their language.[28]

---

[23]Hattori Shirō, ed., *An Ainu dialect dictionary*, p. 8.
[24]See, for example, two recent books by Gyō Shin'ya: *Ainu minzoku teikō shi* and *Yūkara no sekai*.
[25]Ōta Ryū, *Ainu kakumei ron*.
[26]For example, Pon Fuchi, *Ainu-go wa ikite iru*.
[27]For Kayano's writings consult the bibliography.
[28]de Angelis, Girolamo, "Relatione del regno di Iezo," pp. 217–32.

A number of Japanese works on the Ainu were published during the first part of the nineteenth century.[29] The most important of these from the linguistic point of view is a 4,000-word vocabulary of the Ainu language, *Moshiogusa*, first published in 1804. It was compiled by Uehara Kumajirō, a Japanese interpreter. After 1868, Nagata Hōsei, a Japanese official of the Hokkaido government, wrote a short grammar of the Ainu language in Japanese and published it in 1883. Nagata also published the text and translation of a *yukar* epic either in 1882 or 1883.[30] Two Japanese scholars, Kanazawa Shōzaburō and Jimbō Kotora, wrote and lectured on the Ainu language in Japan at the end of the nineteenth century.

Some Westerners also made important contributions to the study of the Ainu language and folklore. One of them was Basil Hall Chamberlain (1850–1935), an English scholar who came to Japan in 1873 and became an early pioneer in the study of the Japanese language. Around 1886 Chamberlain made a number of visits to Hokkaido to study the Ainu language and collect specimens of Ainu folklore. The results of Chamberlain's Ainu studies were published in 1887 (*The Language, Mythology, and Geographical Nomenclature of Japan Viewed in the Light of Aino Studies*) and 1888 (*Aino Folk-tales*). Ethnographical data on the Ainu in the 1880 were published by Romyn Hitchcock ("The Ainos of Yezo, Japan," 1890).

The most substantial contribution by a Westerner to the study of the Ainu language was made by John Batchelor (1854–1944), an English missionary who first came to Japan in 1877. He first came into contact with the Ainu in Hakodate in 1878 and began his study of their language in the same year. Around 1881, Batchelor commenced his missionary work among the Ainu and made translations of portions of the Bible into Ainu. In 1887 Batchelor's 59-page "A Grammar of the Ainu Language" was published in Chamberlain's book.[31] Two years later, in 1889, Batchelor published the first edition of his Ainu-English-Japanese dictionary. The fourth and last edition of it was published in 1938 and contained an expanded section devoted to the grammar, which in the 1938 edition occupies 105 pages. Good examples of Ainu epic folklore collected by Batchelor during the 1880s were made public in papers he delivered to the Asiatic Society of Japan in 1888, 1889, and 1892.[32] Other books published by Batchelor include *The Ainu and Their*

[29]Bibliographies of these works are given in Basil Hall Chamberlain, *The Language, Mythology, and Geographical Nomenclature of Japan Viewed in the Light of Aino Studies*, pp. 137–74, and in Takakura, *Ainu of Northern Japan*, pp. 82–88.
[30]See Kindaichi Kyōsuke, *Ainu jojishi yūkara no kenkyū*, vol. 1, p. 373.
[31]Chamberlain, *Language*, pp. 77–136.
[32]Batchelor, "Specimens of Ainu Folk-lore."

Folk-lore (1901) and *Ainu Life and Lore* (1927). Batchelor's writings on the Ainu language and way of life were the first substantial contribution in English and still retain considerable value to this day, although they must be used with caution since Batchelor was a Christian missionary, not a linguist or ethnologist.

Important studies of the Sakhalin Ainu language and folklore were made by a Pole, Bronislaw Pilsudski, who spent many years in exile in Sakhalin and the Maritime Region. Pilsudski was the elder brother of the famous Polish marshal Jozef Pilsudski. He first came into contact with the Sakhalin Ainu for a brief period in 1896. In 1902 he went again to Sakhalin to collect ethnographic data on them and remained there until 1905. He also made a brief trip to Hokkaido in 1903. During these years he lived in an Ainu village called Ai (Aihama in Japanese) on the east coast of Sakhalin. He married the daughter of the village chieftain and had two children. With the outbreak of the Russo-Japanese War in 1905, he returned to Europe.[33] In 1912 his *Materials for the Study of the Ainu Language and Folklore* was published in Cracow. The book contains the texts of 27 Sakhalin Ainu tales with English translations and notes. It is a work of primary importance in studying the Sakhalin Ainu language and folklore.

Ainu texts were collected by a Russian, Nikolai Aleksandrovich Nevskii, who lived in Japan from 1915 until 1929. A small collection of these texts and Nevskii's Russian translations was published posthumously in Moscow in in 1972.[34] Other Western students of the Ainu culture have included the French ethnologist George Montandon[35] and an English doctor, Neil Gordon Munro (1863–1942), who lived in the village of Niputani during the 1930s.[36]

The greatest contribution to the study of the language and folklore of the Ainu was made by the Japanese scholar Kindaichi Kyōsuke (1882–1971), whose work in this area is of fundamental importance. As a university student in Tokyo, Kindaichi began to investigate the Ainu language in 1904, when he received instruction in the language from Kanazawa at Tokyo Imperial University. In 1906 Kindaichi paid his first visit to the Ainu districts of Hokkaido and became acquainted for the first time with the Ainu epics handed down there.[37] In 1907 he made a field trip to the eastern coast of Sakhalin, the southern part of which was then under Japanese rule, and recorded a

---

[33]Kodama in *Ainu minzoku shi*, vol. 1, p. 61.
[34]Nevskii, Nikolai Aleksandrovich, *Ainskii fol'klor*. Nevskii died in 1945.
[35]Montandon, George, *La civilisation ainou et les cultures arctiques*.
[36]Munro, Neil Gordon, *Ainu Creed and Cult*. Munro's research is especially important.
[37]Kindaichi, *Ainu no kenkyū*, p. 129.

3,000-line Ainu epic. He published this epic with a Japanese translation in 1914.[38] In the summer of 1913, Kindaichi made contacts with a number of Ainu reciters in the village of Shumunkot (Japanese Shiunkotsu) in the Saru river area. One of these, Nabesawa Wakarpa, a male reciter, spent about six months at Kindaichi's home in Tokyo in 1913, and Kindaichi recorded in writing a number of heroic and mythic epics from Wakarpa's repertory. Kindaichi also recorded texts from Nabesawa Taukno, Wakarpa's widow; Sankirotte, a male native of Nikap; Nabesawa Kopoanu, a female native of Shumunkot; and Shikosanke, a female native of Shumunkot. Other informants with whom Kindaichi worked during this period and during the 1920s were: Utekare, a female native of Shin-Piraka; Takahashi Haru, a female of Shin-Piraka, the eldest daughter of Kopoanu; and Nabesawa Yuki, the eldest daughter of Wakarpa and Taukno.[39]

In 1918, Kindaichi was introduced by Batchelor to Imekanu (Japanese name Kannari Matsu, 1875–1961), a member of a prominent Ainu family of Horobetsu in Iburi province. Imekanu was a Christian and worked for many years as a lay missionary in the Episcopal Church under Batchelor. After her retirement from missionary work in 1926, Imekanu began to commit to writing her entire repertory of Ainu epics in the Horobetsu dialect. By her death in 1961, she had filled 72 volumes of notebooks for Kindaichi as well as 52 volumes for her nephew, Chiri Mashiho—a total output of 124 volumes consisting of more than 20,000 pages.[40] From 1959 until 1966, Kindaichi published seven volumes of the texts of Imekanu's epics together with his Japanese translations.[41]

The niece of Imekanu, Chiri Yukie, translated thirteen mythic epics of the Horobetsu region into Japanese. The Ainu texts and Chiri's translations were published in 1923, one year after her death.[42] This was the first publication of Ainu folklore by an Ainu. Chiri, who was a native speaker of Ainu, also provided Kindaichi with much advice concerning the Ainu language.

Kindaichi's writings on the Ainu language and folklore have been extremely influential. His most important work was the two-volume *Ainu jojishi yūkara no kenkyū* [Study of the Ainu Epic *Yukar*], first published in 1931 and subsequently reprinted under two separate titles. The first volume contains a survey of the entire field of Ainu oral literature. The second volume con-

[38]Kindaichi Kyōsuke, *Kita Ezo koyō ihen*.
[39]Kindaichi Kyōsuke, *Ainu no shinten*, p. 4–5.
[40]Kindaichi Kyōsuke, *Ainu jojishi yūkara shū*, vol. 3, p. 2.
[41]Ibid., vols. 1–7.
[42]Chiri Yukie, *Ainu shin'yō shū*.

tains a 233-page grammar of the Ainu epic language and voluminously annotated texts and translations of two versions of the *yukar* epic *Kutune shirka* (the first version obtained by Kindaichi from Wakarpa in 1913, and the second a Horobetsu variant of the same epic obtained from Imekanu). Kindaichi's writings on the Ainu language were collected and published in one volume in 1960.[43]

Chiri Mashiho (1909–61), a nephew of Imekanu and the brother of Chiri Yukie, studied under Kindaichi at Tokyo Imperial University and later obtained his doctorate at Hokkaido University, specializing in Ainu linguistics. Before his untimely death in 1961, he published a number of important scholarly works, and at the time of his death he was working on a classified dictionary of the Ainu language.[44] His most important writings have been collected and published in four volumes.[45] His work on grammar is especially interesting.

Another outstanding disciple of Kindaichi was Kubodera Itsuhiko (1902–71), a native of Hokkaido who devoted himself for many years to collecting Ainu epic texts and ethnographic information from the Saru area of Hidaka, working closely with a number of native informants. In 1960 Kubodera obtained his doctorate from Kokugakuin University in Tokyo for his studies of the Ainu mythic epics.[46] Kubodera succeeded in establishing an extraordinarily good rapport with his native informants, especially with two female informants, Hiraga Etenoa and Hirame Karepia. These two reciters probably had the best repertories of any which have ever been recorded in writing. Hiraga Etenoa was a female native of Shin-Piraka village of the Saru area; she was the daughter-in-law of Utekare, an informant with whom Kindaichi had worked. Hirame Karepia was a female native of Nina village in the Saru area. Besides these two informants, Kubodera also obtained texts from Nitani Kunimatsu (1888–1960), a male native of Niputani village, Saru area; Shikata Shimukani, a female resident of Chikabumi in Ishikari province; Hiramura Kanunmore, a female of Piratori village, Saru area; Hiraga Tumonte, a female of Shin-Piraka, Saru area; Yayashi, a male of Shin-Piraka; and several others. Both Etenoa and Karepia stayed for many months in Kubodera's Tokyo home so that he could work with them intensively. Etenoa stayed in Tokyo from August, 1932, until April, 1933, and Karepia stayed there

[43]Kindaichi, *Ainu-go kenkyū.*
[44]Three volumes of it were published. Chiri Mashiho, *Bunrui Ainu-go jiten.*
[45]Chiri Mashiho, *Chosakushū.*
[46]Kubodera Itsuhiko, *Ainu jojishi shin'yō: seiden no kenkyū.* Ph.D. dissertation, 4 volumes, Kokugakuin University, Tokyo; published by Iwanami.

from January through April, 1936. Nitani Kunimatsu also stayed at Kubo-dera's home from January until April, 1935, and provided Kubodera with much valuable information concerning religious ideology and ritual.

During the 1950s a number of Japanese scholars under the direction of Hattori Shirō conducted a survey of nine Ainu dialects. The results were published in 1964.[47] Tamura Suzuko has studied the grammar of the Saru dialect, and two Americans, George John Simeon and Fred C. C. Peng, have made studies of the language. Emiko Ohnuki-Tierney has studied the folklore of the Sakhalin Ainu and Murasaki Kyōko the dialect of the Sakhalin Ainu.[48]

It is extremely fortunate that Batchelor, Chiri Yukie, Kindaichi, Imekanu, Kubodera, and others were able to commit to writing so many texts of the Ainu folklore. These texts were all written down by them during the period when the Ainu language was still in use, and some of them, such as Imekanu and Chiri Yukie, were native speakers. Since that time, the Ainu language has almost completely disappeared from everyday use, and by the 1950s and 1960s it had become difficult, if not impossible, to collect texts of Ainu folk-lore.[49]

Ainu Oral Literature

Even though the Ainu language has almost entirely disappeared from daily use and the epic tradition has died out with the deaths of the last reciters, we are extremely fortunate in having a substantial body of texts collected, chiefly during the early decades of the twentieth century, by Western and Japanese students. This body of texts reveals that the Ainu epic tradition is one of the richest and most interesting bodies of archaic oral folklore in ex-istence. Writing of the Sakhalin Ainu, Pilsudski said: "The Ainu folklore is, by the general admission of the Far Eastern tribes, exceedingly abundant. The proportion of Ainus acquainted with either one kind or another of these primitive tales is—to my own knowledge—greater than with the Ghilyaks. Their lore of eloquence, of speeches, and of song, is quite astonishing, and has already been remarked by several travellers."[50] Before massive acculturation eloquence *(pawetok)* was regarded by the Ainu as one of the chief manly virtues. Men intoned ritual prayers and greeting formulas, and litigation took

[47]Hattori, *Ainu dialect dictionary.*
[48]For their writings consult the bibliography.
[49]Kubodera, *Ainu jojishi,* p. v.
[50]Pilsudski, Bronislaw, *Materials for the Study of the Ainu Language and Folklore,* pp. ix-x.

the form of interminable arguments (*charanke*), in which both contestants would continue to harangue until one of them either dropped in exhaustion or could think of nothing more to say—victory went to the longer-winded. There was a dichotomy between the colloquial language and the elevated, poetic language used in the epics. The epic language differed even in its grammar from the colloquial, and a number of special linguistic techniques were developed for epic poetry.

For our present purposes, let us divide folklore (oral literature) into the following main genres: (1) the lyric; (2) the epic; (3) the dramatic; and (4) the ritual or ceremonial.[51]

The lyric genre consists of songs which are improvisational, subjective, and emotionally charged. The epic refers to utterances of a narrative type, including both narrative tales and narrative songs of various type. Epics may be mythical, fabulous, heroic, historical, novelistic, didactic, or comical. The ceremonial or ritual utterances include such conventional utterances as prayers, orations, and songs of a public, nonimprovisational nature, such as festival songs or work songs which are collective and have a definite social or communal nature. The lyric, the epic, and the ritual or ceremonial genres exist in abundance among the Ainu, but there is no evidence of any dramatic folklore among the Ainu.

The epic genre is the one which has attained the greatest flowering among the Ainu. If one includes here all types of recited or sung narratives, the Ainu epic literature embraces a vast body of material, greatly overshadowing in its importance and its quantity the lyric and the ritual or ceremonial genres.

The Ainu epic material may be classified in two ways: (1) from the standpoint of its form; and (2) from the standpoint of its content. The following three categories may be distinguished in a formal classification.

(1) Utterances which are pronounced in a monotone or recitative quite similar to ordinary speech ("prose"). The text is recited in a prosaic diction close to that of everyday conversation, no attempt is made to organize the text into verses of any definite length, and archaic phraseology is not prominent. There is a rich tradition of prose tales (*uwepeker*) which are recited in this manner.

---

[51]In this classification I follow V. E. Gusev, *Estetika fol'klora*, pp. 98–163, especially pp. 131–39.

(2) Utterances which are organized into verses of a definite length and sung to definite melodies ("song" or "verse"). Poetic diction with a high density of conventional formulas is used. This style of utterance is used in formal salutations and greetings, prayers, arguments, and in epics.

(3) Utterances which have the stylistic features of (2) but which are sung with the persistent repetition of burdens (*sakehe*). The *sakehe* is a constantly repeated refrain which carries the melody of the epic; the semantically charged text is woven in between the monotonous repetitions of the burden. The narrative text may be interspersed between the repetitions of the burden in various ways; the most common way is for the burden to be repeated after every line of the text. There are cases where more than one burden is used in a single song; at a certain point in the song, there will be a shift from one burden to another.

From the standpoint of content, the epic material may be classified into the following categories:

(1) Mythic narratives. Typically, mythic epics deal with the origins and exploits of deities of various kinds—theriomorphic deities, cult deities, or the culture hero. The deities themselves appear as the speakers, and first-person narration is followed throughout. Mythic epics which are sung with burdens are called *kamui yukar*, and the prose myths are called *kamui uwepeker*. The *kamui yukar* are comparatively short, ranging from perhaps 200 to 1,000 lines in length. The term *oina* is sometimes applied to mythic epics centering around the culture hero.[52]

(2) Heroic narratives. Heroic epics are relatively long. The usual length would be about 5,000 to 7,000 verses, although especially long ones have as many as 15,000 verses. They deal with the deeds of a single hero, who appears again and again in many different epic songs. First-person narration is followed, and the epics are sung without burdens. In one cycle of epics, the *yukar*, the hero is always Poiyaunpe ("little mainlander," "young mainlander"), who dwells at a place called Shinutapka by the river Tomisanpet. Poiyaunpe does battle against the *repunkur* and frequently marries a *repunkur* woman. The details of the story of different *yukar* epics may contradict each other; Poiyaunpe may marry a different woman in different epics or may be

---

[52]The terminology discussed here is that of the Hidaka and Iburi areas. In other areas the terminology is different.

the child of different parents. In another group of epics, the *hau*, the hero dwells at Otasam (or Otashut) and is called Otasam-un-kur (or Otashut-un-kur).

(3) Novelistic narratives. These are narratives dealing with happenings in the lives of human persons other than the two heroes Poiyaunpe and Otasam-un-kur. The narratives may be prosaic (*ainu uwepeker, shisam uwepeker*) or sung (some *kamui yukar* with human speakers and the *menoko yukar*). The *ainu uwepeker* are prose tales telling of the adventures of ordinary Ainu; and the *shisam uwepeker* are tales describing the adventures of Japanese. The *menoko yukar* are "women's epics" having women as their speakers. Some of them are sung with burdens, and others without them. The heroines are usually related to one or the other of the two major heroes of the heroic epics; thus, they are usually called Shinutapka-un-mat or Otasam-un-mat.

(4) Parodies. There is a type of epic narrative, often identified as a "dream epic" *(wentarap yukar)*, which depicts situations that are abnormal. They seem to be fantastic, apocryphal outcroppings of the creative imagination. These are relatively few in number. (Selection 23 is one of these.)

There was a certain amount of give-and-take between the different folklore genres. For instance, even though the *kamui yukar* are by definition mythic epics in which gods are the speakers, some prose tales have been transformed into *kamui yukar* and, even though they have humans as their speakers, are performed in the typical manner of the *kamui yukar* with the monotonously repeated *sakehe* burdens. The Ainu did not draw a clear-cut line between one genre and the others, and heroes identified with a particular genre (such as the *yukar* hero Poiyaunpe) might on certain occasions appear in a different genre (such as the *oina*) where they did not really belong.

Epic reciters (*yukar-kur*) had prodigious memories, and many of them had extremely large repertories drawn from a number of different genres. Naturally, the reciters relied on an arsenal of memorized formulas and phrases which could be used freely whenever they were appropriate. They could, by using a formula (the verb *omommomo*), omit tedious details already well known to the audience. By no means were all of the epic reciters men. The best ones known to us were women, notably Kubodera's informants Hiraga Etenoa and Hirame Karepia. Some of the female reciters also functioned as practitioners of shamanism (*tusu*). The epics were always sung solo by a single reciter without the accompaniment of musical instruments. The reciter would use a block of wood (*repni*)[53] to tap the time on the hearth frame while singing.

It appears that knowledge of the mythic epics was extremely widespread among the general Ainu population. The mythic epics were short and of great importance from the religious point of view. Knowledge of the mythology was considered to enable the possessor to obtain blessings from the good deities and to drive away evil ones. Thus, the performance of mythic epics was not confined to any particular occasion, and they could be sung frequently.

On the other hand, the long heroic epics could not be recited as frequently as the mythic epics. Since the performance could be physically exhausting and last for many hours, sometimes all night, it would be necessary to assemble an audience of listeners who were prepared to listen unhurriedly around the fireplace. While the shorter, less complex mythic epics could be memorized and sung easily by anyone, the memorization of the lengthy heroic epics, with their specialized formulas of diction and antiquated language, would require special skill and long preparation.

The manner of performance of the longer heroic epics has been described by Kubodera.[54] Occasions would be selected during the long winter months, when the people were relatively free from economic activities and tended to become somewhat bored. The singing of the epic would begin by the fireside in the early evening. The reciter would sit by the fireplace, beating time on the hearth frame with his *repni*. The listeners would also each hold a *repni* in their hands, beating time on the hearth frame or on the wooden floor. From time to time, the audience would interject rhythmical exclamations of *het! het!* at certain points in the narrative. In this manner, a striking choral effect would be achieved. The reciter and his audience would be fused into a unity of experience, and the performance would engage the audience's attention so closely that they would scarcely notice the coming of the dawn. It was by no means unusual for the recitation to be still in progress in the morning.

In early days, it was apparently customary for the reciter to lie down on his back by the fireside and sing the narrative while beating time on his

[53]*Repni,* a stick about four to five inches long, means "drumstick." The term is also applied to a shaman's wand.
[54]Kubodera Itsuhiko, "Introduction to Ainu Epic Literature," pp. 154–56.

chest or his abdomen with his hand. The work *Ezo kodai fūzoku* (anonymous, latter half of eighteenth–first half of nineteenth century) preserved at the Hakodate Municipal Library has an illustration showing an Ainu lying on his back and singing an epic while beating time on his abdomen with his left hand (see illustration).[55]

It appears that there were no definite occasions on which recital of folklore was imperative. One supposes that folklore was universally performed on an almost daily basis in the villages and in the mountain hunting lodges. It is well known that the Ainu men were constantly hunting for deer and bear in the mountains and that they lived for long periods in lodges in the mountains. They had no other amusements except to entertain each other with epic folklore. The women, who remained closer to the villages, would also have much time in the evenings to tell tales and sing epic songs. Epics were also performed at important ceremonial occasions such as the bear ceremony, although in these cases it was customary to omit the ending in order to induce the god who was being sent off to return in the future to pay another visit to the humans.

The folklore not only provided entertainment and aesthetic satisfaction to the audience; it also must have played an important role in confirming and strengthening the basic values underlying the traditional society. This role was especially important during the more recent centuries when the Ainu culture was in a process of progressive decline.

Aesthetic Techniques

One of the most striking features of the epic songs is that they consistently use first-person narration. That is, the entire story is told in the first person singular from the point of view of the "speaker," who narrates his experiences subjectively using the pronoun "I." There is no attempt at an objective approach using third-person narration, and we encounter no impersonal Muse or Spirit of Song which intervenes and takes over the narrative. Everything from start to finish is a monologue told by a single speaker. The only exception is in a few cases where there are shifts from one speaker to another, such as in selection 32. Even here, however, the diction remains in the first person singular; only the identity of the speaker is shifted.

[55]Izumi Seiichi, ed., *Ainu no sekai*, illus. no. 95 [n.p.].

At the beginning of every epic song, we have no way of knowing who the speaker is. We cannot even tell whether the speaker is male or female, human or divine. During the course of the narrative, the speaker will describe the circumstances of his or her upbringing and life and will sometimes quote the words spoken by others to him or around him (or her, as the case may be). The name of the hero or heroine will thus be introduced in overheard dialogues or in two-way conversations between the speaker and another character. Since the landscape and events in each epic are viewed through the consciousness of the speaker, sometimes there are hiatuses in the narrative when the speaker loses consciousness or dies. In such cases, the epics use this formula:

rai hene ya	Was I dead?
mokor hene ya	was I asleep?
a-e-kon ramuhu	my mind
shitne kane	was clouded
tanak kane	and dazed.

The story resumes later on when the hero or heroine recovers consciousness or is restored to life.

The reason for this consistent adoption of first-person narration[56] in all of the Ainu epic poetry is not hard to find. As the reader will see himself when reading the selections in this volume, the age-old north Asiatic practice of shamanism is an all-pervasive influence in Ainu life. The words spoken during shamanic seances assume the form of utterances of the deities themselves, borrowing the mouth of the shaman. The idea that first-person narration in the epics was derived from shamanism was first advanced by Kindaichi,[57] and the same idea was applied to Japanese folklore and literature by scholars such as Yanagita Kunio and Orikuchi Shinobu. In the West, a similar theory about the prophetic origins of poetry was developed by Nora K. Chadwick.[58]

Ainu literature is, thus, basically a literature of self-revelation by a speaker. The process of self-revelation is gradual. No matter who the speaker may be, male or female, human or divine, the action always unfolds just as it occurs to the speaker. Not only does the speaker reveal himself by degrees to the audience; he also finds out about himself as the tale progresses. In many cases, the speaker at the beginning of a song does not even know his own

---

[56]I know of no other example in world epic literature where almost every song is told in the first-person singular. In one type of Nenets folk epic, the *yarabts*, first-person narration is used, but third-person narration is used in another type, the *syudbabts*. Z. N. Kupriyanova, *Epicheskie pesni nentsev*, pp. 40–41. See also Péter Hajdú, *The Samoyed Peoples and Languages*, pp. 37–38.

[57]Kindaichi Kyōsuke, *Ainu jojishi: Yūkara gaisetsu*, pp. 391–94, 399–400.

[58]Chadwick, Nora K., *Poetry & Prophecy*.

name or background. His identity and his origins are revealed to him by other characters as the story moves on.

During the performance of the song, the epic reciter in a way assumes a different personality, temporarily becoming the speaker through the use of the first-person pronouns. The psychological mechanism is, one would suspect, rather similar to that of the experiences of a shaman in a trance. The person who is speaking is no longer the reciter, but the personality of the hero or heroine. We must take each revelation on its own terms, that is, as a subjective view into the inner world of a particular god or human. Since the content of an epic song is the autobiography of a particular epic personality, it is quite possible that the epic reciter might refuse, or be unable to provide elucidation about the content, just as a shaman would probably deny any knowledge of the contents of the utterances which had come through his mouth in a trance.

Versification in Ainu song is syllabic. That is, the text is organized into verses (called "mouthfuls") of approximately the same number of syllables. There are no requirements whatever about the sequence or arrangement of syllables within each verse, and no distinction is made between long and short syllables. The number of syllables is irregular. The average length is five syllables, and many verses also have four or six syllables. Occasionally there are verses with three, or even with seven or eight, syllables. In actual performance, each verse is usually followed by a short pause, and in the mythic epics the burden (*sakehe*) is interjected, sometimes after every verse and sometimes sporadically between verses. A verse which is too long can be sung rapidly, and one having too few syllables can be drawn out in singing, or additional sounds or syllables can be added.

Organization of poetic texts into verses of a definite number of syllables is common in folk versification of many peoples. Folk versification of the Turkic peoples is syllabic, and the same principle is also followed by Japanese folk and literary verse. Turkic epic verse is of two types: short verse, having seven or eight syllables, and long verse, having eleven syllables.[59] Japanese poetry, however, has regular alternation between verses of 5 and 7 syllables, the most popular verse form being the *tanka*, a 31-syllable poem with five

[59]Victor Zhirmunsky, writing in Chadwick and Zhirmunsky, *Oral Epics of Central Asia*, pp. 334–39.

verses of 5, 7, 5, 7, and 7 syllables each. Such regular alternation of verse length is entirely unknown in Ainu poetry. It is possible that the Ainu poetry, with its irregular number of syllables and its relative freedom from metrical restrictions, represents an archaic stage of the development of versification.

In Ainu poetry rhyming occurs quite accidentally, as it does in Japanese poetry, but it is not prosodically relevant and not cultivated per se. Alliteration occurs sporadically, and there sometimes appear to be conscious attempts on the part of the reciters to cultivate it, although it is by no means obligatory. A number of the formulas used in the epic songs are clearly alliterative. For example, the *r* and *sh* sounds are repeated in a musical manner in the following formula, which describes the appearance of the posts in the stockade outside a stronghold:

hushko ash rash	The long standing posts—
rash e-makna-kur-	the posts stood bending
roshki kane	up backward;
ashir ash rash	and the newly standing posts—
rash e-sana-kur-	the posts stood bending
roshki kane	up forward.[60]

As is true in all oral poetry, Ainu epic poetry abounds in traditional formulas which are employed by the reciters again and again to express ideas or to depict situations which occur frequently. A reciter will be able to perform a lengthy epic without pause only if he or she knows a large number of such phraseological combinations and is able to build his or her own variations of the formulas by analogy.[61]

In Ainu epic poetry, the use of formulaic diction appears to be more frequent in the lengthier epics than in the short ones, for example, in the mythic epics. In the heroic epics, entire descriptive passages are repeated verbatim in any situation where they fit. Such are, for example, the descriptions of the interior of the hero's native stronghold with its stacks of treasures which "stretch out like a low cliff" and its many suspended swords with their overlapping tassels, the descriptions of the stockade surrounding the hero's stronghold, and the descriptions of the manner in which the hero attires himself before going out on some mission. However, the use of formu-

[60]Hyphens at the ends of verses in the original indicate enjambement, i.e., a part of a lengthy word is carried over to the following verse.
[61]Lord, Albert B., *The Singer of Tales*, pp. 30–67.

laic diction is not confined only to the lengthier heroic epics; we find many formulas in the mythic epics, and typical epic formulas are used even in the prose tales (*uwepeker*), which are narrated, not sung.

The metrical conditions in which formulas are constructed—the organization of the text into verses of four to six syllables in length—impose very few restrictions on formulaic diction, and it is possible to use any formula at any point in the narrative. The only restriction, which applies to the entire body of Ainu poetry, is that the formula must fit into one or more of these verses having approximately the same number of syllables. This metrical requirement has a number of consequences. First, one frequently finds that one verse consists of a single word, a verb or a noun. For instance, the name of the culture hero Okikurmi always occupies one verse. A second consequence is that it is seldom possible to express a complete idea within the limits of a single verse. Some Ainu verbs are quite lengthy incorporative complexes, and in many cases one verse is not long enough to contain the entire verb. Enjambement results when it is necessary to carry over part of the verb to the following line, as can be seen in the example quoted above. Therefore, one will not be surprised to find that many or most of the formulas employed in Ainu epic poetry embrace more than one verse, and that some of them, in fact, are lengthy runs encompassing a large number of verses.

In the following a number of examples of the types of formulas which are encountered in Ainu epic poetry are given. Naturally, since the number of formulas is immense, only a few of the most important formula patterns which the reciters use in reproducing fixed formulas and in evolving their own variations of the models are pointed out. It will be useful to distinguish the following types of formulas in Ainu poetry: attributive formulas, narrative formulas, and formulas of direct discourse.

Under attributive formulas I include all formulas which center around substantives. They include the epithets applied to heroes and heroines, appositions, and stereotyped descriptions applied to individuals, objects, or phenomena. Many of these formulas contain nouns such as *kamui* ("god"), *kane* ("metal"), or *nishpa* ("chieftain") used attributively. For example, magnificent houses are regularly described by the formula *kane chise* ("metal house"); magnificent robes are described as *kane kosonte* ("metal robes");

---

[62]The word *kane*, meaning "metal" or "iron" in Ainu, is derived from the Japanese word for "metal" (*kane*). The use of the word in Ainu attributive formulas was noted also by Pilsudski, who writes: "In some stories and fairy-tales, trees or houses receive this epithet. I suppose this adjective is used, not because the Ainu believe trees or houses can be of iron, nor because they wish to say that these things have the properties of iron, e.g., strength and solidity. I think that in such cases the Ainus express their highest admiration, and wish to say that this tree had the highest quality in any sense. It is known how much iron was prized in ancient times; the Ainus got it with great difficulty from the Japanese and the Manchurians.

even trees are given this description, as *kane sunku* ("metal fir").[62] Magnificent persons or objects are very frequently endowed with the epithet *kamui*, the Ainu word for "god."[63] In the epics we find formulas such as *kamui chacha* ("divine old-man"), *kamui chikirpe* ("divine embroidered-garment"), *kamui ekai-chish* ("divine steep-crag"), *kamui katkemat* ("divine lady"), *kamui kosonte* ("divine robes"), *kamui nupuri* ("divine mountain"), *kamui otop* ("divine locks of hair"), *kamui sarampe* ("divine silken hood"), *kamui shitoki* ("divine pendant necklace"), and many more. The hero's sword is described as *kamui ranke tam*, "god-given sword," and his stronghold as *kamui kat chashi*, "divinely made stronghold." The most common epithet applied to a hero is *kamui-ne-an-kur*, "exalted hero" (literally, "he-who-becomes-a-god"). A highly respected younger brother is always referred to by his adoring elder relatives as *a-reshpa kamui/a-reshpa pito*, "the god whom we are raising, our divine nursling." Highly successful drinking feasts are eulogized as *nishpa iku / nishpa ipe* ("noble drinking feast, noble feast") or as *shisak tonoto* ("matchless drinking feast").

A number of attributive formulas are constructed with participles, which in Ainu are formed with the prefix *chi-*. Some examples are: *chi-e-ranke retar kenna* ("the fallen white snow"), *chi-maka apa* ("the door which opens"), *chi-omap hekachi* ("a lovable baby"), *chi-nuina ape* ("hidden embers"), *chi-tata kewe* ("his mangled corpse"), *chi-ari ape* ("a kindled fire"), or *chi-shina atu* ("its tied cords").

Some of the implements and articles of clothing used by heroes and heroines are referred to with special formulas, such as *tar-ush ikayop* ("quiver with cord attached"),[64] *karimpa-unku* ("bow wound with cherry bark"), and *kina-tuye-hosh* ("grass leggings" or literally, "grass-cutting-leggings"). Women in the epics keep their treasured belongings in women's treasure bags called *sut ketushi* ("grandmother-bag," as it was handed down matrilineally). The culture hero's distinctive accoutrements are described formulaically; they are *o-uhui nikap attush* ("elm bark fiber coat with its hem in flames"), *o-uhui shirka* ("sheath with a flaming tip"), and sometimes also *o-uhui kasa* ("helmet with a flaming rim").

Numbers are often used to form attributive formulas. Special preference is given to the number six, *iwan*, which is sometimes used to mean "many."

De Vries, the first European traveller who gave an account of his journey to Saghalien in 1620, says that the Ainus in Aniva-Bay asked only for iron, and seemed to like it more than silver or gold." (Pilsudski, p. 29). Kupriyanova notes that the word "iron" is frequently used as a metaphorical epithet in the Nenets epic songs ("iron sled," "iron tent," "iron stick for driving reindeer," "iron cap," etc.). Z. N. Kupriyanova, "Epos nentsev" [Epics of the Nenets] in *Spetsifika fol'klornykh zhanrov* (1973) p. 179.

[63] In actual fact, the word *kamui* and its synonym *pito* are both loan words borrowed in ancient times from Japanese.

[64] The quiver is carried slung under the left shoulder by means of a cord passed over the shoulder on the same side.

A large pot is called *iwan at ush shu* ("pot having six cords"). A person wearing many layers of magnificent robes is said to be wearing *kane kosonte | iwan kosonte* ("metal robes, six robes"). The Underworld is said to have sixfold layers and is called *iwan pokna moshir* or *iwan pokna shir* ("sixfold Underworld"). There is also an extended form of the numeral, *noiwan* ("full six, six full, sixfold"). We find such formulas as *tokap rerko | kunne rerko | noiwan rerko* ("night after night and day after day, altogether six full days," literally, "days three-days, nights three-days, six-full three-days"), or *tu noiwan sui | re noiwan sui* ("scores of times, dozens of times," literally "two six-full times, three six-full times").

One of the most frequently used of all the formula patterns in Ainu epic is the parallelism with the numbers *tu* and *re* (or with extended forms of the numerals *otu* and *ore*). *Tu* and *re* are the Ainu numbers two and three, respectively, but in these parallelisms they become indefinite numbers meaning "several," "two or three," "many," "countless," or even "myriads." There are literally hundreds of such formulas. Let me given only a few examples: *tu arka itak | re arka itak* ("many harsh words, countless harsh words," literally, "two harsh words, three harsh words"), *tu atui penrur | re atui penrur* ("many ocean waters, countless ocean waters"), *tu chish teshkar | re chish teshkar* ("many tearful messages, countless tearful messages"), *tu kem poppise | re kem poppise* ("many bloody blisters, countless bloody blisters"), *otu keshto ta | ore keshto ta* ("day after day, day in and day out," literally, "two everyday, three everyday"), *otu ni temkor | ore ni temkor* ("many armsful of firewood, countless armsful of firewood"), *tu okne ipor | re okne ipor* ("many rueful countenances, countless rueful countenances"), *otu tapkan ru | ore tapkan ru* ("many dance steps, countless dance steps"), and *tu tuima kotan | re tuima kotan* ("many distant lands, countless distant lands"). Obviously, the reciters were entirely free to devise their own numerical formulas by analogy with the other formulas of this type.

The second type of formulas which can be distinguished in Ainu epic poetry is what I call narrative formulas. These are formulas which center in verbs and which depict frequently recurring actions, events, and states. Here again I must confine myself to dwelling upon only a few of the more typical patterns of the formulas.

One common pattern used in construction narrative formulas involves the use of at least two verses, the last one of which is a verb of manner, often ending in one of the aspective suffixes (for example, *-kosanu* | *-kosampa*, *-rototke* | *rototo*, *-atki* or *-natara* | *(h)itara*). The final verb is preceded by one of the modal particles: *hawe* (referring to a sound which is made or a statement which is spoken), *humi* (referring to a sound or a feeling), *katu* (referring to an appearance or a visible fact or action), *ruwe* (referring to a state which is visible or a trace which has been left), and *shiri* (referring to a state or situation which is immediately visible), or their derivatives such as *kauko, hau konna, humkan, hum konna, katkan, ruko, ru konna, rukan,* or *shirko.* Several examples will make clear the manner in which these formulas are constructed. (1) The following is a formula describing how the hero drew his sword: *a-tampi humkan* | *nainatara,* "I drew my sword with a clank" (literally, "the sound of my drawing-the-sword | resounded with a clank"). (2) The next formula describes a speaker who is crying noisily: *chish-an hauko* | *charototke,* "the sounds of my crying rang out noisily." (3) This formula describes a woman's gleeful laughter: *wen menoko* | *mina hauko* | *tesesatki,* "the evil maiden's laughter resounded gleefully" (*tesesatki* is a verb of manner meaning "to resound gleefully"—of laughter). (4) A formula describing a large house: *kane chise* | *poro chise* | *ash ru konna* | *meunatara,* "the metal house, the big house, could be seen standing majestically" (more literally, "the appearance of the house as it stood there was majestic"). (5) A formula describing a soul rumbling off through the sky after leaving the body: *kamui inotu* | *hopuni humi* | *keurototke* | *turimimse,* "his life-spirit was heard flying off with an intense rumbling and roaring." (Both *keurototke* and *turimimse* are verbs of manner depicting loud rumbling and roaring noises.) (6) A formula describing how the cords of a flying chariot pull tight with a shrill whistling: *kane ito-at* | *shiyupu humi* | *shiushiwatki,* "the metal cords were heard pulling themselves tight with a shrill whistling" (more literally, "the sounds of the metal cords pulling-themselves-tight resounded with a shrill whistling"). It is clear that this is another very productive pattern allowing the reciter much room for effective improvisation, since the language abounds in onomatopoetic expressions describing different types of sounds, and in verbs depicting very graphically different types of sparkling, glittering, and shining.

A large number of the narrative formulas are constructed on the principle of syntactical parallelism, which was described above in connection with the numerical patterns using *tu* and *re*. Many of the narrative formulas involve the use of synonyms. For example, a curse is pronounced upon an evil swordfish: *e-toi-munin* / *e-toi-ko-pene*, "you will rot in the ground, you will decay in the ground." Onomatopoetic expressions are often compounded to make up parallel verses, as in the following example:

ane chikuni	I knocked him against
ruwe chikuni	the slender trees
a-e-kik humi	and the stout trees,
yaknatara	making cracking noises
rimnatara	and thudding noises.

In other cases, narrative formulas are constructed using the numerals *tu* and *re*. In these cases, the formulas contain verbs, as in the following example.

tu ipe somo a-ki	Many (literally "two") meals I did not eat,
re ipe somo a-ki	countless (literally "three") meals I did not eat

Parallelisms are frequently constructed with contrasting pairs or with pairs of opposites, such as land and sea, near and far, outside and inside, top and bottom.

a-hanke-yashkar	I grabbed at him close up,
a-tuima-yashkar	I grabbed at him from afar.
pokna atui	The bottom [waters of the] sea
chi-kannare	ascended to the top,
kanna atui	and the top [waters of the] sea
chi-poknare	descended to the bottom.
	(Describes a storm at sea in which the waters churn about wildly.)
ya o usat	The ashes around the edges [of the fireplace]
reporaye	he raked out to the center,

rep o usat	and the ashes in the center
yaoraye	he raked out to the edges.
	(Describes the actions of a person who is preparing to make a weighty pronouncement.)

soyun usshiu	The outdoor servants
chi-aunaraye	came running inside
aun usshiu	and the indoor servants
chi-soinaraye	went running outside.
	(Describes the hubbub of the servants upon the arrival of an important person.)

Very often the parallelisms embrace more extensive blocks of text. For instance, the following formula is used to describe the clothing of a character who is wearing many layers of magnificent robes, some fastened under the belt and others hanging loose:

kane kosonte	He wore sixfold
iwan kosonte	magnificent robes
uko-e-kutkor	fastened under his belt,
kane kosonte	and he wore sixfold
iwan kosonte	magnificent robes
opanna-atte	hanging loose.

The following formula describes the state of a hero who is unable to sleep in his bed at night. It seems as if he is being thrust upward and downward at the same time by different spirits:

Sotki asam	It seemed to me
ampa kamui	as if the god ruling
i-e-rikna-kur-	the bottom of the bed
otke pekor	were thrusting me
yainu-an ruwe ne.	upward.
Aman empok	It seemed to me
ampa kamui	as if the god ruling
i-e-rana-kur-	[the area] under the rafters
otke pekor	were thrusting me

yainu-an ruwe ne.	downward.

There is perfect syntactical parallelism between both sentences. Another example may be given.

Reppa chip arke	On the side of the ship
reppa rok kamui	facing the sea,
tu noka orke	I carved
re noka orke	many pictures,
a-e-nuye-kar	countless pictures,
ki ruwe ne.	of the gods dwelling in the sea.
Kimma chip arke	On the side of the ship
kimma rok kamui	facing the mountains,
tu noka orke	I carved
re noka orke	many pictures,
a-e-nuye-kar	countless pictures,
ki ruwe ne.	of the gods dwelling in the mountains.

Thus, parallelism appears to be another very productive technique used in constructing narrative formulas.

The Ainu epic language makes frequent use of incorporation ("polysynthesis"), in which a number of elements are combined to form a lengthy verb having more than five syllables. These incorporative complexes are of great importance in the formulaic diction. In the following examples, all of the incorporative formulas have enjambement.

shi-chupka nehi	he went rumbling
ko-hum-eriki-	upward
tesuitara	toward due east
ainu penram	his body was enveloped
chi-e-urar-ko-	from his chest up
noipa kane	in twisting billows of mist
tar-ush ikayop	I tossed up
a-e-shi-setur-ka-	onto my back
terkere	a quiver with cord attached

pet-etok-ushke	the divine mountain
kamui nupuri	at the source of the river
chi-e-kanto-or-	soared up
soipa kane	into the heavens
chi-kitai-ko-kur-	a pretty little house,
raipa kane	its roof darting
chi-tumam-ko-kur	upward gracefully
yuppa kane	and its sides bound
pirka pon chise	firmly in place
senne moyo	large numbers
nishpa turempe	of noble companion spirits
kotan enka	hovered,
ko-nish-oshirko-	enveloped in clouds,
noipa kane	over the village
hanke ukpe	when [the deer] took grass nearby,
ko-kirau-shika-	he drew his antlers
omare kane	back over his body,
tuima ukpe	and when he took grass far away,
ko-kirau-riki-	he raised his antlers
pumpa kane	up high

In all of these examples, the Ainu verbs formed by means of incorporation require a whole string of English words to translate them. For example, the Ainu incorporative complex *ko-kirau-shika-omare*, which is grammatically a single verb, is translated by eight English words: "he drew his antlers back over his body." The formulas are strikingly similar in their rhythms; compare, for example, the following two formulas:

chi-e-urar-ko-	it is enveloped
noipa kane	in twisting billows of mist
chi-e-kanto-or-	it soars up
soipa kane	into the heavens

A third type of formulas frequently found in Ainu epic poetry is what I call "formulas of direct discourse." These formulas are all used before, in, or after direct discourse. The following are typical formulas used to introduce direct quotations:

itak-an hawe	I spoke
ene okahi	these words
yainu-an humi	This is what
ene okahi	I thought to myself
tuikashike	While doing so,
itak-o hawe	he uttered
ene okahi	the following words

Speeches addressed by one character to another in epic songs begin with monotonous regularity with the following formula:

inkar kusu	See here,
iresu sapo	my elder sister,
itak-an chiki	listen well
e-inu katu	to these words
ene okahi	I have to say!

Direct discourse is usually followed by formulas such as this one:

sekor okaipe	These words
iresu yupi	my elder brother
ye ruwe ne	spoke.

Similar formulas are frequently used to end mythic epics:

sekor okaipe	These things
peurep kamui	a bear-cub god
isoitak	narrated.
sekor okaipe	These things
chironnup kamui	a fox god
yaieyukar	narrated concerning himself.

An interesting, and perhaps unique, feature found in formulaic diction in the Ainu epic songs is that omission of formulas is optional. That is, the reciter can recite a special formula if he or she wishes to omit a formula which is already well known to the audience. The formula consists in the words *an-omommomo*, "I describe in detail."[65] For example, instead of reciting the lengthy descriptive passage about the beauties of the wooden stockade surrounding the hero's stronghold, the reciter can simply say:

a-kot chashi	I describe in detail
pirka ruwe	the beauties
an-omommomo	of my native stockade

It should be noted that, even here, the convention of first-person diction is kept up. It is the epic speaker who is doing the omitting, not the reciter. This formula no doubt is very useful when the reciter feels the need to speed up the narrative.

The epic formulas, which are heavily stocked with archaisms and lengthy incorporative complexes, must have diverged considerably from the colloquial Ainu language used in everyday conversation. The epic language itself was sort of special language, with its own grammar and conventions, cultivated by epic reciters for their own use, and one would suppose that the epic songs would be almost unintelligible to Ainu who had not made a special effort to master the epic diction. Kindaichi and Kubodera found that the reciters themselves no longer understood some of the archaic words and expressions used in the epic songs and were unable to supply any explanations of their meanings.

Very little is known about the techniques by which Ainu epic reciters acquired their repertories of formulas and stories, although it appears that the following three steps were followed by reciters when learning a new epic. First, a skeleton plot of the whole epic would be memorized. This amounted to a sort of catalogue of each of the important events in the epic but contained no details at all. Such catalogues were never recited publicly and were used by the reciters themselves as mnemonic devices only. The next step would be to recite the epic rhythmically in recitative without putting it to a melody. This nonmelodic recitative is called *rupaye*, which means something like "plain reciting." In *rupaye* the reciter maintains a definite beat throughout and actually shapes the verses to fit the required rhythm. After the text of the epic has been constructed by the reciter in recitative, it can be performed

---

[65] For examples of these omissions, see p. 219 and p. 268 in this volume.

publicly in the normal manner, that is, sung to a melody. This is called *sa-ko-ye*, "recite with a melody," "sing to a melody." Epics were never performed publicly in the *rupaye* fashion.[66]

No research has been done about the techniques used by the reciters in combining the words of the test with the melodic lines. In fact, practically nothing at all is known about the melodies used by the reciters. Very few recordings of Ainu epic songs are available.

The People of the Sea (Repunkur)

We have already seen that the ethnonym applied by the Ainu to themselves in their heroic epics was *yaunkur*, "people of the land" or "mainlanders." The Ainu were, indeed, a "people of the land," leading a land-oriented economic life centered in hunting and river fishing.

The dyad *ya* and *rep* ("land" and "sea") is a very productive element in Ainu word formation, and we find countless parallelisms such as *rep ta koikip* ("animals hunted at sea") and *ya ta koikip* ("animals hunted on land") or *rep kush tumi* ("battles passing over the sea") and *ya kush tumi* ("battles passing over the land"). Thus, the word *yaunkur* inevitably forms a parallelism with the word *repunkur*. If there is a "people of the land," the genius of the language requires that there also be a "people of the sea."

The *repunkur*, the "people of the sea" or "islanders" (as contrasted to "mainlanders"), are the enemies of the *yaunkur* in the heroic epics. They are a non-Ainu race of people who are basically sea-oriented. The epics state that they are extremely numerous (in Etenoa's words, *repunkur anak utari inne nep ne kusu*, "since the *repunkur* have numerous kinsfolk") and that there are many powerful shamanesses among the *repunkur* women (to quote Etenoa again, *repun-mat anak nupur hikehe tusu hikehe atpe ne kusu*, "since there are many wizardesses, many shamanesses among the *repunkur* women"). The epics locate the *repunkur* geographically along the northern coastline of Hokkaido facing the Okhotsk Sea, in the Kurile Islands, and on the island of Sakhalin (called Karapto in the epics). The name Santa is also mentioned in the epics in connection with the *repunkur*. Santa is the Japanese Santan, an old name for the Maritime Region around the Amur river and for the peoples living there.

It was Chiri Mashiho who first identified the *repunkur* of the Ainu heroic

---

[66] Mombetsu-chō Kyōdo-shi Kenkyūkai, *Saru Ainu no kayō*, pp. 37–38.

epics with the people who were the bearers of the Okhotsk culture known to archeologists.[67] The following is Chiri's argument:

The antagonists of the Ainu in these wars are a foreign people called the *rep-un-kur*, which means "people from overseas." Among them there appear people from Santan (Santa-un-kur), and among these people from Santan there are some called Tuima-Santa-un-kur (people from distant Santa) who wear their hair behind their backs like cows' tails. This clearly has reference to pigtails, and the people must be from the continent. The heroes who appear in the *yukar* epics are all named after the localities they rule, such as Iyochi, Ishikari, Chupka, Omanpeshka, or Repunshir. Strangely, all of these places appear to be areas within the sphere of the so-called Okhotsk culture, where Okhotsk-type pottery is excavated. In other words, the *yukar* are tales of wars between two peoples: the *yaunkur* ("people of the land," "mainlanders," "natives of Hokkaido"), based in Hokkaido, and the *repunkur*, who came over the seas from the continent and maintained their bridgeheads in various parts of Hokkaido extending from the central part of the Japan Sea coast to the Okhotsk Sea coast. The arena of these wars is a broad area centering around the central, northern, and eastern parts of Hokkaido and including the Kuriles, Sakhalin, Rishiri, Rebun, and the northern Asian continent. The Okhotsk culture is believed to have flourished along the coasts of Hokkaido during a period of about 500 years from 1,300 years ago to about 800 years ago. Thus, one can understand that the contents of the *yukar* deal with the ethnic conflicts which actually took place at that period.[68]

Chiri goes on to say that the invasion of the foreign people forced the Ainu population of Hokkaido to unite and form a confederacy under an overall commander. This solidarity against a common enemy enhanced the consciousness of their ethnic unity and created the basis for the formation of the single people which came to be known later as the Ainu.[69]

The Okhotsk culture of northern Hokkaido, Sakhalin, and the Kurile Islands clearly belonged to a north Pacific cultural complex of groups of hunters of sea animals. The chief occupation of the Okhotsk people was hunting of whales, sea-lions, seals, and dolphins. Fishing and land hunting were also practiced, and implements made of bone and stone, as well as

---

[67] The only substantial description of the Okhotsk culture in English is that of Harumi Befu and Chester S. Chard, "A Prehistoric Maritime Culture of the Okhotsk Sea."

[68] Chiri Mashiho, "Ainu no shin'yō," pp. 5–7. Reprinted in Chiri, *Chosakushū*, vol. 1, pp. 155–222.

[69] Ibid., pp. 6–7.

imported metal implements, are found. Abundant pottery of the Okhotsk type is found at Moyoro, the best-known site, located near Abashiri in Hokkaido. According to Chard, "an arctic or subarctic maritime group," coming originally from the Magadan area on the north shore of the Sea of Okhotsk, moved into southern Sakhalin during the last centuries B.C. and introduced the sea-hunting economy in this area for the first time. In Sakhalin, he says, the newcomers mingled with the local Neolithic population and adopted the pottery of the latter, but always remained close to the sea and retained their original economic pattern. The resulting culture and population then expanded to the northwestern tip of Hokkaido and eventually spread along all the northern shores of Hokkaido. Some of them eventually went up into the Kuriles. In northern Hokkaido, the Okhotsk culture continued until the eleventh to twelfth centuries A.D. and perhaps later. Chard believes that in the Kurile Islands the culture lingered into the second millennium A.D. and that "the Kurile Ainu were the last *cultural* survivors of the Okhotsk people."[70]

R. S. Vasil'evskii points out that there are remarkable similarities between the ancient Koryak culture around the Magadan area and the Okhotsk culture of Hokkaido, Sakhalin, and the Kuriles. He also points to profound connections between the Okhotsk culture and the cultures of the Maritime Region and the lower Amur. His theory is that Paleoasiatic tribes of the lower Amur and Maritime Region were the main components of the people of the Okhotsk culture and that they were also influential in the formation of the closely related ancient Koryak culture. Vasil'evskii connects these peoples with a clearly delineated configuration of cultures of sea hunters stretching across the northern part of the Pacific Ocean from Hokkaido to California. These cultures include the Okhotsk culture, the ancient Koryak culture (continental coast of the Okhotsk Sea, the offshore islands, the coast of Kamchatka), and the early cultures of the Aleutian Islands, Kodiak island, and western Alaska. The Eskimo cultures of northern Asia and northern and northwestern Alaska, he says, are outside the realm of these cultures.[71]

It is very possible that this north Pacific culture complex, stretching along the North Pacific Rim, was an important formative element in the Ainu culture. It is known that the Okhotsk people lived in close proximity with

[70] Chard, Chester S., "Time Depth and Culture Process in Maritime Northeast Asia," p. 215, and personal communication dated March 7, 1975. As to the lower limit date of the Okhotsk culture, Befu and Chard write: "It is not impossible for the Okhotsk culture to have lasted until the 13th or the 14th century A.D. in Hokkaido and perhaps even later in the Kuriles. The discovery of 10th-century Japanese swords at Moyoro suggests that the culture was still thriving in Hokkaido after the 10th century." Befu and Chard, "Prehistoric Maritime Culture," p. 15.
[71] Vasil'evskii, Ruslan Sergeevich, *Proiskhozhdenie i drevnyaya kul'tura koryakov* pp. 180–99.

the Ainu or their ancestors for many centuries. Intermarriage must have taken place between the two peoples, and the Ainu language may have been enriched by borrowings from the Paleoasiatic language spoken by the Okhotsk people. Thus, the Ainu would seem to occupy the westernmost position in a chain of related cultures stretching across the Pacific from Hokkaido to Alaska, the Pacific Northwest, and California.

The reasons for the disappearance of the Okhotsk culture have not been explained. If the Okhotsk culture died out during the thirteenth or fourteenth century, it might be possible to explain its disappearance in terms of the inroads of the Mongols, who expanded their power to the Maritime Region during the first half of the thirteenth century. They are said to have invaded Sakhalin five times during this period.

The epics may shed some light on the fate of the Okhotsk people. Although there is frequent mention of warfare between the *yaunkur* and the *repunkur*, or rather between Poiyaunpe and the *repunkur*, at the same time the Ainu epic heroes frequently marry *repunkur* women. In the epic Poi-Soya-un-mat (selection 32) the hero Otasam-un-kur finally marries a *repunkur* shamaness, Kunnepet-un-mat, even though she is "an enemy offspring, a woman of the enemy race." In the *yukar* epic "Kotan Utunnai" (selection 33) the hero Poiyaunpe marries Shipish-un-mat, a bellicose *repunkur* woman who is also a shamaness. In the epic *Kutune shirka* the hero Poiyaunpe is himself part *repunkur*. That is, a *repunkur* chieftain from a place called Omanpesh had formerly fought side by side with Poiyaunpe's father, and both men had married each other's sisters. Thus, Poiyaunpe's mother was a *repunkur*. When Poiyaunpe himself goes to do battle at Omanpesh, he finds relatives there. The young chieftain of Omanpesh recalls that they are cousins and decides to fight on Poiyaunpe's side. Poiyaunpe refers to the young chieftain and his sister as *repunkur yupi* (*repunkur* elder brother) and *repunkut tureshi* (*repunkur* younger sister). In the same epic Poiyaunpe marries the *repunkur* woman of Ukampeshka who has the nickname Nisap Tasum (Sudden Illness). Other such examples of intermarriage between *yaunkur* and *repunkur* could be mentioned.

It is quite probable that the epics reflect a complex historical process of interaction between two different peoples, one a land-oriented group of hunters and river fishers, and the other a sea-oriented group engaged in hunting of sea animals. At times the two peoples must have lived peacefully side by side; at others there must have been hostility and warfare between them. The frequent references to intermarriage probably indicate that in the end the "people of the sea" were absorbed by the Ainu. The conclusion of Etenoa's version of the epic *Kutune shirka* seems to point to such a peaceful conclusion. The following is a synopsis of the final passages of her version of the epic:

> Finally, the hero hears a rumor. On the opposite side of the bay, his enemies of old have come sailing up in a large fleet and are building a village there. They say that they are unable to compete with Poiyaunpe and desire to cast their lot in with him and to fight on his side. They are preparing wine and treasures as gifts to present to him. Hearing this rumor, the hero laughs silently to himself and continues to do his carving, his eyes focused on a single spot.

The hero Poiyaunpe thus gives his tacit consent to a merging of the *yaunkur* with the surviving remnants of their old enemies, the *repunkur*.

Women in the Ainu Epic Tradition

An extremely important economic and social role was played by women in the traditional Ainu society. The society was split into two parts, with strictly defined tasks being assigned to each sex. The labor to be performed by the men was hunting and fishing. The men were to perform religious rituals, entertain guests, and fight in case of warfare. All the other daily tasks fell to the lot of the women, who gathered the firewood, prepared the meals and clothing, raised the children, collected wild food plants, and cultivated a few agricultural crops. Not only were the women quite able to support themselves; it even appeared that it was they who were supporting their husbands.[72]

Men who were able to do so would have concubines (*pon mat*) in various places. The concubines would support themselves and would depend on the husband only for those tasks which were tabooed to women, such as hunting and worship. Far from being costly to the man, concubines would increase

---

[72] Kindaichi, *Ainu no kenkyū*, p. 30.

his wealth by weaving and embroidering garments for him. The men who had the largest number of concubines were the wealthiest.[73]

While men specialized in praying to the gods, women were practitioners of shamanism (*tusu*). Some of the epic reciters with whom Kindaichi worked were shamanesses. The heroines who appear in the epic literature are almost always depicted as being shamanesses. The conventional formula in the epics describing a shamaness with her companion spirits (*turenpe*) hovering around her is the following:

sara turenpe	Her visible companion spirits
kapap sai kunne	flocked about her
e-pishkanike	darkly
kurunitara,	like a bunch of bats,
mukke turenpe	and her invisible companion spirits
e-kimui-kashi	twinkled
nochiu meru ne	over her head
ko-teunin kane	like stars flashing.

During the period of decline of the Ainu culture, it was the women who remained in the villages and kept the traditional culture alive. Consequently, during this period the women tended more often to have good repertories of epics than the men, and thus most of the outstanding reciters known to us are women.

The Ainu social organization was unusual in the fact that women traced their ancestry separately from the men. The male line (*ekashi ikir*) was traced and recognized only by the males, and the female line (*huchi ikir*) only by the females. This curious male-female dichotomy ran through every aspect of Ainu society and has been much remarked upon. B. Z. Seligman, writing on the basis of Munro's discoveries, remarks that in each group the members of each sex recognized their own kinship obligations and rendered each other mutual aid. "The Ainu [social] system has double unilineal elements, in that both matriliny and patriliny are recognized, but it is unsal in that each sex acknowledges only the line of its own sex."[74] There was exogamy in matrilineal descent; males and females descended from females of the same matrilineal kin group could not marry each other.

---

[73] Ibid., pp. 30–31.
[74] B. Z. Seligman, writing in Munro, *Ainu Creed and Cult*, pp. 157–58.

The matrilineal kin group was identified by means of secret girdles (*upsor kut*) which must never be shown to any man. These girdles were reputed to have magical powers. They could be used by women to calm storms, hold back tidal waves or fires, and repel pestilence deities.[75] A woman could not marry any man whose mother wore the same type of girdle as she did. Each mother made the girdle for her daughter and instructed her in how to make and wear it. The women were organized into various *kut* groups associated with the following deities: the Goddess of the Waters (Wakka-ush-kamui); the bear (*kimun kamui*); the killer whale (*repun kamui*); the wolf (*horkeu kamui*); the fox (*chironnup kamui*); the eagle (*kapachir kamui*); the racoon-dog (*moyuk*); and the hare (*isepo kamui*).[76]

Women wearing the same types of girdles were members of the same female kinship group (*huchi ikir*) and had a high degree of solidarity. They had obligations to come to each other's assistance in cases of illness, childbirth, and death. When a woman died, her body could be prepared for the funeral only by women of the same *kut* group (*shine upsor*). It was believed that women belonging to certain *kut* groups inherited abilities such as the ability to shamanize, to practice midwifery, or to recite epics. They inherited such skills and did not need to learn them.

Women belonging to the same *kut* group tended to become dispersed geographically, since obviously the mother-in-law and daughter-in-law living in the same house were always of different kinship groups. In case of divorce, the female children would remain with the mother and the male children with the father. Matrilineal property was inherited by female descendants only. The epics mention women's treasure bags (*ketushi*, *sut ketushi*) in which women stored the property they inherited from their mothers and grandmothers.

Other interesting women's customs include the practice of tatooing around the lips. The tatooing began when a young woman was around the age of thirteen, and she became marriageable when it was completed. When a woman came of age, she would begin to wear a one-piece shift (*mour*) tied around the neck with cords or buttons to conceal her breasts.

A separate "woman's house" (*menoko chise*) was built in some areas of Hokkaido for a young woman of marriageable age. She would sleep alone there

[75] Ibid., p. 143. The existence of the secret girdles was discovered by Munro during the course of his medical practice among the Ainu during the 1930s and was unknown until that time.
[76] Ibid., pp. 142–43.

and would be able to receive male visitors. Marriage was by mutual consent, and when a young couple decided to marry they would be given their own separate house. The epics mention an interesting practice concerning marriage. The woman cooks a meal, evidently of cereal, for the man. The man eats half of the bowlful and gives the remainder of the bowl to the woman. If the woman eats the remainder of the food in the bowl, this signifies that she consents to marry him.

Widows were expected to cut their hair short and wear widow's hoods (*chish konchi*) which concealed their faces (see selection 29). Mourning lasted for a number of years, sometimes as long as three. Either the husband or the wife could ask for a divorce. If the husband was to blame, he would be required to pay indemnities to the wife (see selection 2).

A form of psychoneurosis called *imu* was common among Ainu women. It consisted in fits of hysteria, usually accompanied by the repetition of certain sounds or actions. When a woman was surprised by something, she would act compulsively, repeating nonsense syllables over and over or doing or saying the opposite of what was asserted or requested by others. The fits were regarded as amusing by other members of the community, and the epic texts depict them humorously (see selection 5). Women who had fits of *imu* were said to be predisposed to becoming shamanesses.[77] However, it is not clear whether *imu* was a necessary stage which women had to pass through before they become shamanesses.

Women play very prominent roles in the heroic epics. The heroines fight in battle along with the heroes. In some cases, as in "The Epic of Kotan Utunnai," the hero states that he is amazed at a woman's valor in battle. Sometimes separate women's battles will be fought out in the sky concurrently with the men's battles on the ground.

A familiar theme in the epics is that of the enemy woman who is a powerful shamaness and who turns against her own kinsfolk, casting her lot in with the hero Poiyaunpe. Typical heroines of this type are Shipish-un-mat in "The Epic of Kotan Utunnai" and Nisap Tasum in *Kutune shirka*. The following is a synopsis of that part of *Kutune shirka* in which the story of Nisap Tasum is told. (The version is that of Hiraga Etenoa, recorded in writing by Kubodera in February and March, 1933.)

---

[77] Munro, *Ainu Creed and Cult*, p. 108; Chiri, Mashiho, "Jushi to kawauso," pp. 55–58. An identical disorder is reported by Czaplicka among the natives of Siberia. Czaplicka, *Aboriginal Siberia*, pp. 315–16.

The hero is resting after a battle, and his female relatives are just beginning to treat his wounds when, suddenly, he hears a god coming from the land of the *repunkur*. A voice cries out, bringing the following message: "I am the servant woman of Ukampeshka-un-mat, the younger sister of Ukampeshka-un-kur. When you were previously doing battle at Omanpesh, both Ukampeshka-un-kur and his younger sister were to have gone to fight against you, but the younger sister secretly sympathized with you and refused to fight against you. She announced that she had a sudden stomachache and that she was unable to accompany her brother into battle. However, there being many potent wizardesses among the *repunkur*, it was discovered that Ukampeshka-un-mat was secretly in love with Poiyaunpe. Ukampeshka-un-mat was taken prisoner and is now being tortured in a place called Shisuye-Santa Kari-Santa." The servant woman begs the hero to go and rescue the lady, who is known by the nickname Nisap Tasum (Sudden Illness).

The hero immediately forgets his pain, pushes aside the women, and goes out. Jumping into the water, he swims along through the ocean until he arrives on the sandy beach at Shisuye-Santa Kari-Santa. He extracts the many sharp points from his own body (he had been wounded with them in a previous battle) and prays to his companion spirits to restore him to his former bodily condition. His wounds are healed by revivifying winds which come blowing down.

The hero walks inside the stockade on top of the cliff. Inside the house a feast is in progress. The hero peers through the window. The chieftain of Kari-Santa Shisuye-Santa is the host of the feast, and the guests include the hero's old enemies. There is a creaking among the rafters. Ukampeshka-un-mat (Nisap Tasum) is hanging there naked and is being subjected to the stream torture. She addresses her tormentors, telling them to kill her quickly. If she dies, she says, it will make no difference to the land. "Sooner or later, after I have died, the lord of the *yaunkur* will fight to avenge me, and all of you will die."

At the feast, two women are asked to shamanize. The first woman is unable to. The second woman shamanizes and prophesies that everyone at the feast will be slain. At this moment, the hero decides to reveal himself. He comes stamping fiercely inside, and the assembled guests at the feast fall silent.

The hero demands to be given something to eat and drink. He is served. The creaking in the rafters continues. He sees Nisap Tasum being tortured there and goes and cuts her down. Restoring her spirits with wine, he speaks to her. As the hero continues to give Nisap Tasum wine to drink, the assembled enemies begin to deride him.

At this point, the hero begins to run around on all fours on the floor. The gods on the sheath of his sword, *Kutune shirka*, come to life, and the hero himself is transformed into a supernatural fox (*sak kimotpe*). As the fox barks, clouds of mist come streaming forth from its mouth. He kills many of the enemies with his claws, and many more warriors rush into the house to join the fighting. The hero sets the house on fire, and Nisap Tasum also cuts down many of the warriors who are coming in through the doorway. He smashes all the ancestral treasures, which go winging their way up into the air with muffled rumblings. A powerful wind comes blowing down, and they all rush outside just before the house tumbles down inflames. The hero and Nisap Tasum continue to fight outside until the very last enemy has been slain.

After the battle, the hero and Nisap Tasum sit down to rest. Nisap Tasum addresses the hero, saying that she was motivated nobly in what she did, that she had been persecuted all her life by the evil *repunkur*, and that she is ashamed that her bosom (*upsor*) had been laid bare to the hero's sight. She says that she will be happy after death if he will deign to slay her with his own blade. The hero ignores her request and flies up into the air, heading toward his native stronghold. Nisap Tasum, apparently pleased, follows after him. They arrive home at Shinutapka.

After they return home, the hero and Nisap Tasum are welcomed exuberantly by the hero's relatives, who perform a ritual (*ukewehomsu*) to celebrate the hero's safe return and to welcome Nisap Tasum.

Much emphasis in the epics is placed on a woman's "bosom" (*upsor*). The secret girdle is called "bosom girdle" (*upsor kut*), and women belonging to the same kinship group (*huchi ikir*) are said to be of the "same bosom" (*shine upsor*). For a man to see a woman's body, or perhaps her girdle, was tantamount to raping her, and he would have to marry her or kill her (or she kill him). In some epics, when there has been a shipwreck and bodies are washed ashore, other women will run ahead to cover up the bodies of the women who may be lying injured or unconscious so that they will not accidentally be seen by the men.

It is possible to conclude from these facts, and also from the epics in this volume, nearly all of which were recited by women, that Ainu women had a highly developed culture of their own which differed from that of men and contained many elements which were kept strictly secret from them. Most of the studies of the Ainu which have been written in the past have overlooked this aspect of Ainu culture, since female informants were unwilling to provide any information about the women's secrets.

Conclusion

As we have seen, the epic poetry of the Ainu reflects the social conditions and world-view of the traditional Ainu society of past centuries, specifically the period before the Ainu were subjugated by the Japanese around the years 1669 to 1672. Like the wood carvings made by the Ainu men and the weaving and embroidery done by the women, the oral literature shows high aesthetic qualities and has a long history of development obviously going back over many centuries.

The ideas which are expressed in the epics and which, in fact, formed the basis for the traditional Ainu way of life, are extremely archaic and share many common features with the ideology which was prevalent among the Paleoasiatic peoples of northeast Asia until recent times. The bear cult and bear ceremonialism, in particular, appear to be of the greatest antiquity. The Ainu epic tradition, with its extremely archaic mental patterns and modes of diction, is one of the purest and most beautiful surviving examples of the oral literatures of the hunting and fishing peoples of northeast Asia.

Bibliography

Ainu bunka [Ainu culture]. 2v. (Nos. 106, 107 of *Kōgei*) 1942.

Ainu Bunka Hozon Taisaku Kyōgikai, comp., *Ainu minzoku shi* [Ethnography of the Ainu], 2v. Tokyo: Daiichi Hōki Shuppan, 1969.

Angelis, Girolamo [Hieronymus] de. "Relatione del regno di Iezo," in *Relatione di alcune cose cavate dalle lettere scritte ne gli anni 1619, 1620 & 1621 dal Giappone*. (Photographic reproduction) Roma: 1624.

Batchelor, John. *The Ainu and Their Folk-lore*. London: Religious Tract Society, 1901.

———. *An Ainu-English-Japanese Dictionary*. 4th ed. Tokyo: Iwanami, 1938.

———. *Ainu Life and Lore: Echoes of a Departing Race*. Tokyo: Kyobunkwan, 1927.

———. "Specimens of Ainu Folk-lore," read March 14, 1888. *Transactions of the Asiatic Society of Japan*, vol. 16, part 2, pp. 111–54. (Reprinted 1915)

———. "Specimens of Ainu Folk-lore," read Dec. 4, 1889. *Transactions of the Asiatic Society of Japan*, vol. 18, part 1, pp. [25]–86. April, 1890.

———. "Specimens of Ainu Folk-lore," read April 28, 1892. *Transactions of the Asiatic Society of Japan*, vol. 20, part 2, pp. 216–27. Jan., 1893.

Befu, Harumi, and Chester S. Chard. "A Pre-historic Maritime Culture of the Okhotsk Sea." *American Antiquity* 30, no. 1 (July, 1964): 1–18.

Bowra, C. M. *Heroic Poetry*. London: Macmillan, 1966.

Chadwick, Nora K. *Poetry & Prophecy*. Cambridge: University Press, 1952.

Chadwick, Nora K., and Victor Zhirmunsky. *Oral Epics of Central Asia*. Cambridge: University Press, 1969.

Chamberlain, Basil Hall. *Aino Folk-tales*. [London?] The Folk-lore Society, Publications No. 22, 1888. Reprint. Nendeln / Liechtenstein: Kraus Reprint Limited, 1967.

———. *The Language, Mythology, and Geographical Nomenclature of Japan Viewed in the Light of Aino Studies*. Tokyo: The Imperial University, 1887. (Memoirs of the Literature College, Imperial University of Japan)

Chard, Chester S. "A New Look at the Ainu Problem." *VIII International Congress of Anthropological and Ethnological Sciences*, Tokyo: 1968, pp. 98–99.

———. *Northeast Asia in Prehistory*. Madison: University of Wisconsin Press, 1974.

———. "Time Depth and Culture Process in Maritime Northeast Asia." *Asian Perspectives* 5 (2), winter 1961: 213–16.

Chekhov, Anton. *The Island, A Journey to Sakha-*

lin. Tr. by Luba and Michael Terpak. New York: Washington Square Press, 1967.

Chiri, Mashiho. *Ainu bungaku* [Ainu literature]. Tokyo: Gengen Sha, 1955.

———. *Ainu-go nyūmon* [Introduction to the Ainu language]. Sapporo: Nire Shobō, 1956.

———. "Ainu no shin'yō [Ainu god-songs]." *Hoppō bunka kenkyū hōkoku* 9 (March, 1954): 1–78.

———. "Ainu no shin'yō [Ainu god-songs] (2)" *Hoppō bunka kenkyū hōkoku* 16 (March, 1961): 1–34.

———. *Bunrui Ainu-go jiten* [Classified dictionary of the Ainu language]. Tokyo: Nihon Jōmin Bunka Kenkyūsho, 1953–62. vol. 1. *Shokubutsu hen* [Plants], 1953; vol. 2. *Dōbutsu hen* [Animals], 1962; vol. 3. *Ningen hen* [Human beings], 1954.

———. *Chosakushū* [Collected works]. 4v. Tokyo: Heibonsha, 1973–74.

———. "Jushi to kawauso [The magician and the otter]." *Hoppō bunka kenkyū hōkoku* 7 (1952): 47–80.

———. "Karafuto Ainu no shin'yō [God-songs of the Sakhalin Ainu]." *Hoppō bunka kenkyū hōkoku* 8 (March, 1953): 185–240.

Chiri, Mashiho and Oda Kunio. *Yūkara kanshō* [Appreciation of the *yukar*]. Tokyo: Gengen Sha, 1956.

Chiri, Yukie. *Ainu shin'yō shū* [Collected Ainu god-songs]. Tokyo: Kyōdo Kenkyū Sha, 1923.

Coon, Carleton S. *The Hunting Peoples.* Boston: Little-Brown, 1971.

Czaplicka, M. A. *Aboriginal Siberia, A Study in Social Anthropology.* Oxford: Clarendon Press, 1969. [First published 1914]

Egami, Namio. *Yūrashia hoppō bunka no kenkyū* [Studies of the cultures of northern Eurasia]. Tokyo: Yamakawa Shuppansha, 1951.

Ergis, Georgii Ustinovich. *Ocherki po yakutskomu fol'kloru* [Essays on Yakut folklore]. Moscow: Nauka, 1974.

Fujimoto, Hideo. *Ainu kenkyū shi—aru dammen* [History of Ainu study—a cross-section]. Sapporo: Miyama Shobō, 1968.

———. *Ainu no haka* [Ainu graves]. Tokyo: Nihon Keizai Shimbun, 1964.

Geroicheskii epos narodov SSSR [Heroic epics of the peoples of the USSR]. 2v. Moscow: Khudozhestvennaya Literatura, 1975.

Gusev, Viktor Evgen'evich. *Estetika fol'klora* [Aesthetics of folklore]. Leningrad: Nauka, Leningradskoe Otd., 1967.

Guss, David M. "The Power is Great: God Songs and Epics of the Ainu." *Alcheringa,* new series, vol. 3, no. 1 (1977): 21–38.

Hajdú, Péter. *The Samoyed Peoples and Languages.* 2d ed., rev. Bloomington: Indiana University, 1962.

Hallowell, A. Irving. "Bear Ceremonialism in the Northern Hemisphere." *American Anthropologist,* n.s., vol. 28, no. 1, (Jan.-March. 1926): 1–175.

Hattori, Shirō, ed. *An Ainu Dialect Dictionary with Ainu, Japanese and English Indexes.* Tokyo: Iwanami, 1964.

Heibonsha. *Fudoki Nippon* [Geographical account of Japan]. 1958. vol. 6, "Hokkaidō."

Hitchcock, Romyn. "The Ainos of Yezo, Japan." *Smithsonian Report of the United States National Museum*, 1890. Washington, D. C., pp. 429–502.

———. "The Ancient Pit-dwellers of Yezo." *Smithsonian Report of the United States National Museum*, 1890. Washington, D.C., pp. 417–27.

Howard, B. Douglas. *Life with Trans-Siberian Savages*. London: Longmans, Green, 1893.

Howell, Richard W. "The Classification and Description of Ainu Folklore." *Journal of American Folklore* 64, no. 254 (1951): 361–69.

———. "The Kamui Oina: A Sacred Charter of the Ainu." *Journal of American Folklore* 65, no. 258 (1952): 379–417.

Izumi, Seiichi, ed. *Ainu no sekai* [World of the Ainu]. Tokyo: Kashima Shuppankai, 1968.

Kayano, Shigeru. *Hono-o no uma* [The horse in flames]. Tokyo: Suzusawa, 1977.

———. *Ore no Niputani* [My Niputani]. Tokyo: Suzusawa, 1975.

———. *Uepekere shūtaisei* [Complete collection of *uwepeker*], vol. 1. Tokyo: Arudoo, 1974.

Kindaichi, Kyōsuke. *Ainu bungaku* [Ainu literature]. Tokyo: Kawade Shobō, 1934.

———. *Ainu bunka shi* [Ainu culture]. Tokyo: Sanseidō, 1961.

———. *Ainu-go kenkyū* [Studies of the Ainu language]. Tokyo: Sanseidō, 1960.

———. *Ainu jojishi Itadori-maru no kyoku* [Ainu epic Kutune Shirka]. Tokyo: Seiji Sha, 1944. (Reprint of vol. 2 of his *Ainu jojishi: Yūkara no kenkyū*)

———. *Ainu jojishi: Yūkara gaisetsu* [Outline of yukar, the Ainu epic]. Tokyo: Seiji Sha, 1943. (Reprint of vol. 1 of his *Ainu jojishi yūkara no kenkyū*)

———. *Ainu jojishi: Yūkara no kenkyū* [Studies of yukar, the Ainu epic]. 2d ed. Tokyo: Tōyō Bunko, 1967. 2v. (Reprint of the 1931 edition)

———. *Ainu jojishi: Yūkara shū* [Collection of yukar, the Ainu epics]. 8v. Tokyo, Sanseidō, 1959–68.

———. *Ainu Life and Legends*. Tokyo: Board of Tourist Industry, Japanese Government Railways, 1941. (Tourist Library 36)

———. *Ainu no kenkyū* [Studies of the Ainu]. Tokyo: Yashima Shobō, 1925.

———. *Ainu no shinten* [Sacred texts of the Ainu]. Tokyo: Yashima Shobō, 1943.

———. *Ainu seiten* [Ainu sacred books]. Tokyo: Sekai Bunko Kankōkai, 1923.

———. *Gakusō zuihitsu* [Essays from a scholar's window]. Tokyo: Jimbun Shoin, 1936.

———. *Kita Ezo koyō ihen* [An old song from Northern Ezo]. Tokyo: Kyōdo Kenkyū Sha, 1914.

———. *Kita no hito* [Man of the North]. Tokyo: Seiji Sha, 1942.

———. *Yūkara* [Yukar]. Tokyo: Shōka Sha, 1936.

———. *Yūkara* [Yukar]. Tokyo. Iwanami, 1936. (Iwanami bunko)

Kindaichi, Kyōsuke, and Chiri Mashiho. *Ainu*

gohō gaisetsu [Outline of Ainu grammar]. Tokyo: Iwanami, 1936.

Kindaichi, Kyōsuke and Sugiyama Sueo. *Ainu geijutsu* [Ainu art]. Tokyo: Daiichi Seinen Sha, 1941–43.

Kitagawa, Joseph M. "Ainu Bear Festival (iyomante)." *History of Religions* 1, no. 1 (1961): 95–151.

Kreinovich, Erukhim Abramovich, *Nivkhgu, zagadochnye obitateli Sakhalina i Amura* [Nivkhgu, the enigmatic inhabitants of Sakhalin and the Amur]. Moscow: Nauka, 1973.

Kubodera, Itsuhiko. *Ainu bungaku josetsu* [Introduction to Ainu literature]. Tokyo: Tokyo Gakugei Daigaku, 1956. (Tokyo Gakugei Daigaku Kenkyū Hōkoku 7, special number)

———. *Ainu jojishi: Shin'yō, seiden no kenkyū* [Studies of Ainu mythic epics *kamui yukar* and *oina*]. 4v. Ph.D. dissertation, Kokugakuin University, Tokyo, 1960; Tokyo: Iwanami, 1977.

———. *Ainu no bungaku* [Ainu literature]. Tokyo: Iwanami, 1977.

———. *Ainu no mukashi-banashi* [Ainu tales]. Tokyo: Miyai Shoten, 1972.

———. "Introduction to Ainu epic literature" Tr. by Donald L. Philippi, n.d. Typescript.

Kupriyanova, Z. N. *Epicheskie pesni nentsev* [Epic songs of the Nenets]. Moscow: Nauka, 1965.

Levin, Maksim Grigor'evich. *Ethnic Origins of the Peoples of Northeastern Asia*. Toronto: University of Toronto Press, 1963.

Levin, Maksim Grigor'evich and L. P. Potapov, eds. *Istoriko-etnograficheskii atlas Sibiri* [Historico-ethnographical atlas of Siberia]. Moscow–Leningrad: Izd-vo Akademii Nauk SSSR, 1961.

———. *The Peoples of Siberia*. Chicago: University of Chicago Press, 1964.

Lord, Albert B. *The Singer of Tales*. Cambridge: Harvard University Press, 1964.

Maraini, Fosco. *Gli iku-bashui degli Ainu*. Tokyo: Istituto Italiano di Cultura in Tokio, 1942.

Matsuyoshi, Sadao. *Hokugai no higeki* [Tragedy of the northern boundaries]. Tokyo: Yūzankaku, 1960.

Mitsuoka, Shin'ichi. *Ainu no ashiato* [Traces of Ainu footprints]. 7th ed. Shiraoi: Miyoshi Shoten, 1962.

Mombetsu-chō Kyōdo-shi Kenkyūkai. *Inonno itak* [Ainu prayers]. Mombetsu, 1966.

———. *Kutune shirka*. Mombetsu, 1965.

———. *Saru Ainu no kayō* [Songs of the Saru Ainu]. Mombetsu, 1966.

Montandon, George. *La civilisation ainou et les cultures arctiques*. Paris: Payot, 1937.

Munro, Neil Gordon. *Ainu Creed and Cult*. London: Routledge & Kegan Paul, 1962.

Murasaki, Kyōko. *Karafuto Ainu-go* [Sakhalin Ainu language]. Tokyo: Tosho Kankōkai, 1976.

Nabesawa, Motozō. *Ainu no jojishi* [Ainu epics]. Mombetsu: Mombetsu-chō Kyodo-shi Kenkyūkai, 1969.

Nevskii, Nikolai Aleksandrovich. *Ainskii fol'klor* [Ainu folklore]. Moscow: Nauka, 1972.

Nippon Hōsō Kyōkai. *Ainu dentō ongaku* [Ainu

traditional music]. Tokyo: Nippon Hōsō Shuppan Kyōkai, 1965.

Ohnuki-Tierney, Emiko. *The Ainu of the Northwest Coast of Southern Sakhalin.* New York: Holt, Rinehart & Winston, 1974.

———. "Another Look at the Ainu—A preliminary report." *Arctic Anthropology* 11, suppl. (1974): 189–95.

———. "Concepts of Time among the Ainu of the Northwest Coast of Sakhalin." *American Anthropologist* 71 (1969): 488–92.

———. "A Northwest Coast Sakhalin Ainu World View." Ph. D. dissertation, University of Wisconsin, 1968.

———. "Regional Variation in Ainu Culture." *American Ethnologist* 3, no. 2 (1976): 297–330.

———. *Sakhalin Ainu Folklore.* Washington, D. C.: American Anthropological Association, 1969. (Anthropological studies, no. 2)

———. "Sakhalin Ainu Time Reckoning." *Man* 8, no. 2, (1973): 285–99.

———. "The Shamanism of the Ainu of the Northwest Coast of Southern Sakhalin." *Ethnology* 12, no. 1 (Jan. 1973): 15–29.

———. "Spatial Concepts of the Ainu of the Northwest Coast of Southern Sakhalin." *American Anthropologist* 74 (1972): 426–55.

Ōta, Ryū. *Ainu kakumei ron* [Theory of the Ainu revolution]. Tokyo: Shinsei Sha, 1973.

Pilsudski, Bronislaw. *Materials for the Study of the Ainu Language and Folklore.* Cracow: Imperial Academy of Sciences, 1912.

Pon, Fuchi, *Ainu-go wa ikite iru* [The Ainu language is alive]. Tokyo: Shinsen Sha, 1976.

Robins, R. H. *General Linguistics, An Introductory Survey.* London: Longmans, 1964.

Rothenberg, Jerome, ed. *Shaking the Pumpkin; Traditional Poetry of the Indian North Americas.* New York: Doubleday, 1972.

———. *Technicians of the Sacred: A Range of Poetries from Africa, America, Asia, & Oceania.* New York: Doubleday, 1968.

Sakurai, Kiyohiko. *Ainu hishi* [Secret history of the Ainu]. Tokyo: Kadokawa, 1967.

Sarashina, Genzō. *Kamera kikō: Ainu no shinwa* [Camera journey: Ainu myths]. Tokyo: Tankō Shinsha, 1967.

Savage Landor, A. H. *Alone with the Hairy Ainu. Or, 3,800 Miles on a Pack Saddle in Yezo and a Cruise to the Kurile Islands.* London: John Murray, 1893.

Shin'ya, Gyō. *Ainu minzoku teikō shi* [History of Ainu national resistance]. Tokyo: San'ichi Shobō, 1972.

———. *Yūkara no sekai* [World of the *yukar*]. Tokyo: Kadokawa, 1974.

Shoolbraid, G. M. H. *The Oral Epic of Siberia and Central Asia.* Bloomington: Indiana University, 1975.

Simeon, George John. "The Phonemics and Morphology of Hokkaido Ainu." Ph. D. dissertation, University of Southern California, 1968.

Spetsifika fol'klornykh zhanrov [Specifics of folklore genres]. Moscow: Nauka, 1973.

Stephan, John J. *Sakhalin, A History.* Oxford: Clarendon Press, 1971.

Sugimura, Kinarabukku. *Kinarabukku yūkara shū* [Collected *yukar* of Kinarabukku]. Asahikawa: Asahikawa Sōsho Hensan Iinkai, 1969.

Takabeya, Fukuhei. *Ainu no jūkyo* [Ainu dwellings]. Tokyo: Shōkokusha, 1943.

Takakura, Shin'ichirō. *The Ainu of Northern Japan: A Study in Conquest and Acculturation.* Tr. by John A. Harrison. Philadelphia, 1960. (Transactions of the American Philosophical Society, n.s., vol. 50, part 4)

——. *Ainu kenkyū* [Ainu research]. Sapporo: Hokkaidō Daigaku Seikatsu Kyōdō Kumiai, 1966.

Tamura [née Fukuda], Suzuko. "Ainu-go Saru hōgen no dōshi no kōzō [Morphological structure of verbs in the Saru dialect of Ainu]." *Gengo kenkyū* 30: 46–64.

——. "Ainu-go Saru hōgen no fukujoshi to shūjoshi [Adverbial particles and final particles in the Saru dialect of Ainu]." *Gengo kenkyū* 39: 21–38.

——. "Ainu-go Saru hōgen no jodōshi [Verbal particles in the Saru dialect of Ainu]." *Minzokugaku kenkyū* 24, no. 4: 67–78.

——. "Ainu-go Saru hōgen no meishi [Nouns in the Saru dialect of Ainu] – 1." *Waseda Daigaku Gogaku Kyōiku Kenkyūsho Kiyō* 3: 33–59.

——. "Ainu-go Saru hōgen no meishi [Nouns in the Saru dialect of Ainu] – 2." *Waseda Daigaku Gogaku Kyōiku Kenkyūsho Kiyō* 5: 37–57.

Torii, Ryūzō. *Études archéologiques et ethnologiques. Les Aïnou des Iles Kouriles.* Tokyo: Journal of the College of Science, Imperial University of Tokyo, 1919.

Uehara, Kumajirō. *Ezo hōgen Moshiogusa* [Vocabulary of the Ezo dialect]. 1804. (Facsimile reproduction, Sapporo: Kōnandō Shoten, 1969)

Vasil'evskii, Ruslan Sergeevich. *Proiskhozhdenie i drevnyaya kul'tura koryakov* [Origin and ancient culture of the Koryaks]. Novosibirsk: Nauka, Sibirskoe Otd., 1971.

Voprosy izucheniya eposa narodov SSSR [Problems of study of the epics of the peoples of the USSR]. Moscow: Izd-vo Akademii Nauk SSSR, 1958.

Waley, Arthur. "Kutune Shirka, the Ainu epic." *Botteghe oscure* vii (1951): 214–36.

Watanabe, Hitoshi. *The Ainu Ecosystem: Environment and Group Structure.* Tokyo: University of Tokyo Press, 1972.

Yamada, Hidezō. *Hokkaidō no kawa no na* [Names of Hokkaido rivers]. Rev. ed. Sapporo: Moreu Raiburarii, 1971.

Zhirmunskii, V. M. *Tyurkskii geroicheskii epos* [Turkic heroic epics]. Leningrad: Nauka, Leningradskoe Otd., 1974.

Part I
Songs of Gods

Introduction to Part I

The twenty-five selections in this part are songs sung by *kamui* of various types, and the native term for this genre of the epic folklore is *kamui yukar,* "god epic."

In the traditional world-view of the Ainu, all species of non-human beings are endowed with supernatural characteristics and are called *kamui*. The dictionary definition of "god" is no doubt inadequate, but there is no other convenient equivalent for *kamui*, which is actually a loan word borrowed from the Old Japanese *kamï*, meaning "god." The *kamui* are gods in the Paleolithic sense, not in the Western sense. That is, they are non-human beings with supernatural attributes who live in thoroughly anthropomorphic fashion in their own god-worlds, where they are invisible to human eyes, but who also share a common territory with the humans and pay frequent visits to the humans in disguise. Animals are such gods in disguise.

The Ainu are extremely liberal in their use of the word *kamui*. Besides being used as a noun meaning god in the sense discussed, it can also be used as an adjective meaning "magnificent" or "splendid." In the epics we find "divine embroidered garments" (*kamui chikirpe*), "divine robes" (*kamui kosonte*), "divine pendant necklaces" (*kamui shitoki*), and "divine winds" (*kamui mau*). The magnificent locks of wavy hair of epic heroes are called "divine hair" (*kamui otopi*), and highly respected human women are called "divine ladies" (*kamui katkemat* or *kamui moiremat*). Strongholds (*chashi*), old men (*chacha*), and armor (*hayokpe*) are deified and called *chashi kamui, chacha kamui,* and *hayokpe kamui*. In the epics, a younger brother who is being raised by his older relatives is respectfully called "god whom we are raising, our divine nursling" (*a-reshpa kamui a-reshpa pito*). In this case, the word *pito,* also a loan word from Old Japanese (meaning "human being"), is used as a synonym for *kamui*. The word *kamui* also means "bear." Thus, *yuk chikoikip kamui chikoikip* is a common couplet meaning "game animals, both deer and bear." *Kamui menoko* ("god woman") may mean either "goddess" or "she-bear."

At first glance, it would seem that the Ainu use of the word *kamui* with its troublesome polysemantism is hopelessly confusing and that no clear distinctions are made, semantically or otherwise, between animals, humans, man-made implements, and gods. All animals, all plants, and even human artifacts are impartially called *kamui*. The epithet *kamui* is even applied to highly respected human beings. However, the Ainu obviously are capable of making the necessary distinctions between different orders of being, and they have a series of coherent beliefs about the nature of reality.

In the Ainu world-view, the world is a common territory shared between different species of beings. The humans (*ainu*) are one of these species and are totally dependent for their survival on the other types of beings with which they share the world. Continued human existence was made possible by rituals and beliefs implying social relationships with the natural world, the *kamui*. This system has been called, with penetrating insight, "the system of social solidarity between man and nature" by Watanabe.[1]

The human-*kamui* relationship is one of interdependence. The non-human species in nature also depend on the humans for their well-being, and the traditional world-view is based on the fundamental concept that the world is a space shared by interdependent species. Humans and gods are more or less equals, with the humans having a slight advantage over the gods. True, the gods can do some things that ordinary humans cannot. They have supernatural powers, can move from place to place swiftly, can fly through the air, and can change their forms at will. Among the humans, only shamans have such powers. But in certain matters the humans are superior to the gods. The gods fear the humans, depend on them, and are subject to their power. The gods admire the humans and wish very much to visit the human homeland (*ainu kotan, ainu moshir*). The gods can enhance their prestige in their communities when they are worshiped and are given presents by the humans. In fact, the wealth of the gods consists of the presents they receive from the humans.[2]

The humans also depend on the gods. They are guarded and protected by the good deities, who surround the humans inside and outside the house and who have the responsibility for watching over them and warding off evil from them. The most important deity in this respect is the ancient Fire God-

---

[1] Watanabe, Hitoshi, *The Ainu Ecosystem*, pp. 69–78.
[2] The ideas on the human-god relationship were developed in greatest detail by Kindaichi. See, for example, his *Ainu jojishi: Yūkara gaisetsu*, pp. 3–15.

dess (*kamui huchi*) who dwells in the hearth of every Ainu home. She acts as the intermediary between humans and gods and is prayed to first by the humans every time they address prayers to any deities. There are evil deities (*wen kamui, nitne kamui*) who envy the good fortune and happiness of the humans and of the good deities and seek to harm them both. These evil beings also desire to have for themselves the presents which the humans offer to the good deities. They steal away the souls of the food (the fish and the game), spread diseases, and cause famines. The evil deities can succeed in their wicked schemes only when the vigilance of the good deities is diminished. Exactly like human beings, the good deities are rather absentminded, and their attention can easily wander. Calamities may occur if they are not minding their business of looking after the affairs of the humans. This is why it is so important for the humans to master the techniques of attracting and holding the attention of the good deities and of invoking the aid of extremely powerful deities who can be called on in emergencies to ward off evil influences. Ainu men were specialists in these techniques, and all of their activities were accompanied or preceded by prayers and rituals.

The gods are anthropormorphic through and through. No matter whether they live in the human homeland (the plains, the meadows, the rivers, the seas, the mountains, the forests, or inside the houses of the humans), in the skies, in far-away lands, or in the Underworld, the lives of the gods follow the human pattern closely. When they are at home in their god-worlds, they have human form. Their appearance is human-like, but more majestic than that of ordinary humans. They build themselves houses to live in; they form their own communities; they wear clothing; they pray to the gods; they fight battles; they love their spouses and children; and they like to brew wine and invite their friends and relatives to drinking feasts. They love to dance and sing and to listen to epics. In fact, their tastes, their likes and dislikes, correspond exactly to those of humans. At the same time, their worlds are separate from the world of the humans, and there is a certain strangeness about humans for them. The gods especially dislike the smell of humans, which they seemingly cannot tolerate. They hide themselves from the humans by wrapping themselves in black or white clouds, but if they choose they can reveal themselves to humans in their true form, anthropomorphic but extremely majestic. Or if they wish they can appear in their disguises as animals or plants.

The presents of wine and of *inau* which the gods receive from the humans are their prized treasures. The *inau* are elaborately whittled sticks of willow or other wood with beautifully fashioned curled shavings. The Ainu make great numbers of these ritual artifacts, and there are a great many different varieties of them, each variety having its specific purpose and being intended for a certain deity to whom it is especially acceptable.[3] The Ainu attribute supernatural powers to these man-made artifacts, which are regarded as being messengers to gods, intermediaries between humans and gods, and sometimes even as gods themselves. (A god made by human hands appears in selection 9). The gods prize the gifts of *inau* given to them by the humans in exactly the same way that the Ainu prize their own household treasures, which consist of imported Japanese goods. A god who returns from a visit to the humans laden with many presents of wine and of *inau* has his prestige greatly enhanced. This dependence of the gods on the humans for presents is strikingly similar to the attitude of the Ainu toward the Japanese.

The gods admire the beauties of the human homeland and long to come and visit it, but many of them seldom have an opportunity to make this visit. When they come on their visits to the humans, the gods do not come only for sightseeing purposes; they come also with business in mind. The key word for this in Ainu is *irauketupa*, a verb with the following meanings: (1) to make one's livelihood, to practice a profession or business; (2) to go trading, to visit for the purpose of trading, to go on a business trip; (3) to strike a profitable transaction.[4] This verb is applied both to humans going on trading expeditions and to gods who come to visit the land of the humans in the guise of animals. When the gods come to the world of humans, they come because they wish to receive presents of *inau* and wine. The exchange of presents of *inau* and wine for animal fur and flesh is thought of as a "business transaction." This god-human transaction is at the very basis of the Ainu religion, which expresses it most spectacularly in the bear ceremony.

At home in their own country, the gods have clothing racks where they hang up their different costumes. When they come to visit the human homeland, they always come in their disguises. If they do not intend to trade, they

---

[3] Munro's chapter on the *inau* is especially interesting. Munro, *Ainu Creed and Cult*, pp. 28–43.
[4] Quoted from my unpublished manuscript of an Ainu-English dictionary.

will put on a worthless old coat, but they will put on their best costumes if they want to make a transaction. These costumes are called *hayokpe*, which may mean "armor" as well as "disguise" or "costume."[5] The *hayokpe* is a disguise which is material and perceptible to the humans and which is put on by the god because it is desirable and economically useful to the humans. For example, the god of the mountains (*kimun kamui*), the representative of the mountain game, comes wearing a bear costume (selection 9). The god of the sea (*repun kamui*), the ruler of the food animals in the ocean, comes in the guise of a killer whale (selection 6). Another important deity, the guardian spirit of the land (*kotan-kor-kamui*) comes disguised as an owl (selection 12). Pestilence deities (*pa-kor-kamui*) come in the form of flocks of little birds (selection 26) when they come for their gruesome type of *irauketupa*.

The *hayokpe* worn by a god friendly to the humans is a present brought with him to leave with his human friends. It is not the human hunter who chooses and kills a bear or a deer. It is a god masquerading as an animal who chooses the hunter, voluntarily allows the hunter to kill what appears to be an animal, and gives the hunter the animal disguise as a present. The grateful hunter in exchange presents the god with *inau* or with the curled shavings which are equally potent. The presents given by the humans to the gods make up the wealth of the gods, and the presents left by the gods among the humans enable the latter to survive and to carry on their economic activities. When the god of the mountains comes on a visit, he will leave behind his warm bear's fur, his tasty meat, his marrow and blood, and his internal organs. The humans can make clothing of the fur or use it for trading; they will reverently and joyfully consume the flesh, the marrow, the blood, and the organs; and they will dry the gall, which is a valuable trade commodity used for medicinal purposes.

When a god's *hayokpe* is broken, the god's spirit is released. By slaying the "animal," the humans set free the spirit of the god trapped inside the disguise and enable him to return to his own world. The bear ceremony illustrates this most clearly. After the humans have killed the bear, they lay the bear's head in state and make offerings of food, wine, and *inau* to the god. An elaborate feast is held, and the spirit of the god remains for several days as an honored guest among the feasting humans. The god is seated in the place of

[5] See also note 4, selection 12.

honor at the head of the fireplace (the *ror*), just under the sacred window (*rorun puyar*). During the god's sojourn, the divine visitor delights in watching the humans feasting and dancing and in hearing their songs and epics. Simultaneously, another non-human convocation is going on; the god is being entertained by the gods who dwell inside the human house, especially by the Fire Goddess. For the Ainu, feasting and drinking are important cultic acts by which solidarity with the supernaturals is reaffirmed and strengthened.

After the feast is over, the divine visitor is sent home (*arpare, omante, hopunire*) to his own world. This is what is known as "ritual dismissal." The bear ceremony is called *iyomante*, "sending-off," that is, a farewell ceremony for a departing guest. After his send-off, the god returns home laden with many gifts from the humans. Upon his arrival, he finds his house filled with gifts from the humans. The gifts have been delivered mysteriously in his absence. The more of these presents a deity receives, the more renowned will he be in the society of the gods, just as an Ainu will have more social prestige the greater the amount of trade goods he manages to accumulate.

After returning to his native land, the god will gather together his friends and relatives from near and far and will hold a magnificent feast, using the gifts of wine and food that he has received as presents from the humans. He will speak admiringly of the wonders of the land of the humans. He will tell the gods how well he was treated by the humans and will distribute one or two of the human *inau* to each guest. The gods will all praise him and wish to go to visit the human homeland for themselves. The continuing round of visiting and exchanging of presents must be maintained in order for the humans to enjoy prosperity.

The World of Gods

This section introduces the reader to the world of the gods as they describe it in their own terms. This world occupies the extreme edge of the spectrum of god-human communication, one in which there is little or no human involvement. Some of the gods lead rather dull lives, having no excitement except attending drinking feasts, and others involve themselves in exciting adventures. The humans appear here only peripherally as suppliers of wine and *inau*. But even here, in their own god-worlds, the gods for the most part live in the human manner, and their interpersonal relationships are recognizably of the human type.

This section contains five selections, all from the two most important reciters from the Saru region of Hidaka: Hiraga Etenoa and Hirame Karepia.

1. Song of *Kararat* (Carrion Crow) Goddess

This *kamui yukar* was recorded in writing on October 28, 1932, by Kubodera from the reciter Hiraga Etenoa. It was sung to the burden *Hetkuna ō*. Kubodera mentions that it might also be sung with the burden *Hetuina*. The literal meanings of both the burdens are unclear.

A crow goddess amuses herself by performing the "dance of the glittering treasures, dance of the glittering metals" (*tama kin tapkar, kane kin tapkar*). When she does this dance, acorns and chestnuts come dropping down from her hands. News of this dance of hers spreads among the gods, and she begins to be invited to the drinking feasts of the gods.

The Ainu distinguished between two types of crows: the hondo jungle crow (*Corvus coronoides*), which was disliked and called *shi-pashkur* or *shi-e-pashkur* ("dung-crow," "dung-eating-crow") and the carrion crow (*kararat, Corvus corone*), which was regarded as auspicious. Kayano gives a tale in which a human's life is saved by a carrion crow. (Kayano, *Uepekere shūtaisei*, pp. 63–75).

The text is Kamui Yukar 47 in Kubodera's *Ainu jojishi: Shin'yō, seiden no kenkyū*, pp. 218–20.

I lived
in the Upper Heavens,
dwelling
among the gods.
However,
whenever I would hear
the sounds of feasting,
the sounds of drinking
of the gods
who had received [presents of]

human *inau*
and human wine,
I would always
be longing to have them.

I longed for them
so very much that,
when I would get lonely,
I would stand up and
would do

the dance of the glittering treasures,
the dance of the glittering metals
on the floor at the head of the fireplace.[1]
Then acorns would come dropping down
from one of my hands,
and chestnuts would come dropping down
from my other hand.
Thanks to this,
I was able to amuse myself,
and this was the way
I continued to live
on and on
uneventfully.

Then news spread
among the gods
that I was doing this,
and only then
did the gods
become aware for the first time
of my existence.
After that,
when wine was delivered
from the humans,
I was invited for the first time,
and I was able
to attend a drinking feast.

I drank, and
o how very
delicious
was the wine!
As I drank,
my heart
was very

mellowed by the wine,
mellowed by the liquor.
At that time
I did
the dance of the glittering treasures,
the dance of the glittering metals,
moving up along the floor
and down along the floor.
As I danced,
acorns came falling down
from one of my hands,
and chestnuts came falling down
from my other hand.
Then the gods
began to race each other
to pick up
the chestnuts
and to pick up
the acorns
on the floor.
Sounds of loud laughter,
sounds of great merriment
rose up all at once.
While this was going on,
the God Ruling
the Upper Heavens
spoke these words:

"I did not know
until now
that the weighty deity[2]
the *kararat* goddess
had her dwelling
so very close by,
near my own house.

---

[1] *Rorui-so*, the expanse of floor at the *ror*, the section of the house located at the head of the fireplace near the sacred window (*rorun puyar*). It lies at the opposite end of the house from the entrance and is the place of honor in the house.

[2] *Pase kamui*. A god who is important, of great consequence. The Ainu word *pase* literally means "heavy."

One of the reasons
why I invited
the *kararat* goddess
was because I wished
to apologize to her,
but look
how mellowed by the wine
are her spirits!''
Thus did he speak.

The peerless feast
wore on to its conclusion.
After that,
I have remained
in my own house.
Ever since then,
whenever the gods
are worshiped
by the humans
and wine is delivered,
there is not a banquet,
not a drinking feast
from which I am
ever omitted.
I am always invited
and attend every feast,
and as I drink,
my spirits are
mellowed by the wine.
After that
I do
the dance of the glittering metals,
the dance of the glittering jewels
among the guests at the feast,

and acorns fall down
from one of my hands,
and chestnuts fall down
from my other hand.
The gods
race each other
to pick up
the chestnuts
and the acorns.
Sounds of loud laughter,
sounds of great merriment
rise up all at once,
and I take
delight in all this
as I attend
all the noble drinking feasts,
the noble feasts.

This is the way
I continue to live
on and on.
Whenever wine
or *inau*
are delivered
from the humans,
I am given
portions of *inau*
and portions of wine,
and this enhances
my glory as a deity.
This is the way
I continue to live
on and on
uneventfully.

2. Song of the Fire Goddess

This *kamui yukar* was recorded in writing on September 6, 1932, by Kubodera from the reciter Hiraga Etenoa. It was sung to the burden *Apemeru koyan koyan, matateya tenna*. The first words of the burden mean "fire sparks rise-rise" and are derived from the name of the Fire Goddess, Apemeru-ko-yan-mat, "Fire-sparks-Rise-Woman."

The Fire Goddess dwells in the fireplace of every Ainu home and acts as an intermediary between the Ainu and all the other gods. Worship of this goddess is central in all Ainu religious life. Whenever prayers are addressed to any god, the first prayer and the first *inau* are offered to her. Women are said to regard her as their own ancestor. The Fire Goddess is usually called *kamui huchi* ("god grandmother," Elderly Goddess) or *ape huchi* ("fire grandmother"), but her full name is Apemeru-ko-yan-mat Unameru-ko-yan-mat, "Fire-sparks-Rise-Woman Cinder-sparks-Rise-Woman."

In this song, the husband of the Fire Goddess has been stolen away by the Goddess of the Waters (Wakka-ush-kamui). The Fire Goddess vanquishes the other goddess in a contest of magic powers but spares her life. The husband later returns sheepishly and offers "indemnity" (*ashimpe*) to the Fire Goddess. The Fire Goddess ignores the repentant husband but allows him to stay. The role of woman as the guardian of the family hearth and the relatively independent position of women in Ainu society seem to be emphasized in this song. The Fire Goddess definitely is stronger than her husband in every way.

The text is Kamui Yukar 1 in Kubodera's *Ainu jojishi: Shin'yō, seiden no kenkyū*, pp. 42–47.

Doing nothing but needlework,
I remained with my eyes
focused on a single spot,
and this is the way

I continued to live
on and on
uneventfully.

Then one day
my wedded husband,
my honored husband
went outside
holding in his hands
silver wiping sticks
six in number,
and ordinary wiping sticks
six in number.[1]
After that,
he did not come back
for a long time,
for a very long time.
Nevertheless,
I thought to myself:

"Am I
a deity with weak powers?"[2]

Thinking this,
I paid no attention.
As always,
I did nothing but needlework,
remaining with my eyes
focused on a single spot.
I continued
in this way
for a very long time,
but my beloved husband
did not return

for entirely too long a time.
I thought this
most strange.
Then I stared at
the needle I had been sewing with.[3]
When I looked,
this is what I found:
The Goddess of the Waters
had fallen in love with
none other than
my beloved husband,
my wedded husband.
For this reason,
she had sent for him
and had shut him up
at her place.
This is what the matter was.

Therefore,
I stuck my needle through
the handiwork I was doing
and put it aside.
After that,
I girded myself
with a single sedge stalk.
I arranged my hair
up high
with a silken hood.
I slipped on my feet
a pair of fleeting clogs,
and I slipped on my hands
a pair of fleeting gloves.
I stuck into the front of my robes
a metal fan.[4]

---

[1] Blocks of wood (*hoyaikeni* or *hoyaikep*) used for the same purpose as toilet paper. Because the husband is such an exalted deity, he uses six blocks of silver as well as six wooden ("ordinary") blocks. The husband, in other words, went outside to go to the privy.

[2] The goddess asks herself the rhetorical question: "Why should I, being a powerful deity, be thrown into confusion?" Powerful deities (*nupur kamui*) were slow to respond, and only weak deities (*nupan kamui*) could be rushed into action.

[3] To divine.

[4] The word "metal" may also be used as an adjective meaning "magnificent." It is not clear whether a "metal fan" is meant here, or a "magnificent fan."

Then
I set out,
and I arrived at
the house of
the Goddess of the Waters.
When I went inside,
this is what I found:
On the right-hand side of the fireplace,[5]
the Goddess of the Waters
was sitting by the fireside.
To the left[6]
of the divine lady
was sitting
my beloved husband,
my wedded husband.
I stepped along
the left-hand side of the fireplace.[7]

I was so
terribly angry that
I seized in my hands
the pot-hook hanging [over the hearth]
and shook it
back and forth
again and again.
While doing this,
I uttered
these words:

"Look here,
o divine lady,
Goddess of the Waters!
Listen to
what I have to say.

Since you have dared
to do such a thing,
let us compare
our magic powers!
If I lose,
I will give you
right away
my wedded husband,
my beloved husband,
since you have done this
because you want to marry him.
If you lose,
then you will
never see
my beloved husband,
my wedded husband [again]!''

As I said this,
I took out
the metal fan
and remained standing
rooted to the spot
on the floor
on the left-hand side of the fireplace.
On one side of the fan,
the metal fan,
were painted
many pictures,
countless pictures
of scorching rays of sunlight,
of lethal rays of sunlight.
On the other side of the fan
were painted
many pictures,

---

[5] The *shiso*, the side of the fireplace on the right when viewed from the *ror* (the section in front of the sacred window), is where the head of the house sits.

[6] In the place of honor next to her, as if he were her husband.

[7] *Harkiso* (also called *hekari-so*), the side of the house where guests are seated.

countless pictures
of many columns of flames,
of myriads of columns of flames.
I took out
this fan.
I challenged to battle
the Goddess of the Waters,
the divine lady.

Then
she took out
a metal fan
which was like this:
On one side of the fan
were painted
many pictures,
countless pictures
of frost-laden clouds.
On the other side of the fan
were painted
many pictures,
countless pictures
of summer rainstorms.
She took out
this fan.

She pointed toward me
the part
of the fan with the pictures
of the frost-laden clouds.
Slowly
she fluttered it
in my direction.
As she did this,

a fierce
winter sleet storm
came raining down.

However,
I took out
my metal fan
and pointed toward her
the part of it with pictures
of the scorching rays of sunlight,
the lethal rays of sunlight.
Lethal rays of sunlight,
scorching rays of sunlight
came blazing down.
After a while,
the Goddess of the Waters
was about
to die of sunstroke
at any moment.
Unable to bear it any longer,
she pointed toward me
the side of her fan
with the pictures
of the summer rainstorms.
Fierce
summer rainstorms
came pouring down.

When that happened,
I pointed toward her
the side
of my metal fan
with the pictures
of many columns of flames,

of myriads of columns of flames.
Slowly
I fluttered
the metal fan
up high and down low.
As I did this,
fierce showers
of red rainbow-like sparks
rained down,
and many columns of flame,
myriads of columns of flame
came raining down
onto the floor.
The walls
burst into flames,
and the hems
of the robes worn
by the Goddess of the Waters
burst into flames.
The beautifully embroidered garments
made by the divine lady
which were
weighing down
her long clothing racks
burst into flames.

When this happened,
the Goddess of the Waters
apologized,
speaking these words:

    "Truly,
    what I did was wrong,
    my deeds were wrong,

and this is why
I am now being
punished so cruelly.
But
I apologize!
O most weighty deity,
o divine lady,
please calm
your anger against me!"

When I heard
her say this,
I reflected carefully,
turning various matters over in my mind.
This is what I thought to myself:

    "In the beginning,
    when we were sent down
    from the Upper Heavens
    to the land of the humans,
    we were sent down
    in order to rule
    the land of the humans.
    In spite of this,
    she has acted
    with brazen disrespect
    toward me.
    Nevertheless,
    no matter how I may punish her,
    no matter how angry I may be at her,
    it is not for me
    to kill her in a miserable manner."

Thinking this,

I plunged head first
through the door hangings.
Departing in anger,
I came home
to my house.
After that
I continued
to live on
doing nothing
but needlework.
Then one day
the door opened.
I looked,
and this is what I saw:
My beloved husband,
my wedded husband
came walking in
carrying
a bundle wrapped in a sedge mat.
He put down
that sedge mat
at the head of the fireplace.

Nevertheless,
I did not want
even to turn around
or to glance that way.
I stayed there
without even
turning toward him.
He stared fixedly
down into the center of the hearth
and remained for a time
without saying anything.
Then he opened

that sedge mat
and spread out [its contents]
at the head of the fireplace.
It contained
many precious treasures,
divinely made treasures.
There was a glittering
brightness over
the treasures.
Taking out
the many precious treasures,
he said these words:

"My beloved wife!
Since what I did
was wrong,
I would not dare
come home
without an indemnity.[8]
Thus I offer these
as payment
so that I may come home."

Though he spoke these words,
I did not breathe a word
in reply to him.
After a while,
without saying a word,
he folded up
that sedge mat
and put it
on the stacks of sacred vessels.[9]
After that,
he remained [at home].

---

[8] *Ashimpe*, "fine," "indemnity." The husband apologizes for his infidelity and offers payment of treasures as a penalty.

[9] *Iyoikir*, the piles of household heirlooms or treasures lining the north wall of the house. They consisted mostly of lacquered tubs, boxes, and utensils of Japanese manufacture.

3. Song of Wolf Goddess

This *kamui yukar* was recorded in writing by Kubodera from the reciter Hira-ga Etenoa on the same day as the preceding selection, September 6, 1932. It was sung with two burdens: *Heurur heurur* and *Uɔkar kanto*. Except for the word *kanto* (sky, heaven), both the burdens are semantically unclear.

Wolves (*horkeu*) figure prominently in Ainu mythic songs and tales. They were not regarded as being harmful predators by the Ainu. In fact, the wolves inhabiting Hokkaido in the past caught the plentiful deer for food and did not trouble the Ainu, who admired them greatly for their intelligence and skill at hunting. The Wolf God of the Upper Heavens (*rikun kanto ta horkeu kamui*) is a favorite character in epics, and sometimes the younger sister of this Wolf God is the mother of the *yukar* epic hero Poiyaunpe. She is a goddess of very beautiful appearance who wears white robes. (See below, p. 208.)

The wolf goddess in this song is living with her cubs in the land of the humans. She is attacked by an evil monster bear (*wen arsarush*). The cubs cry out to summon their father from the Upper Heavens. He arrives and defeats the monster bear, and the wolves go home to the Upper Heavens.

The text is Kamui Yukar 27 in Kubodera's *Ainu jojishi: Shin'yō, seiden no ken-kyū*, pp. 158–59.

I was among my cubs
on a meadow beside a brook.
This was the way
I continued to live
on and on until

One day
downstream

noises were heard.
I looked and saw
an evil monster bear,
a vile demon bear,
with his lower fangs
jutting out beyond
his upper jaw,
with his upper fangs

jutting out beyond
his lower jaw,
and with his inner gums
exposed.
The evil monster bear,
the vile demon bear
came this way.
As soon as he caught sight of me,
he glared at me
with his eyes wide open.
Then he attacked me.

After that
we fought each other,
rolling over each other
and rolling under each other
as we wrestled
on the meadow beside the brook.
We took turns
seizing each other by the teeth
and shaking each other about,
as we wrestled together
going in this direction and that.
As we continued to fight,
I bit out
small chunks of flesh
and large chunks of flesh
of the evil monster bear.
In his turn
he bit out
small chunks of my flesh
and large chunks of my flesh.
We continued
to take turns doing this.

The evil monster bear
had
ordinary heart strings[1]
six in number
and metal heart strings
six in number.
I also
had
ordinary heart strings
six in number
and metal heart strings
six in number.

We each continued
to take turns
in cutting
the other's ordinary heart strings
one by one
and the other's metal heart strings
one by one.
As we continued fighting each other,
by this time
I still had left
one heart string,
an ordinary heart string,
and one heart string,
a metal heart string
which he had been unable to get at.
The evil monster bear,
he also
still had left
one heart string,
a metal heart string,
and one heart string,

---

[1] *Sampe-at*, cords on which the heart is suspended. The bear has six ordinary strings and six metal strings. Each one of these must be cut before he can be killed.

an ordinary heart string,
which I had been unable to get at.

"Hear us,[2]
our father,
who must be
in the Upper Heavens,
in the high skies!
Come quickly
to rescue
our mother!
An evil monster bear,
a vile demon bear
looks as if he is
about to kill
our mother.
Our father,
come quickly
to rescue
our mother!"

The gods my children
cried out these words.

Then,
right away,
the Wolf God,
the most weighty deity,
came down
from the Upper Heavens.
In an instant
he gave a mighty kick
to the evil monster bear,
the vile demon bear
and kicked him down
to the Underworld,
the dank land.

Afterward,
we went home
to the Upper Heavens
together with
our cubs.

[2] At this point the burden changes to *Uokar kanto*, which continues to the end.

4. Song of Spider Goddess

This *kamui yukar* was recorded in writing by Kubodera from the reciter Hiraga Etenoa on the same day as the two preceding selections, September 6, 1932. It was sung with the burden *Nōpe*. The significance of the burden is not clear.

Spider goddesses (*yaoshkep kamui*) are worshiped by women. Some shamanesses have them as their companion spirits (*turen kamui, turenpe*), and spiders are also invoked to assist childbirth. The name of the spider goddess is Ashketanne-mat, "Long-Fingered-Woman." The long fingers of the spider are evidently connected with the practice of midwifery.

In this song, Big Demon (*poro nitne kamui*) who dwells behind the Cloud Horizon (*nishoshitchiwi*) comes to marry Spider Goddess. Spider Goddess easily repels the intruder, who turns out to be incredibly stupid and boorish. After the battle is over, Spider Goddess returns to her needlework as if nothing had happened. The Ainu goddess can overcome male marauders easily by using her superior shamanistic powers. Here we have undoubtedly a reflection of the social role of women as shamanesses.

The text is Kamui Yukar 4 in Kubodera's *Ainu jojishi: Shin'yō, seiden no kenkyū*, pp. 55–58.

Doing nothing but needlework,
I remained with my eyes
focused on a single spot,
and this is the way
I continued to live
on and on until

One day

from far out at sea
a god was heard coming this way
with a loud roaring
and rumbling.
After a while
he stopped his chariot[1]
over
my house.

[1] Ainu gods are said to fly through the sky riding aboard vehicles called *shinta*, which is the common word for "cradle." The Ainu cradle consists of a wooden frame with rails at the sides. Cords are attached to it at four places, and it is suspended from a rafter or a branch. The cradle is swung back and forth like a swing to put the baby to sleep. The "chariots" in which the gods fly through the sky, emitting fierce rumblings, are clearly patterned after these cradles. I follow Batchelor's precedent in adopting the word "chariot" for this cradle-like vehicle for want of any better English equivalent. (Batchelor, *Ainu Life and Lore*, p. 291)

All around
it grew silent.
Then after a while,
the voice of a god
came ringing out.
This is what he said:

"Greetings,
o goddess dwelling
in this place.
Listen to
what I have
to say.

"Behind
the Cloud Horizon
there dwells
Big Demon,
and he has fallen in love
with you
and you alone.
Because of this,
he is now
getting ready
to come here.
I have come [to warn you]
because I was
worried about you
in case Big Demon
should arrive
unexpectedly."

The voice of the god
rang out with these words.

Nevertheless.
I thought to myself:

"Am I
a deity with weak powers?"[2]

Thinking this,
I paid no attention.

After that,
doing nothing but needlework,
I remained with my eyes
focused on a single spot,
and this is the way
I continued to live
on and on
uneventfully until

One day
a god was heard moving shoreward
with an even louder
roaring
and rumbling.
After a while
he stopped his chariot
over
my house.
The voice of a god
came ringing out.

"It was not
a lie
that I told you, but
you, weighty goddess,

---

[2] The same response as that of the Fire Goddess. See note 2, selection 2.

seem to have
doubted me,
for you do
nothing about it
even while Big Demon
is on his way here.
This is why
I have come here
to give you
a warning.''

At these words,
I turned and looked,
and true enough,
Big Demon
was on his way.
Thus,
at my sitting place
I set in waiting
Thin Needle Boy.
In the middle of the fireplace
I set in waiting
Chestnut Boy.
At the window
I set in waiting
Hornet Boy.
In the water barrel
I set in waiting
Viper Boy.
Above the doorway
I set in waiting
Pestle Boy.
Above the outer doorway

I set in waiting
Mortar Boy.
After that
I transformed myself
into a reed stalk[3]
and waited.

Just then,
outside the house
there was the sound of a voice.
Without hesitation
some sort of being
came in,
wiggling its way through
the narrow doorway.
The one who came in
was surely
the so-called
Big Demon,
he who dwells
behind
the Cloud Horizon.
He stepped along
the right-hand side of the fireplace[4]
and sat down
at my sitting place
on the right-hand side of the fireplace.
He started to dig up
the hidden embers in the fireplace,
uttering these words
while he did so:

    ''I thought that

---

[3] A contest of magic powers is coming. Spider Goddess transforms herself into a stalk of reed and hides in the thatching of the wall. She will watch as her six servants deal with Big Demon.

[4] I.e., the visitor is acting as if he were master of the house.

the goddess dwelling
in this place
was here
just a moment ago,
but now she is gone.
Where could she
have gone?''

Saying these words,
he dug up the embers.
When he did that,
there was a loud snap
in the middle of the fireplace.
Chestnut Boy
popped into
one of the eyes
of Big Demon.
When that happened,

   ''*Haí*, my eye!''

he cried, and
fell over backward.

When he did that,
Needle Boy
jabbed him
in the flesh on his rump.
When that happened,

   ''*Haí*, my eye!
   Haí, my rump!''

he cried, and
stood up and
went
toward the window.

Then Hornet Boy
stung him
in one of his eyes.
After that,

   ''*Hai*, my eyes!
   Hai, my rump!''

he cried, and
went
toward the water barrel.

Then Viper Boy
bit
Big Demon
on one of his hands.

When that happened,
Big Demon cried:

   ''*Haí*, my hand!
   Haí, my eyes!
   Haí, my rump!''

Crying this,
he went out.
Then Pestle Boy
tumbled down

on top of the head
of Big Demon.

Then Big Demon
moaned in pain,
crying:

> "*Hai*, my eyes!
> *Hai*, my hand!
> *Hai*, my rump!
> *Hai*, my head!"

Crying this,
he went outside,
Then when he went out
through the outer doorway,
Mortar Boy
tumbled down
on top of his head.

Right away
Big Demon
was heard moving off dying
with a loud rumbling
and roaring.[5]

When it was all over,
everything grew quiet all around.

After that,
I came out
by the fireside
and did nothing but needlework,
remaining with my eyes
focused on a single spot,
and this is the way
I live on and on
uneventfully.

This tale was told by Spider Goddess.[6]

---

[5] When gods die, they rumble away noisily across the sky.

[6] The final formula was added by Kubodera. These formulas, which are usually spoken, rather than being sung, are appended at the ends of some of the mythic epics to identify the speaker who is telling the story.

5. Song of Young Killer Whale

This *kamui yukar* was recorded in writing by Kubodera from the reciter Hirame Karepia on February 19, 1936. It was sung with the burden *Inahō*. The meaning of this burden is not clear.

Just as the bear (*kimun kamui*) is the supreme land deity, so is the killer whale (*repun kamui*) worshiped as the supreme sea deity. Whales which were washed ashore were regarded as gifts sent to the humans by the killer whale. The Ainu no doubt admired the killer whale for its ability to kill whales. One of the female kinship groups is associated with the killer whale.

In this song, a young killer whale hero is being raised by his elder sister (his "foster sister"), who addresses him with the respectful term Young Offspring (Wariunekur) applied to the epic heroes. The elder sister punishes him for his pranks, and he cries ceaselessly day and night. One day a shoal of whales comes, and the elder sister and the young killer whale both rush outside. The sister harpoons a rorqual, and the young hero a little whale. After that, they have a whole house full of blubber to eat. The behavior of the killer whale siblings when they are at home is so human that the sister even has an attack of *imu* when she is surprised by her little brother.

The text is Kamui Yukar 18 in Kubodera's *Ainu jojishi: Shin'yō, seiden no kenkyū*, pp. 128–30.

My elder sister
raised me,
and we lived on.
She raised me with
a little toy bow
and little toy arrows,
and we lived on.

Turning around
toward the head of the fireplace,
I would shoot arrows
at the small wine-tubs
and the big wine-tubs.
Turning around
toward the foot of the fireplace,

I would shoot arrows
at the big pots
and the small pots.
Laughing gleefully
to myself,
I would jump and skip about
on one side of the fireplace
and on the other side of the fireplace.

Then, one day,
my elder sister
was weaving a mat.
Turning
her back to the fire,
she would weave one row of weft.
Turning around
to face the fire,
she would weave another row.
While she was doing this,
I shot [an arrow] with mighty force
at the cord tying up her sleeves.
It was amazing
how very
startled she was by this.
She went into a fit of *imu*,[1]
saying these words:

> "It breaks at the top,
> it breaks at the bottom!"

My foster sister
spoke these words
in her fit of *imu*.

When I laughed at her,
she got angry
and sprang up.
She threw me down
onto the floor.
She hit me hard
again and again
with her fists.

I was angry
and began
to cry.
I continued to cry
both night
and day.
Then my elder sister
brought in
armful after armful
of firewood.
She kindled a fire next to me.

> "You irritate me,
> o Young Offspring![2]
> If you cry like this,
> how will you ever grow strong?
> Stop this crying,
> please stop!"

My foster sister
uttered
these words,
but in spite of that
I still kept on
kicking my feet

---

[1] *Imu* is a form of psychoneurotic behavior common among Ainu women. When surprised by something, the woman will act compulsively, such as repeating nonsensical syllables over and over. The fits are regarded as humorous by other members of the community. Women who have fits of *imu* are said to be predisposed toward becoming shamanesses. See also p.47

[2] *Wariunekur*, a title applied in epics to youthful (human) heroes. See note 1, selection 21. Here the young killer whale god is treated exactly as if he were a human hero.

as I cried and cried.

Then one day,
my foster sister
said these words:

"A shoal of whales is coming!
O Young Offspring,
stop your crying
and come quickly!"

Saying these words,
she took in her hands
a pretty harpoon
and dashed outside.
Only then
did I jump up.
I grasped in my hand
a pretty little harpoon
and hurried outside.

I went down to the beach.
I looked out and saw that,
true enough,
a shoal of whales,
a big flock of whales,
was coming this way.

My elder sister
harpooned
a rorqual
and hauled it ashore.
Just then,
a little whale

came along,
splashing with his tail
and paddling with [the fins on] his chest.
I harpooned him with a mighty thrust.

After that,
the little whale
redoubled his strength,
and he pulled me
half-way into the water.
Now I redoubled my strength,
and I thought
I had hauled
the little whale
half-way ashore.
But then
the little whale
redoubled his strength,
and pulled me into the water.
We continued
to struggle together
back and forth
in a mighty contest.

At this time,
my foster sister
bent backward
and bent forward
with laughter.

"I told you,
Young Offspring
that you would be weak
from all that crying.

Now look at you!
One little whale
is too much for you to manage!''

Saying this,
my foster sister
came along,
laughing as she came.
Taking hold of
the pretty little harpoon,
she hauled
that little whale
up onto the sandy beach.

Then
my foster sister

busily set about
cutting up the whales.
We carried home
so much blubber
that our house
was full of it,
and on and on
uneventfully
we lived,
feeding ourselves with it.
This is why
I tell the story about it.

These words
were spoken
by Young Killer Whale.

The World of Gods and Humans

This section contains fourteen selections describing various types of experiences shared by gods (non-human beings) and humans. Gods save humans from famine and tell them how to prevent famines in the future; bears come on visits to the land of the humans; gods bless certain humans and punish others; and the culture hero Okikurmi chastises evil deities. The human-god interaction involves mutual assistance and mutual instruction: Gods help and teach humans, and humans, through their culture hero, help and teach gods.

As mentioned before, food animals are gods in disguise and must be treated with religious reverence (*oripak*) and given presents. The performance of the necessary ritual acts for the "animals" is a religious act essential for human survival, and the very existence of the human community depends on the observance of these rituals by all hunters and fishers. For instance, the salmon are given presents of *inau* symbolically by the observance of a certain rite. No matter whether they have been caught in nets, speared, or trapped in fish traps, the salmon must be individually beaten over their heads with a special type of decorated club (*i-sapa-kik-ni*, "head-beating-club"). This is tantamount to giving them *inau*. The deer are also given individual presents of curled wood shavings, which are considered to have the same potency as the actual *inau*. If the humans neglect to perform these hunting and fishing rituals, the souls of the animals will go home in tears and will complain of mistreatment to their species rulers (the "masters" of the game or of the fish). Famine will invariably result (see selections 7 and 8).

Similar patterns of thought apply to the treatment of spirits of dead ancestors. They also are entertained and given offerings of wine and food which enable them to give their own feasts and enhance their prestige in the land of the dead. A different welcome is given to evil deities, such as the gods of pestilence and disease, when they come to visit. These deities are told that there is famine among the humans, that the village is empty, and that there is nothing to eat but certain types of food known to be abhorrent to these particular deities. They are demonstratively given offerings of these foods. This is supposed to induce them to go elsewhere and seek out victims among humans who are in better circumstances.

This section contains seven selections from Hiraga Etenoa, three selections from Chiri Yukie, two selections from Hirame Karepia, one from Nabesawa Wakarpa, and one from his wife Nabesawa Taukno. Chiri Yukie was a native of Horobetsu in Iburi province; all the other reciters mentioned are from the Saru region of Hidaka province.

6. Song of a Killer Whale

The text and Japanese translation of this *kamui yukar* in the Horobetsu dialect were published by Chiri Yukie in her *Ainu shin'yō shū* (1923), pp. 86–101. It was sung with the burden *Atuika tomatomaki kuntuteashi hm hm!* The meaning of the burden is not entirely clear, but *atui ka* means "on the sea" and *kuntu* evidently means "immense."

A young killer whale shoots a rorqual and her young and tosses them ashore by the village of Otashut. The humans in the village worshipfully receive the whales and send presents to the killer whale.

The young killer whale has twelve elder brothers and twelve elder sisters (six long elder brothers, six long elder sisters, six short elder brothers, and six short elder sisters). The elder brothers and sisters are inept at hunting whales, and the young killer whale finds them ridiculous.

My six elder brothers,
the long elder brothers,
my six elder sisters,
the long elder sisters,
my six elder brothers,
the short elder brothers,
and my six elder sisters,
the short elder sisters
raised me,
and I lived on.
I would sit
on a seat,
a movable seat,[1]
in front of the rows of treasures

and would concentrate
on carving on sheaths
and carving on scabbards.
This was
the only work
I ever did
as I lived on.

Everyday,
in the morning
my elder brothers
would take their quivers on their backs
and would go outside
along with my elder sisters.

---

[1] *Chituye amset. Amset* is a seat, bed, or movable platform. Epic heroes are raised on such a platform, where they sit during the day and sleep at night. *Chituye amset*, literally "cut seat," seems to mean a movable seat, one which can be taken from place to place. Movable platforms 6 feet by 4 and 14 inches high were noticed in every Ainu house by Isabella Bird in 1881. They were placed at the head of the fireplace, and guests sat and slept on them. Isabella Bird, *Unbeaten Tracks in Japan* (New York, 1881), II, 89, quoted by Richard W. Howell, "The Kamui Oina," p. 399.

In the evening,
they would come home
empty-handed
with discouraged looks
on their faces.
My elder sisters,
looking tired,
would cook food
and serve it to me.
They themselves also
would eat.
After the meal
was finished,
my elder brothers
would start
to work their hands busily
at making arrows.
As soon as their quivers were full,
since they all
were tired,
they would go to bed,
and there would be the rumbling
sounds of their snoring.

The following morning,
they would get up
at the first cracks
of dawn.
My elder sisters
would cook food
and serve it to me.
After they all
had finished eating,
once again they would take their quivers

on their backs
and would go off somewhere.

Again, in the evening,
they would come back
empty-handed
with discouraged looks
on their faces.
My elder sisters
would cook food,
and my elder brothers
would make arrows.
This was what they did
all the time.

One day again
my elder brothers
and my elder sisters
took their quivers on their backs
and went outside.
I continued for a while
to make
carvings on treasures.
Then I stood up
on the seat.
I took in my hands
a little golden bow
and a little golden arrow.
I went outside
and looked around.

I saw the calm sea
stretching out smooth into the distance.
Far at the eastern tip of the ocean

and far at the western tip of the ocean
were many whales
splashing about
as they played.
Far at the eastern tip of the ocean,
my six elder sisters,
the long elder sisters
would make a circle,
and my six elder sisters,
the short elder sisters
would drive whales
inside the circle.
My six elder brothers,
the long elder brothers,
and my six elder brothers,
the short elder brothers
would shoot at the whales
inside the circle,
but the arrows would pass under
the whales
or would pass over them.
So this was what
they had been doing
day after day!

I looked and saw,
at the middle of the ocean,
a rorqual
together with her young
splashing about
in this direction
and in that direction
as they played.
After I saw them,

I fixed
the little golden arrow
to my little golden bow
and shot it
from far off.
With this one arrow
I shot down with mighty force
both of them at once,
both the whale and her young.

Then
I cut in two
one of the whales.
I tossed
one of the halves of this whale
into the circle
formed by my elder sisters.
Then
I put under my tail
the [remaining] one
and a half whales,
and moved shoreward
in the direction of
the land of the humans[2]
until I reached
the village of Otashut.[3]
I pushed ashore
the one
and a half whales
just below the village.

After that
I went homeward,
gently submerging

[2] The country where the humans live, the human world, is called *ainu moshir*, which also means "Ainu land." The name for the country inhabited by the Ainu, as distinguished from that inhabited by their enemies, is *yaunkur moshir*, "country of the people of the land."

[3] Otashut is a common place name in both Hokkaido and Sakhalin. It is said to mean "stretch of sand extending from the sea's edge up to the grass upland."

[and emerging]
on the surface of the ocean.
As I moved along,
some sort of creature
came running up
alongside me,
panting hard
for breath.
When I looked,
I saw that it was
a sea wren.
Panting heavily,
he said these words:

    "Tominkari-kur,
    Kamuikari-kur,
    Iso-yanke-kur,[4]
    o mighty warrior,
    o weighty deity!
    Why on earth
    have you cast ashore
    such magnificent game
    for the miserable humans,
    the wretched humans?
    The miserable humans,
    the wretched humans
    are using axes
    and sickles
    to chop the meat
    and hack the meat
    of the magnificent game.
    O mighty warrior,
    o weighty deity,
    go quickly

and take back
the magnificent game!
Even when game
is cast ashore for them
in such abundance,
the miserable humans,
the wretched humans
act like this
without even
thanking you for it!''

When he said this,
I laughed at him
and spoke,
my voice ringing out.
These are the words I spoke:

    "Since I have given it
    to the humans,
    it now
    belongs to them.
    If it belongs
    to the humans,
    what difference does it make
    if they hack at it
    or chop it up
    with sickles
    or with axes?
    Why shouldn't they
    do anything they want with it
    when they eat it
    if it belongs to them?''

When I said this,

---

[4] These three names are used in prayers and mythic epics of the Horobetsu region to refer to the killer whale. The first word (Tominkari-kur) probably means "He who watches over the treasures." The second word (Kamuikari-kur) probably means "He who watches over the gods." The third word (Iso-yanke-kur) means "He who casts game ashore." Whales washed ashore are believed to be presents cast ashore for the humans by the killer whale. *Iso*, translated as "game" in this epic, means any type of prey granted as a boon to humans. Here it is used consistently to mean "whales."

the sea wren
was much
discomfited, but
I paid not
the slightest
attention to him.
Gently submerging
[and emerging]
on the surface of the ocean,
I went on
and arrived
at my native ocean
just before
the sun set.

I looked and saw
my elder brothers,
all twelve of them,
and my elder sisters,
all twelve of them,
uttering shouts
in unison
and milling around
in confusion together
at the eastern tip of the ocean.
They were having a difficult time pulling
that half of a whale.
Feelings of wonder
rose up in me.[5]

Paying no attention to them,
I returned
to my own home
and sat

on my seat.

After that,
I turned around
and looked back toward
the land of the humans.
I saw that
the menfolk
and the womenfolk,
all decked out
in their festive garb,
were doing joyful dances,
were doing dances of rejoicing
all around
the one
and a half whales
that I had cast ashore.
On the grassy downs
above the sandy beach
they had spread out
ornamented sedge mats.
On them [was seated]
the village chieftain
of the village of Otashut,
wearing sixfold robes
fastened under his belt
and sixfold robes
hanging loosely.
On his head he wore
a sacred headgear,
an ancestral headgear.
In his belt he wore
a god-given sword.
Godlike in appearance,

[5] Evidently meant ironically. Chiri Yukie translates this as "I was really exasperated." The young killer whale hero is surprised and amused at the utter ineptitude of his elder brothers and sisters.

he was worshiping,
raising his hands
up high.
The humans
were shedding tears
of joy over the game.

What was this
the sea wren
had said
about the humans
using axes
and sickles
to chop up
the whales I had cast ashore?
Instead, the village chieftain
and the village people
had taken out
their sacred swords,
which they had kept stored away
from of old as their most cherished treasures.
They were using them to cut up the meat
and were carrying it away.

After that,
there was no sign at all
of the return
of my elder brothers
and my elder sisters.

When two or three days
had gone by,
something caught
my eye

at the window.
I looked
and saw that
on the window,
the sacred window[6]
there was standing
a metal wine-cup[7]
filled
to the brim
with wine.
On top of it was
a winged libation wand.[8]
Turning this way and that,
it spoke a message.
This is what it said:

"I am
the chieftain
of Otashut.
With full reverence
we make
this offering of wine."

It went on in detail
about how the chieftain
of the village of Otashut
thanked me
on behalf of
all his people.

"Tominkari-kur,
Kamuikari-kur,
Iso-yanke-kur,
o weighty deity,

---

[6] *Rorun purai* (or *rorun puyar* in the Saru dialect), the sacred window at the head of the fireplace said to face in an eastern direction or toward the upstream. The spirit fence (the fence of clustered *inau*) is located a few steps outside this window.
[7] This may mean either "metal wine-cup" or "magnificent wine-cup."
[8] *Kike-ush-pashui*, a special type of libation wand ("moustache-lifter") with curled shavings attached to it. The family mark is carved on it. This libation wand is regarded as a messenger from humans to the gods, and it accompanies the offering of wine to the god and speaks the message from the humans.

o mighty warrior,
it is no one but you
who has taken pity on us
like this
just when there was famine
in our village
and we were
so short of food
that we didn't know what to do!
Thank you
for having
given life to
our village!
We are so delighted with the game
that we have brewed
a little wine,
and here we make
an offering of thanks
to the weighty deity,
together with
a few little *inau*.''

The winged libation wand
uttered these words
in its oration
as it turned this way and that.

After that
I stood up,
picked up
the metal wine-cup,
and raised it
and lowered it.
I removed the lids

from six wine-tubs
on the floor at the head of the fireplace
and poured
a little
of the delicious wine into each.
Then I set
the metal wine-cup
on the window.
After that,
I sat down
on my seat.
When I looked up,
that wine-cup,
along with the libation wand,
had vanished completely.

After that,
I continued
to make
carvings on sheaths
and carvings on scabbards.
Then by and by
I happened to look up
and saw that
the inside of the house
was filled with
beautiful *inau*.
White mists
were hovering
inside the house,
and flashes of white light
were glittering.
It was a delightful sight,
and my heart leaped with pleasure.

After that,
another two or three days
went by.
Now at last
outside the house
it sounded as if
my elder brothers
and my elder sisters
had come home, pulling
that whale,
uttering shouts
in unison.
Feelings of wonder
rose up in me.

When I looked at them
as they came
inside the house,
my elder brothers
and my elder sisters
were very tired,
and their faces
looked withered and wan.
They came inside.
When they saw
so many *inau*,
they were amazed
and made gestures of worship
again and again.

In the meantime
the six wine-tubs
on the floor at the head of the fireplace
had become

brimming full,
and the aroma of the wine,
the beloved beverage of the gods.
wafted about
inside the house.

After that,
we decorated
the inside of the house
with beautiful *inau*.
We invited
the gods from far away
and the gods nearby.
We held
a peerless wine feast.
My elder sisters
cooked the whale
and served it
to the gods.
Then the gods
ate, uttering
cries of gratitude.

When the drinking feast
had reached its mid-point,
I stood up
and told the tale
of how I had been moved to pity
when famine broke out
in the land of the humans,
of how I had cast game ashore,
and of how the evil deities
had been jealous
when I had prospered

the humans,
and the sea wren
had spoken
slanders to me.
I told them in detail
about exactly how
the village chieftain
of the village of Otashut
had thanked me,
and how the winged libation wand
had come
to deliver the message.
As I pronounced my oration,
the gods
shouted out in unison
cries of *het! het!*
and grunts of *hum! hum!*
Their voices rang out
as they praised me.

After that again
we resumed
our peerless wine feast.
From one end of the festive mats
to the other end of the festive mats,
the gods
performed *tapkar*
and *rimse*,[9]
their voices resounding beautifully.

Half of
my elder sisters,
carrying
wine flagons,

wound their way around
among the guests.
Half of them
mingled with
the goddesses
and sang festive songs,
their voices resounding beautifully.

When two or three days
had gone by,
the drinking feast came to an end.
When I gave
two or three
of the beautiful *inau*
to each of the gods,
the gods
bowed down low,
bending their waists over double,
and made gestures of worship
again and again.
They all
returned
to their own home.

Afterward,
as always
I have lived with
my six elder brothers,
the long elder brothers,
my six elder sisters,
the long elder sisters,
my six elder sisters,
the short elder sisters,
and my six elder brothers,

[9] *Tapkar* is a slow, stately man's dance performed during drinking feasts by the guests one at a time. Sometimes one or two women would support the male dancer by dancing along behind him. *Rimse*, in the dialect of the Horobetsu Ainu, is a group dance performed by both women and men at festivals and feasts; the dancers form a circle and dance around toward the left, singing in unison. These dances could only be performed by dancers dressed in their best festive costumes. There was a belief that they were performed for the gods, who delighted in watching the humans do their dances. A mountain god, out of his desire to witness the Ainu dances again, might visit the Ainu village once more in the form of a bear. (Chiri Mashiho, *Chosakushū*, v. 2, pp. 48–52, 64–74)

the short elder brothers.

Whenever the humans
brew wine,
every time
they worship me
and always send me
presents of *inau*.

Now
the humans
are living
in peace
free from all
hunger
and troubles, and
my heart is at ease.

7. Song of the Goddess of the Waters

This *kamui yukar* was recorded in writing by Kubodera from the reciter Hiraga Etenoa on September 19, 1932. It was sung with the burden *Petru a petru*. The word *petru* is no doubt the same as the word *petaru*, meaning "watering place," that is, the place by the river where water is drawn. The Goddess of the Waters is sometimes called Petru-ush-mat, meaning "Woman-Dwelling-in-the-Watering Place."

The Goddess of the Waters, Wakka-ush-kamui ("Goddess-Dwelling-in-the-Water"), was worshiped by being given offerings of *inau* by the river and at the spirit fence (*inau san, nusa san*) outside the house. A special cluster of *inau* dedicated to the goddess was set aside at the right-hand end of the spirit fence, as viewed from the sacred window. In this song the goddess is also called Petorush-mat (*pet-or-ush-mat*), apparently meaning "Woman-Dwelling-in-the-River." Petru-ush-mat and Petorush-mat are no doubt variants of the same word.

In this song, the Goddess of the Waters, together with the Goddess of the River Rapids (Chiwash-kor-kamui), saves the human race from famine and tells them how to prevent famines in the future by observing the proper hunting and fishing rituals. The role played by the culture hero Okikurmi in this mythic epic is secondary. He appears only as a supplicant on behalf of the human race. Variants of this song were obtained by Kindaichi from Taukno and by Kubodera from Hiramura Kanunmore and Nitani Kunimatsu.

The text is Kamui Yukar 81 in Kubodera's *Ainu jojishi: Shin'yō, seiden no kenkyū*, pp. 368–75.

Doing nothing but needlework,
I remained with my eyes

focused on a single spot,
and this is the way

I continued to live
on and on.

Then one day
something dark appeared
at the window.
I looked and saw
on the window sill
a large wine-cup
filled [with wine]
to the brim.
On top of the wine-cup
there was
a winged libation wand.
That libation wand
went leaping and hopping
on the window sill,
turning around
in this direction
and in that direction.
As it did this,
the winged libation wand,
while it turned this way and that
on the wine-cup,
spoke a message.
These were its words:

    ''The god Okikurmi
    has sent me
    to speak this message:

    'Famine has broken out
    in the human homeland,[1]
    and I have been assisting

my kinsfolk
by giving them
all the food I had,
but by this time
even I
have become
hard pressed.
Nevertheless,
I have brewed wine
with the only food I had,
with the last grains I had,
and I am now
invoking your aid
with wine
and with *inau*.
O Goddess of the Waters,
o Petorush-mat,
come to our assistance,
I pray!'

    ''This is the message
    which the god Okikurmi
    sent me to bear.''

This was the message
spoken by
the winged libation wand.
So I stood up
and put six wine-tubs
at the foot of the fireplace
and put six wine-tubs
at the head of the fireplace.[2]
After that,
I picked up

---

[1] *Ainu kotan*, same as *ainu moshir*. The words *ainu kotan* may also mean ''Ainu village,'' but in this case it means the land or world of the humans.

[2] The *ror* (head of the fireplace) is the section of the house by the sacred window (*rorun puyar*) farthest away from the entrance. The foot of the fireplace (*útur*), the section of the house near the entrance, is separated from the *ror* by the fireplace.

that wine-cup
and emptied its contents
into those wine-tubs.

After that,
two or three days
passed by, and
I invited
the Goddess of the River Rapids.[3]
I invited
the Owl God.[4]
I invited
the God of the Game.[5]
I invited
the God of the Fish.[6]

After that,
the invited guests
were ushered in with much ceremony.
At that time,
I seated
the Owl God
in back of
the big wine-tub.[7]
I seated opposite him
the Goddess of the Hunt.[8]
I seated facing each other
the God of the Game
and the God of the Fish.

After that,
I began to wind my way about
among the guests
to pour wine to them.

After a while,
I began to speak,
saying these words:

"See here,
God of the Game,
and God of the Fish!
I have something to say
that both of you
and all the gods
must hear.
What I have to say is this.

"Famine has broken out
in the human homeland,
and the god Okikurmi
is hard pressed by it.
For this reason,
he has brewed wine
with the last grains he had,
with the only food he had,
and he has sent
presents of wine
and presents of *inau*
to my abode
because he wishes,
by means of *inau*
and by means of wine,
to invoke the aid
of the God of the Game
and the God of the Fish.
This is why
I have invited
all of you

[3] Chiwash-kor-kamui
[4] Kotan-kor-kamui, literally "god who rules the land" or "god who rules the village."
[5] Yuk-kor-kamui, the master of the animals (chiefly the deer).
[6] Chep-kor-kamui, the master of the fish (chiefly the salmon).
[7] This is the position of the chief guest (*sake-iyush-kur*). He is seated with his back toward the north wall, facing the wine-tubs.
[8] Hashinau-kor-kamui.

weighty deities.
Give your consent,
I pray you,
to this request of mine!''

When I said this,
the God of the Game
remained silent
for a time.
Then he spoke these words:

    ''When my kinsfolk [the deer]
go to pay visits
to the humans,
the humans say:
'Spring venison!
Bah, who can ever
eat such meat?'
Saying this,
they throw away
my kinsfolk
with utter contempt
without any *inau*,
and they come home in tears.
I am angry
because of this,
and I have shut up
all of my kinsfolk
in the storehouse.''

Thus spoke
the God of the Game.
The God of the Fish
spoke these words:

''When my kinsfolk [the fish]
go there
to do business,[9]
the humans
kill the fish
by beating them
with rotten wood.
They say:
'Who would ever eat
such ragged-tailed fish?'
They throw them away
with utter contempt,
and my poor kinsfolk
come home in tears.
I am angry
because of this, and
I have shut up
all of my kinsfolk
in the storehouse.''

These words
were spoken by
the God of the Fish.

In the meanwhile,
the two of us—
the Goddess of the River Rapids
and I—were performing
many different songs and dances.
During this while,
the Owl God
remained
with his eyelids
shut tight over each other.

---

[9] The word is *irauketupa*, "to transact business," "to go on a business trip." Animals visit the land of the humans in order to make a definite transaction. In exchange for the bodies they leave, they want to receive presents to take home with them. See above, p. 62.

I pondered
within my heart
what might be the cause for this.
It turned out that
a hair from the head
of a human woman
had gotten into the wine,
and this way why
the Owl God
was angry.

Therefore,
I started to speak,
saying these words:

    "O what a gangling
    hobgoblin of a woman
    am I!
    I did not
    even know that
    a hair of mine
    had gotten into the wine.
    And the Owl God
    had gotten angry,
    thinking that it was
    a hair from the head
    of a human woman!"

When I said this,
the Owl God
popped his eyes open
and spoke these words:

    "O, I see!

One of the magnificent tresses
of Petorush-mat,
the exalted lady,
was in the wine!
And all the time
I was angry,
thinking that it was
a hair from the head
of a human woman!"

Thus did he speak.
In the meanwhile
the two of us—
the Goddess of the River Rapids
and I—continued performing
many different songs and dances.
While we were dancing
my soul [left my body and]
went off.
It went
to the home of
the God of the Game
and opened
the doors of the storehouse
of the God of the Game.
After that
herds of small deer
and herds of large deer
came running out all at once.
They went skipping and jumping together
over the mountain slopes,
the herds of small deer
by themselves,
and the herds of large deer

by themselves.
Then, turning back,
my soul
returned and
came back into
my mortal body.

In the meantime,
the soul of
the Goddess of the River Rapids
[left her body and] went outside.
It went on until
it came to
the home of
the God of the Fish.
It opened
the doors
of the storehouse
of the God of the Fish.
It took down
the baskets with fish in them.
It scattered them
over the river fishing beds.
As soon as it did this,
the fish were
so abundant
in the river fishing beds
that it seemed as if
the schools of fish on the bottom
were rubbing against the rocks
and the schools of fish at the top
were scorched by the sunshine.

During all this while,

the two of us—
the Goddess of the River Rapids
and I—still kept on performing
many different songs and dances.
As we did them,
all of the gods
were watching us
with smiles
on their lips.
After a while,
both the God of the Fish
and the God of the Game
found out that
the two of us—
the Goddess of the River Rapids
and I—had gone
to their homes in their absence,
had opened
the doors of their storehouses,
and had let out
the deer
and the fish.
Although they found it out,
there was nothing
they could say about it,
and they kept silent
as if nothing had happened.

Then
we got on with
the peerless wine feast.
After that,
all the gods
expressed

their gratitude
and went home.

After that,
I did nothing but needlework,
remaining with my eyes
focused on a single spot,
and this was the way
I continued to live,
on and on,
uneventfully.
As time went on,
I spoke in a dream
to the god Okikurmi:

    "When the deer
    went to pay visits
    to the humans,
    they were treated badly
    and went home
    to the God of the Game
    saying
    that they were angry
    because of this.
    This is why
    the God of the Game,
    wishing to avenge
    his kinsfolk,
    shut them up in his storehouse.
    The souls of the food
    did he shut up in his storehouse.

    "[The same thing was true] also
    of the God of the Fish.

When the humans
killed the fish,
they would kill them by beating them
with rotten wood.
The right way
to kill fish
is to cut
willow trees
and to make.
pretty *i-sapa-kik-ni*.[10]

"The salmon
are to be killed
with these.
But they were killing them
by beating them
with rotten wood.
The God of the Fish
was angry
because of this,
and shut up the souls of the food
in his storehouse.
This was the cause
of the famine
in the human homeland.

"However,
your wine
and your *inau*
arrived at my abode.
Using them,
I invited
the God of the Game
and the God of the Fish,

---

[10] "Head-beating-sticks," clubs for beating the fish over the heads. A willow branch about 1.5 inch in diameter is cut to a length of about 1 foot 5 inches. A square-shaped grip is whittled at one end, removing the bark. The bark is left on the remaining half of the stick. At approximately the middle, where the grip part comes to an end, curled wood shavings are made. It was believed to be necessary to beat the salmon on the heads with these clubs to enable them to return to the land of the gods joyfully with presents of *inau*. The beating with the special club was equivalent to giving them presents of *inau*.

as well as
the Goddess of the Hunt
and the Owl God,
and we had a drinking feast.
During the drinking feast,
while the gods
were enjoying themselves,
this is what we did.
The Goddess of the River Rapids
opened
the doors of the storehouse
of the God of the Fish,
and I
opened
the doors of the storehouse
of the God of the Game.
Thanks to this,
there is now
plenty of fish
and deer.
For this reason,
from now on,
you must command
your kinsfolk—
you must
command them
never to do
these things again
from now on.

"One thing more—
You must apologize
both to the God of the Game
and to the God of the Fish

and must worship them
with *inau*
and with wine
on behalf of
your kinsfolk.
You must also
express your gratitude
to the Goddess of the River Rapids."

These words
I spoke in a dream
to the god Okikurmi.
I continued to live
on and on
uneventfully.
Then,
both the God of the Game
and the God of the Fish
expressed
their gratitude to me.
This is what they said:

"Petorush-mat,
o exalted lady,
thanks to you
our kinsfolk
are being treated well."

They expressed
their gratitude.

Okikurmi also
worshiped me,
expressing

his reverence
with wine
and with *inau.*
The God of the Fish
and the God of the Game
also expressed
their gratitude.

The god Okikurmi
worships me,
expressing

his gratitude
with wine
and with *inau,*
and I live on
with my glory as a deity
enhanced thereby.

These words
were narrated
by Petorush-mat,
the exalted lady.

8. Song of the Owl God

The text and Japanese translation of this *kamui yukar* in the Horobetsu dialect were published by Chiri Yukie in her *Ainu shin'yō shu*, pp. 74–85. It was sung with the burden *Konkuwa*. The meaning of the burden is not immediately clear.

The speaker in the song is the Owl God, identified in the title supplied by Chiri as *kamui-chikap kamui* ("god-bird god," "owl god"). At the end of the song the speaker is identified as *kotan-kor-kamui-kamui ekashi* ("god-ruling-the-land, god grandfather," the Owl God, the elderly god). In this song, the Owl God is residing in the land of the humans, of which he is the guardian. At the very end of the song, his work completed, he ascends into the heavens, leaving "a most mighty warrior, a youthful warrior" (*shino rametok, upen rametok*) behind him to watch over the human homeland. According to Kindaichi, there are considerable differences in religious belief about the Owl God from one area to another. In the Saru region of Hidaka, the Owl God is not accorded the same degree of daily worship as in other regions. In Iburi, and even more so in Ishikari, Tokachi, Kushiro, and Kitami, the Owl God is regarded as the second most important cult deity in daily worship, following after the Fire Goddess. In these latter regions, the Goddess of the Hunt (Hashinau-uk-kamui) is not the object of any particular religious cult (Kindaichi, *Ainu no shinten*, p. 120).

The term *kotan-kor-kamui*, applied to the owl, means "god ruling the land." This seems to indicate that in earlier periods the owl was regarded as being responsible for ruling or watching over the human homeland. In a whole series of culture hero epics, the culture hero is pictured as marrying the younger sister of the Owl God (see selection 24).

The other personages who appear in the song include a crow boy (*pashkur okkayo*), a mountain jay (*metot-eyami*), and a dipper boy (*katken okkayo*). The crow is the hondo jungle crow (*Corvus coronoides*), which was despised by the Ainu. The dipper (the Siberian black-bellied dipper, *Cinculus pallasii pal-*

lasii) was regarded as a particularly auspicious bird by the Ainu and frequently appears in epics as a messenger. The Owl God has an important message to sent to the heavens. The first two would-be messengers, the crow and the mountain jay, fall asleep while listening to the Owl God recite the message. The third messenger, the dipper, listens without tiring to the entire message and then flies off immediately to deliver it. The message has to do with famine which has broken out among the humans. The reply brought back by the dipper tells the reasons why famine has occurred. The Owl God teaches the humans in their dreams how to observe the proper hunting and fishing rituals in order to prevent recurrences of famine in the future. The necessary observances are the same as those enjoined in selection 7.

Like all the mythic epics recorded in Chiri's book, this song is most interesting from the aesthetic viewpoint and has many delightful touches.

"Long ago,
when I used to speak,
my voice
would ring out
like the buzzing
at the center of the handgrips
of bows wound with cherry bark,[1]
but now
I feel old,
I feel feeble.
O for someone
who is eloquent
enough to be trusted
with a message!
If only there were such a one,
I would send him as a messenger
to the heavens
bearing five

and a half messages!"

While saying these words,
I beat time
on top of the lid
of a wine-tub with a hoop around it.

Then someone [appeared]
at the door
and said:

"Who but me
is eloquent
enough to be trusted
with a message?"

I looked and saw
that it was

[1] The bows would snap with a buzzing sound when the warriors would twang the strings. The Owl God compares his own voice with this snapping sound.

Crow Boy.
I invited him in.
Then
I beat time
on top of the lid
of the wine-tub with a hoop around it
while I recited
the message which
Crow Boy
was to bear.
Three days went by.
While I was just reciting
the third message,
I looked up and saw that
Crow Boy
had dozed off, nodding his head,
behind the hearth frame.
When that happened,
I flew into
a terrible rage.
I thrashed Crow Boy,
feathers and all,
and killed him.

Then once again,
I began to beat time
on top of the lid
of the wine-tub with the hoop around it,
saying these words:

    "If only there were someone
    who might be trusted
    with a message,
    I would send him as a messenger

to the heavens
bearing five
and a half messages!"

Then again someone [appeared]
at the door
and said:

    "Who but me
    is eloquent
    enough to be
    sent as a messenger
    to the heavens?"

I looked and saw
that it was
Mountain Jay.
I invited him in.
Then once again
I began to beat time
on top of the lid
of the wine-tub with the hoop around it
while I recited
the five
and a half messages.
Four days went by.
While I was just reciting
the fourth message,
Mountain Jay
dozed off, nodding his head,
behind the hearth frame.
I got angry,
thrashed Mountain Jay,
feathers and all,

and killed him.

Then once again
I began to beat time
on top of the lid
of the wine-tub with the hoop around it,
saying these words:

> "O for someone
> who is eloquent
> enough to be trusted
> with a message!
> If only there were such a one,
> I would send him
> to the heavens
> with five
> and a half messages!"

Then someone
came inside
with a respectful manner.
I looked and saw that it was
Dipper Boy.
Godlike in appearance,
he sat down
on the left-hand side of the fireplace.
When that happened,
I began to beat time
on top of the lid
of the wine-tub with the hoop around it
while I intoned,
both night
and day,
the five

and a half messages.
When I looked, I saw that
Dipper Boy
was listening
intently,
with no signs at all
of weariness.
[I went on]
day after day
and night after night,
altogether
for six days and nights.
Finally,
as soon as I had finished reciting,
he flew out right away
through the smokehole
and went flying off
toward the heavens.

Now, the import
of the message was this.
There was famine
in the land of the humans,
and the humans
were on the verge of starving to death
at any moment.
When I looked
to see what was the reason
that this had happened,
I found that it was because
the God of the Game
and the God of the Fish
in the heavens
had taken counsel together

and decided not to send any deer
and not to send any fish.
No matter what the gods
said to them,
they would not pay
the slightest attention.
Thus, when the humans
would go into the mountains
to hunt,
there were no deer,
and when they would go
to the rivers
to fish,
there were no fish.
Seeing this,
I became angry,
and this was why
I sent a message
to the God of the Game
and the God of the Fish
in the heavens.

After that,
day after day
went by.
Then there was heard
a pattering
in the skies,
and someone
came inside.
I looked and saw
Dipper Boy,
now looking even more
beautiful than before.

The features of a warrior
stood out majestically
on his countenance.
He intoned
the message in reply.

This was the reason
why the God of the Game
and the God of the Fish
in the heavens
had withdrawn the supply of deer
and withdrawn the supply of fish
until this day.
When the humans
hunt deer,
they beat the deer on their heads
with pieces of wood.
When they skin them,
they throw away
the heads of the deer
and leave them right there
in the woodlands.
When they catch fish,
they beat the fish on their heads
with pieces of rotten wood.
The deer
come home
naked
and in tears
to the God of the Game.
The fish
come home
to the God of the Fish
holding in their mouths

pieces of rotten wood.
The God of the Game
and the God of the Fish,
indignant at this,
took counsel together
and decided to withdraw the supply of deer
and to withdraw the supply of fish.
However,
the God of the Game
and the God of the Fish
said that
they would provide plenty of game
and provide plenty of fish
if the humans
would treat the deer well
and would treat the fish well
after this.
This message
he recited in detail.

After I heard this,
I praised
Dipper Boy.
I looked and saw that,
true enough,
the humans
had been treating the deer badly
and treating the fish badly.

After that,
I taught
the humans
in their sleep,
in their dreams

that they must not
do such things
after this.
The humans also
suddenly became
aware of this.

Ever since then,
they decorate
their *i-sapa-kik-ni*
beautifully like *inau*
and use these to kill the fish.
When they hunt deer,
they decorate beautifully
the heads of the deer
and give them *inau*.
As a result,
the fish
come home
with rejoicing
to the God of the Fish,
holding in their mouths
beautiful *inau*.
The deer
come home
with rejoicing
to the God of the Game
with their heads newly decked out.
The God of the Game
and the God of the Fish
are overjoyed at this, and
they provide plenty of fish
and plenty of deer.
The humans

live now
free from all
troubles
and hunger.
Having seen this,
my heart is at ease.

As for me,
I am now old
and feeble,
and I have been
desiring to go
to the heavens, but
in the land of the humans,
over which I watch,
should there be famine,
and should the humans
be on the verge of starving to death,
I could not

ignore this
and go away,
and this is why
I have remained
until now.
But now
there are no troubles
to worry about,
and I am now going
to the heavens,
leaving behind me
a most mighty warrior,
a youthful warrior,
to watch over
the land of the humans.

Thus recounted the Owl God, the elderly god,
before he went to the heavens, they say.

9. Song of a Bear

This *kamui yukar* was recorded in writing by Kubodera from the reciter Hiraga Etenoa in 1932. It was sung with the burden *Howēwē hum*. The burden clearly represents the sound of a bear's cry. Songs of bears very often have similar burdens: *Ho wēi ho wēi; Uēwewe wē; Weiwei inou; Wēwa hum*. No doubt these all had similar melodies.

The bear appearing in this song calls himself *nupuri-kor-kamui*, "god ruling the mountain." These gods are gentle, wise, and friendly toward the humans. When they appear in human form, they wear black robes. Other types of bears are ferocious, unreasonable, and violently inclined toward the humans; they are known as monster bears (*arsarush*). However, even bears of a benevolent type could behave themselves violently toward humans on account of a misunderstanding, as is true in this case.

The song gives the whole scenario for human-bear relationships: the hunting magic practiced by the hunters in the mountains, the eery night spent by the fireside in the mountains, the trip down to the human village, the magnificent bear ceremony, the welcome given the visiting deity by the Fire Goddess, the ritual dismissal, the delivery of piles of presents from the humans, and the feast held by the god after his return to his own country. One can understand how central was this bear ceremonialism in the life of the Ainu.

Other bears appear in selections 10, 15, and 31.

The text is Kamui Yukar 6 in Kubodera's *Ainu jojishi: Shin'yō, seiden no kenkyū*, pp. 61–72.

I am
a Mountain God.[1]
My wedded wife,

She of the Shiny Fur—
so much did I respect her
that I did not even allow her to fetch water

---

[1] *Nupuri-kor-kamui.*

or even to kindle a fire.
We lived
on and on,
and finally
a lovely little baby
was born to us.
On and on
we continued to live.
Then, one day,
this is what
I thought to myself:

"If I were to leave home,
I would be worried
about things at home in my absence.
Nevertheless,
I want to go and visit
the god ruling
the Lower Heavens,
for he and I
have become
the greatest of friends."

Thus,
I gave parting instructions
to She of the Shiny Fur,
my wedded wife.
I went
to pay a visit to
the god ruling
the Lower Heavens.
After I arrived
at the abode
of the god ruling

the Lower Heavens,
we began to enjoy
pleasant conversation,
and we remained
day after day
occupied in this way.
As time went on,
even though I was worried
about things at home in my absence,
the god ruling
the Lower Heavens
was so exceedingly
talkative
that I was quite
unable to carry out my intention
of leaving for home.

Then, one day,
all of a sudden
Uncle Crow [appeared and]
kept pecking
and scratching
at the post by the doorway.
This is what he said:

"O Mountain God,
o most weighty deity!
Are you blind
to such a degree?
After you left,
She of the Shiny Fur,
your wedded wife,
decided that she wanted
to visit the humans.

She left behind
your little baby.
She closed up tightly
the windows
and the door
and tied them shut
with leather thongs,
and left him behind.
Ever since then,
that little baby,
your little baby
jumps at the windows
and jumps at the door,
the sound of his weeping
ringing out noisily.
He continues
to scream out in distress,
calling for his mother dear
both night
and day.
Can it be,
o Mountain God,
that you are blind
to such an extent?''

When I heard
Crow Boy,
Uncle Crow
say these things,
I flew into
a frenzied rage
at the mere
hearing of them.
I sprang up.

At the head of the fireplace
I got up
and went rushing
toward the doorway.
I plunged head first
through the middle of the door [hangings].
After that
I went down,
with blasts of wind
whirling in my ears.

I darted down
onto the yard
of my own home.
This is what
I heard.
Inside the house
my little baby
was crying,
his cries ringing out noisily.
Just then,
I headed
toward the doorway.
When I tried
to go inside,
the doorway
was tied shut
with leather thongs.
Then
I cut
the leather thongs.
Breaking down
the doorway,
I went inside.

My little baby
was shrieking and weeping,
was jumping and crying.
He was jumping
at the windows.
Just then,
I rushed toward him.
Picking up
my little baby,
I tossed him up
onto my back
and tied up tightly
the carrying cords.
After that
I went outside,
intending
to go down to
the human village
and to ravage
the human village.

After this,
I went down
along the course
of our native river,
with blasts of wind
whirling in my ears.
As I was going down,
Light-Footed-One
Swift-Footed-One[2]
came dashing out
from somewhere.
He ran around and around
at a distance from me

and stretched his tail
far out
while barking to bewitch me.

Just then,
from behind a tree,
the top of a bow
could be seen protruding.
Overjoyed,
I rushed
toward it.
A pretty little arrow
lodged itself with a thump
on my body.
Two young men
went running away
from behind the tree.
After that,
I began to chase
right after them.

As I went on,
Light-Footed-One,
Swift-Footed-One
stretched his tail
far out
while barking to bewitch me.
He slipped through
right under my neck
and kept running in circles
around and around me.
I got angry
at this
and began to try

---

[2] Names applied to the fox (*chironnup kamui*). Foxes are believed to bark for the purpose of casting spells or bewitching. Here the fox is trying to bewitch the bear.

to strike at
Light-Footed-One,
Swift-Footed-One,
but he slipped
through my hands.
I continued to strike at him
and miss him again and again.
I was quite unable
to get at him.

When I had been doing this
for some time,
the God of Aconite Poison[3]
came dashing out [and said]:

"The Fire Goddess
has sent me
to bear this message:

'O weighty deity,
please come to pay me
a peaceable visit,
and let us meet
to enjoy
peaceful conversation!'

"I have come
to bring this message
from the Fire Goddess."

Thus spoke
the God of Aconite Poison, but
I still continued to strike out violently.
Light-Footed-One,

Swift-Footed-One
still continued
to stretch his tail
far out
while barking to bewitch me
as he ran around and around
at a distance from me
and came dashing up
closer and closer to me.

Just then,
the Resin God[4]
came dashing out.
He and the God of Aconite Poison
working together
wrapped themselves around
my hind limbs
and my fore limbs
and seized me with their hands.
I tumbled down
and lay outstretched
majestic and godlike.
I lost all consciousness
of what was happening.

After sleeping for a while,
I opened my eyes,
and this is what I saw.
I was sitting
on a tree branch,
with my hands and legs
hanging down limply,[5]
and at this point
I regained consciousness.

---

[3] *Shuruku-kamui.* Aconite poison (*shuruku, shurku*), obtained from the root of the wolfbane (*Aconitum subcuneatum* Nakai), was used to poison arrows. The poison god enters the hunted animal, depriving him of his freedom of movement.

[4] *Unkotuk kamui.* Fir or spruce resin is used to attach the arrowhead to the arrow shaft.

[5] A conventional formula applied to the soul after it has left the corpse. The soul of the Mountain God looks down uncomprehendingly on the corpse it has just left, not recognizing that the carcass of the bear is his own.

Underneath me
a big old he-bear
was lying outstretched
majestic and godlike.
On top of
that he-bear
a little bear-cub
was playing.

Just then,
those same young men
came walking back
together.
They whispered
to each other,
saying:

> "It seemed
> as if this was
> a benevolent deity,
> but what was the meaning
> of his behavior just now?"[6]

As they were
whispering these things
to each other,
the dogs
went chasing after
the bear-cub, but
those young men
beat them off soundly.
The bare-fanged ones [the dogs]
went running away.
Afterward,

they picked up
the bear-cub.

Then they began
to prepare[7]
the he-bear
and worshiped him.
Then they whittled wing-shaped notches
on a stick of wood with sharpened endings.[8]
They stood it up
by the side of
that bear.
The young men
worshiped it by rubbing their hands together,
[saying]:

> "Do you deities enjoy yourselves
> by conversing together!
> It has already
> become dark by now,
> and since it is
> too late
> to move the bear,
> we will leave him here.
> When morning comes,
> we will come back.
> Then we will bring
> the weighty deity [the bear]
> down to the village.
> Do you deities both
> watch over each other!"

While saying
these things,

[6] The hunters had thought that the bear wished to be taken by them and wondered why the bear seemed to be so enraged.

[7] An animal carcass is prepared for ritual dismissal according to ancient tradition. The brains and eyeballs are removed from the bear's head, which is stuffed with wooden shavings.

[8] This describes the whittling of a "club *inau*" (*shutu inau*), also called "winged *inau*." It is an *inau* with flaps known as "wings" cut on the stem. In this case, the club *inau* is set up to watch over the bear's carcass overnight. The humans are able to impart souls to the deities they fashion with their hands. Later on, the *inau* god appears to the bear's soul and spends the night with him in pleasant conversation.

they cut
a stick of wood
with sharpened endings,
stood it up
by the side of
that bear,
and worshiped it by rubbing their hands
together.
Then
they put the bear-cub
on their backs
and went down the mountain.

After they were gone,
I wondered
what was the purpose
for which they had
made this [stick of wood]
and left it there.
I continued
to stare steadily
at it, but
once, for a moment.
I looked away.
Then [when I looked again],
a blazing bonfire
had been kindled
and was burning
by the side of
that bear.
A young man
was sitting
by the fire.
He began to speak,

saying these words:

     "O weighty deity,
     come down
     beside the fire,
     and let us enjoy ourselves
     in conversation!"

Thus did he speak.
Therefore,
I went down
beside the fire,
and we began
to engage in pleasant conversation.
While we were conversing,
birds
and different demons
would come
to steal the meat.
Then that young man
would stand up
with a club
and would go running
all around me,
beating off soundly
and chasing after
those creatures who had come
to steal the meat.
We continued to do this
for a long time until
finally
morning came.

     Then

the fire
was gone,
though I was sure
that a fire had been burning right there.
That young man also
was gone.
There was standing there [only]
a stick of wood with sharpened endings.

Thus,
I went up
onto the tree branch
and remained there.
Just then,
many people were heard
coming this way with a noisy clamor.
A large crowd of people
came this way.
Then they began
to skin
that bear.
When they had finished,
the large crowd of people
went down the mountain
bearing the meat on their backs.
The elder one of
those [two] young men
carried on his back
the bear's head
with the skin still attached to it.
So I jumped down
from the tree branch
onto the bundle
of the man who was carrying

the bear's head.
When I did this,
he could hardly walk,
and he was having such a hard time
that I [got off his back and] went
walking down
by his side.

We walked downhill
until we came upon
a human village,
a populous village.
At the center of the village,
an immense house[9]
was seen standing
majestically.
I was seated
in the middle of
the spirit fence,
the *inau* fence
just east of the house.

After I had remained
there for a while,
the Fire Goddess,
wearing sixfold layers
of magnificent robes
fastened under her girdle
and sixfold robes
hanging loosely,
came outside
hobbling along
on a crooked staff,
a magnificent staff.

[9] Literally, "a house the size of a mountain"

"I thank you
for having come to pay me
a peaceable visit,
for it is
just such conduct
for which a weighty deity
wins praise!"

Speaking these words,
she came outside.
After that
I was invited inside.
I went inside
and was seated
under the sacred window.[10]
My wedded wife
was already there
before me.

After that
crowds of young men
and crowds of young women
gathered together.
Those who were making dumplings
went running about
this way and that.
Those who were whittling *inau*
were plying their whittling knives
together this way and that.
They continued to make *inau*
until now
it was time
for me to be dismissed.[11]

I was given
one bundle of *inau*
and one bundle of dumplings
and went outside.
After that
I went on my way
until I came back
to my own home.
I went inside.
Before I had arrived,
bundles of dumplings
and piles of *inau*
had been delivered in
through the window.
The floor at the head of the fireplace
was filled up
with all the many dumplings
and the many *inau*.

After that,
I remained there
for two or three days.
Then She of the Shiny Fur,
my wedded wife,
came along
after me.
She came back
loaded down with
much wine,
many *inau*,
and dumplings too.

After that,
I sent out messages everywhere

10 *Rorun puyar.* A visiting god is seated in state, at the *ror*, the most sacred place in the house.
11 *Hopunire*, to give ritual dismissal to, to send off.

to the gods dwelling nearby
and the gods dwelling far away
and invited them [to the feast].
The invited guests
were ushered in with much ceremony.
Then we began
to hold
the delightful banquet.

My wedded wife
spoke these words:

> "So exceedingly
> did I long to have
> the human wine
> and the human *inau*
> that I went to visit
> the humans.
> Then my beloved husband,
> getting angry,
> came down
> intending
> to ravage
> the human village.
> Were he ever
> to do such a thing,
> however weighty
> a deity he might be,
> he would be kicked down
> to the dank country,
> to the Underworld.
> The Fox God,
> worried about this,
> bewitched you,

my beloved husband,
and thanks to this
your heart was calmed.

> "Since I was afraid of you,
> you were given dismissal
> first.
> After that,
> I requested
> the humans
> to raise
> our little baby.
> Thus,
> I had to wait
> while the wine was being brewed,
> and I was delayed
> on this account.
> This is why
> I have come back
> after [the return of]
> my beloved husband.
> We are now
> holding this banquet
> for all of the gods
> with the wine
> and the dumplings.
> I implore you,
> my beloved husband,
> do not punish me!''

My wedded wife
spoke these words.
All of the gods
also scolded me.

After that
I made many
worshipful gestures
again and again.
Afterward,
all of the gods
left for home,
expressing
their thanks.

After that,
we lived on
uneventfully.
After some time
had gone by,
our dear little child
came back
from the humans
carrying on his back
much wine

and many *inau*.

Once again
we invited
the gods dwelling nearby
and the gods dwelling far away.
The invited guests
were shown in with much ceremony.
After that,
the peerless feast
went on magnificently.
All of the gods
expressed
their thanks
and left for home.

These things
were recounted
by a Mountain God.

10. Song of the Daughter of the Mountain God

This *kamui yukar* was recorded in writing by Kubodera from the reciter Hirame Karepia on February 17, 1936. It was sung with the burden *Weiwei inou*. Like the burden of selection 9, this burden clearly is meant to indicate the sound of a bear's cry.

The speaker is a she-bear, the daughter of a Mountain God (*nupuri-kor-kamui kor matnepo*). Although she comes from a family of benevolent bears who are supposedly friendly toward the humans, she has an evil disposition, and her only thought is that she wants to kill a human. One day she slips out and accomplishes her dream: she kills a human woman. At the demand of the Fire Goddess, the bear maiden goes and restores the dead human woman to life. In spite of her evil deeds, the humans are grateful to the bear maiden and give her a splendid ritual dismissal. The bear maiden repents of her evil conduct and warns other she-bears against doing such evil deeds in the future.

The didactic formula at the end ("I bid you, o she-bears, do not, on any account, do such deeds as these!") is of a type frequently encountered in the *kamui yukar*. In this case the instruction is given by one deity to other deities; in other cases, the humans, through their culture hero, impart instruction to gods. Evil conduct is punished, whether the guilty one is a god or a human.

The text is Kamui Yukar 10 in Kubodera's *Ainu jojishi: Shin'yō, seiden no kenkyū*, pp. 94–98.

I lived together with
my mother,
my father,
my little elder brother,
and my big elder brother.

Ever since I was little,
I had always thought
these things to myself:

"Somehow or other, I wish

that I could see a human!
How I would love to kill one!''

I thought nothing but this
as time went by.

When we would go to bed,
my mother
and my father
would always put me to bed
between both of them.
During the daytime,
they would forbid me
to go outside,
and they would keep watch
over me all the time.
Whenever my little elder brother
and my big elder brother
were about to go outside,
this is what they would say:

"Be sure to keep careful watch
over our younger sister!"

Saying these words,
they would go out.
After that,
they would go on visits
to the humans
and would come back
loaded down
with bundles of *inau*,
bundles of dumplings,
and bundles of wine.

We would invite
the gods nearby
and the gods far away
and would hold
peerless banquets, and
this is the way
we lived
on and on.

Then, one day,
my elder brothers
went outside
and were gone.
Slipping out
when my mother
and my father
were not looking,
I dashed outside
and went down the mountain.

There was a big woodland by a river.
I went down toward it.
I twisted my voice
into subtle melodies of a song
deep within my throat,
and I continued
to bite off
carelessly
the tips of the stalks
of the hawkweed.

"How I wish I would see a human!
How I would like to fight one!
How I would like to kill one!"

Thinking these thoughts,
I walked downhill until
the sound of a song
was heard rising up.
Hiding myself
behind a tree,
I looked and saw
a human woman
walking this way,
a basket with a carrying cord attached
tossed up on her back.
She was twisting her voice
into subtle melodies of a song
deep within her throat.

I sprang toward her
with a roar, and
she ran away.
As she whirled around,
she began to speak,
saying these words:

"O weighty deity,
listen, I pray you,
to what I have to say!
I am
the only daughter
of the village chieftain,
and his only child.
We are both
feeding ourselves
on nothing but
herbs and grasses.
I have come here

to gather lily bulbs.[1]
Do not, I pray you,
[kill me],
mistaking me for someone else!"

As she spoke
these words,
I knocked her over.
I attacked her
and killed her utterly.

After that,
I went homeward
along the woodland by the river,
licking my paws.

When I went inside
the dwelling of
my father
and my mother,
they both spoke the same words:

"Where on earth
could our worthless daughter
have gone?
Look at the way
she has come back—
is it possible that
she has done
some evil deed?"

Saying
these things,
they scolded me.

[1] *Turep*, edible bulbs of the lily plant (*Cardiocrinum Glehni* Makino) growing in shady woods and pounded to make starch.

After a while,
when the day
had come quite to an end,
a message
arrived
from the Fire Goddess.

"Your evil daughter
has killed
a young human woman,
the only child
of a human chieftain,
who lived with her
and depended on her for his food.
Restore her
to life!
If this is not done,
no matter whether
you are the Mountain God,
you, together with
your kinsfolk,
will be kicked down
to the utterly evil country,
the dank country!"²

These words
arrived
as a message
from the Fire Goddess.
[Then my father said]:

"There now! What did I say!
Our worthless daughter,
you went off somewhere,

were gone for a while,
and then came back.
If you did
this evil deed,
go then
and restore
the human woman to life!
If you don't do it
right away,
with my own hands
I will kick you down
to the utterly evil country,
the land of bogs!"

As he said
these words,
blows rained down on me from all sides.
Weeping,
I stepped
outside.

After that,
licking my paws
and weeping,
I went downhill along
that big woodland by the river.

Before I got there,
a large crowd of people
had already come up
and carried
that woman away.
I licked and licked
the blood spattered

² The Underworld

on the leaves of grass.

Then once again
I started to go downhill,
weeping as I went.
I made my way
just east of a village,
a populous village.
In the center of the village
there was a big house.
From within it
the sounds of wailing
were soaring upward.

At that,
I broke through the window
and went inside.
The people who were sitting
all around
the dead woman
sprang up
and ran away.
At that time,
the village chieftain
began to speak,
saying these words:

> "If the weighty deity
> has come here
> because she was worried
> about the wounds she herself inflicted,
> it must mean that
> she has come
> in order to restore

my daughter
to life for me.
Let all the humans
remain carefully
respectful!''

When he said this,
all of the humans
remained
with their heads
hanging down very low.
Then
the humans
undressed
that woman.

After that,
I began to lick
the wounds over and over
from one end to the other.
While doing so,
I blew silently
many puffs of breath[3]
onto them,
while I continued
to lick the wounds again and again
from one end to the other.
As I did this,
the smaller wounds
and the larger wounds
gradually closed up,
and after a while
they healed back again.
Finally,

---

[3] Women (usually shamanesses) blow puffs of breath (*husse*) out of their mouths to drive away evil or to heal the sick and wounded.

I restored her
to her previous form.

After that,
she raised herself up on her elbows.
After that,
I went out
through the window.
Then the humans
tipped their quivers
and shot me with their arrows.
Immediately,
the God of the Aconite Poison
wrapped himself around my legs,
and I became an animal carcass.

After that,
they invited me
inside the house.
At that time,
the Fire Goddess,
wearing sixfold robes
fastened under her girdle
and sixfold robes
hanging loosely,
came walking up
and beat me mightily.

    "You who are
    the daughter of
    a weighty deity,
    what is this you have done?
    From now on,
    it will be well

    if you
    repent,
    if you have
    a godlike disposition,
    a peaceful disposition!''

Saying this,
she beat me mightily.
Nevertheless,
I was decorated with
splendid *inau*
and many different foods
and was given dismissal.[4]

I went homeward,
and when I went inside
my own home,
on the window sill [there was]
a big wine-cup,
filled [with wine]
to the brim.
The winged libation wand
recounted the message
from the beginning
and brought the message
to the end.
Turning about this way and that,
it spoke the message.

My father
put six wine-tubs
at the head of the fireplace
and emptied
that wine-cup into them.

---

[4] That is, I was given splendid offerings and given ritual dismissal (*hopunire*).

Piles of *inau*
were delivered.
We invited
the gods nearby
and the gods far away.
After that,
the peerless drinking feast
went on magnificently.
All of the gods
spoke these words:

    "Even though you,
    o daughter
    of the weighty deity,
    did deeds
    meriting slight words
    of disapproval,
    now on the contrary
    you are being praised
    in this way
    by the humans
    and the gods.
    This being the case,
    we rejoice in you!"

Saying these words,

they drank the wine.
All the gods
went off in different directions.
After they were gone,
I repented,
thinking to myself:

    "What [evil] spirit
    could have bewitched me,
    that I could
    possibly have done those things?"

And so I have continued
to live
on and on
ever since.

Thus, I bid you,
o she-bears,
do not, on any account,
do such deeds as these!

These words
were spoken
by the daughter
of the Mountain God.

11. Song of an Elderly Eagle

This *kamui yukar* was recorded in writing by Kubodera from the reciter Hiraga Etenoa on September 28, 1932. The burden is not recorded; the reciter stated that she had "forgotten" the burden to which the song was performed. Does this mean that the burden had some sacred significance for women and could not be divulged to men?

The speaker in the song is an eagle (*kapachir*). The story is simple but rich in possible meanings. Two women come along and refuse to pick out the lice from the eagle's head. The eagle curses them and predicts that one of them will marry a crow (*pashkur*, the type of crow despised by the Ainu) and the other will marry a rat. Two other women come along. These women pick out the lice from the eagle's head. The eagle blesses them and predicts that one of them will marry a sea god (*repun kamui*, a killer whale) and the other will marry a mountain god (*kimun kamui*, a bear). The prophecies come true, and the eagle is brought presents regularly by the two women who have married the killer whale and the bear.

No doubt this song was of especially deep significance for women, since there were women's kinship groups associated with the eagle, the killer whale, and the bear.

The text is Kamui Yukar 46 in Kubodera's *Ainu jojishi: Shin'yō, seiden no kenkyū*, pp. 215–17.

Having lice
and lonely as well,
I was sorely distressed
and lived on.
On and on
I lived

uneventfully
until

One day
downstream
there were voices.

I looked and
saw that it was
two women
coming this way
carrying axes
to cut firewood.

So
I told them
to pick out my lice.
They were afraid of me
and went running away.
I got angry
at this.

      "One of the women
      will have a crow
      for a husband;
      one of the women
      will have a rat
      for a husband,"
      I said.

After that
on and on
uneventfully
always lonely
I continued
to live
until

One day
downstream
there were voices.

I looked, and it was
two women
carrying axes
coming this way
to cut firewood.

So
I told them
to pick out my lice,
and they put down
the axes they were carrying
and walked up beside me.
Then
they picked out my lice;
turning my little head
this way and that way,
they picked out my lice.
To thank them for it,
I spoke and
said these things:

      "One of the women
      will have a killer whale
      for a husband;
      one of the women
      will have a bear
      for a husband,"
      I said.

After that
those women
went away and were gone.

After that

I lived on
and on until
I looked and,
true enough,
of the women who had not picked out my lice,
one of the women
had a crow for a husband,
and one of the women
had a rat for a husband,
I saw.

After that
I lived on and
I looked and saw
one of the women
who had picked out my lice
coming this way
bearing a present for me
of a bundle of blubber.
She said this:

    "Just as the weighty god
    did say,
    truly enough,
    I have a killer whale
    for a husband and here
    I have come
    bearing a present to you
    of a bundle of blubber," so
    she said.

After that
she went away and was gone.

After she was gone,
on and on
uneventfully
I lived
until

One time
the other woman
came this way
bearing a present to me
of a bundle of bear's meat.
She said this:

    "Just as the weighty god
    did say,
    truly enough,
    I have a bear
    for a husband and here
    I am coming
    bearing a present to you
    of a bundle of bear's meat,"
    so saying,
    she came this way.

After that
she went away and was gone.
After that
on and on
I lived
and during all this time
until they grew old
those women—
one of the women
would come bearing blubber

and one of the women
would come bearing
bear's meat
until they grew old.
They took turns
doing it until

Now finally

I have grown old
and I am now
ascending to
the heavenly skies. So

Said
an elderly eagle.

12. Song of the Owl God

The text and Japanese translation of this *kamui yukar* in the Horobetsu dialect were published by Chiri Yukie in her *Ainu shin'yo shū*, pp. 2–23. The burden given by Chiri is *Shirokanipe ranran pishkan,* which means "Silver droplets sprinkle down all around." This is the refrain spoken by the Owl God at various places in the course of the song. Evidently the burden is not repeated after each line.

The speaker is the Owl God, identified in the title supplied by Chiri as *kamui-chikap kamui.* In the text of the song he is also referred to by his other name *kotan-kor-kamui* ("god-ruling-the land"). For a discussion of the Owl God, see introduction to selection 8. Concerning the owl as a dispenser of blessings, Chamberlain records the following story:

> There are six owls,—brethren. The eldest of them is only a little bigger than a sparrow. When perching on a tree, it balances itself backwards, for which reason it is called "The Faller Backwards." The youngest of the six has a very large body. It is a bird which brings great luck. If anyone walks beneath this bird, and there comes the sound of rain falling on him, it is a very lucky thing. Such a man will become very rich. For this reason the youngest of the six owls is called "Mr. Owl."
>
> [The rain here mentioned is supposed to be a rain of gold from the owl's eyes.]—(Translated literally. Told by Penri, 16 July 1886.)[1]

Two variants were collected by Dr. Kubodera from the Saru region, one from Hiraga Tumonte and the other from Nitani Kunimatsu. In both these Saru variants the speaker is a *kesorap,* a fabulous bird with speckled feathers, rather than an owl. In the variant of Nitani Kunimatsu, the burden is *Akishkato apishka,* but within the text of the song the bird is made to sing: *Shirotani-pe ran ran, konkani-pe ran ran* ("Silver droplets sprinkle down, golden droplets sprinkle down").

---

[1] Chamberlain, Basil Hall, *Aino folk-tales*, p. 54.

In the variant from Hiraga Tumonte, the bird is shot down by a human man who used to be wealthy but is now poor. Being ignorant and ineloquent, he was victimized by false litigation, and all of his treasures were taken away from him. The *kesorap* pities him and imparts some of his, the bird's, eloquence to the poor man. This enables the poor man to take back all his possessions, and he becomes much wealthier than he had ever been before. This song contains the idea that eloquence, given as a blessing by a god, leads to prosperity. Litigation among the Ainu took the form of prolonged oratorical contests (*charanke*), in which the more eloquent of the two litigants emerged victorious.

In the variant from Nitani Kunimatsu, the bird is shot down by a little boy who is raised by his grandmother. The boy's father and mother used to be prosperous but had died in the prime of life. The bird blesses the boy, who becomes wealthy.

In Chiri's variant no reasons are given to explain why the poor boy's family had become impoverished. Social discord is mentioned, and it is necessary for the poor boy's father to ask the other villagers for a reconciliation. The narrative seems to reflect some sort of upheaval which occurred in the Ainu society, perhaps as a result of the breakdown of the highly stratified society at the end of the Middle Ainu Period (on this point, see the Introduction, pp. 9–12).

On the other hand, it is possible that the variants obtained from the reciters in the Saru region may be more archaic in contents than the Horobetsu version published by Chiri. Chiri was highly literate and came from a Christian family, and her version may have been somewhat influenced by modern patterns of thought. However, like the other texts in her book, the song is very aesthetically pleasing.

"Silver droplets sprinkle down all around,   this song,
Golden droplets sprinkle down all around"   I came down
                                                 along the river.
Singing   While I passed

over
a human village,
I looked down
below me.
It seemed that
those who used to be poor
were now rich,
and those who used to be rich
were now poor.

By the seashore,
human children
were playing together
with little play bows
and little play arrows.

"Silver droplets sprinkle down all around,
Golden droplets sprinkle down all around"

Singing
this song,
I passed
over
the children.
Then they ran along
underneath me,
speaking these words:

"What a beautiful bird!
It is a little owl!
Come,
let's shoot arrows at it!
He who shoots
that little bird,

the little owl,
he who is first to take him
will be
a true warrior,
a real chieftain!"

Saying this,
the children
of those who used to be poor
but were now rich
fixed
little golden arrows
to their little golden bows
and shot them at me.
I let the little golden arrows
pass under me
and pass over me.

At that time,
in the midst
of the children,
one little boy
holding in his hands
an ordinary[2] little bow
and ordinary little arrows
was standing among them.
When I looked at him,
I could tell
from his clothes
that he appeared to be
the child of a poor family.
But
when I gazed
at his eyes,

[2] I.e., wooden

he seemed to be
the offspring of a well-born family.
He stood there among them
like a bird of a different breed.

He also
fixed
an ordinary little arrow
to his ordinary little bow
and took aim at me.
Then the children
of those who used to be poor
but were now rich
all laughed at him
and spoke these words:

    "Confound you,
    poor boy!
    If that little bird,
    the little owl
    does not even take
    the little golden arrows
    belonging to us,
    why ever should
    that little bird,
    the little owl,
    take
    an ordinary arrow,
    an arrow of rotten wood,
    belonging to a poor boy
    like you?"

Saying this,
they all kicked

the poor boy
and beat him.
Nevertheless,
the poor boy
paid not the slightest
attention to them
and took aim at me.
When he did this,
I was seized
by feelings of sympathy for him.

    "Silver droplets sprinkle down all around,
    Golden droplets sprinkle down all around"

Singing
this song,
I circled around
slowly
in the heavenly skies.
The poor boy
planted one of his legs
far away
and planted his other leg
nearby.
He bit hard
on his lower lip
and took aim. Then,
he released [the arrow] with a snap.
The little arrow
gleamed brightly
as it came this way.
At that time
I stretched out
my hand

and grasped
that little arrow.
I fluttered about again and again.
I plunged downward,
with blasts of wind
whirling in my ears.

When I did this,
those children
all came running.
Kicking up
fierce sprays of sand,
they raced toward me.
At the very moment when
I tumbled down
onto the ground,
the poor boy
was the first one
to reach me
and grab me.

When that happened,
the children
of those who used to be poor
but were now rich
came running up
afterward.
Spilling out
many words of abuse,
countless words of abuse,
they all pushed
the poor boy
and beat him.

"The despicable boy,
the poor boy
has beat us
at what we were trying
to do first!"

When they said this,
the poor boy
bent his body over me
and clutched me to his belly.
He continued doing this
for a very long time, and then
darted out
from the crowd.
Then
there were the sounds of running
with hurried steps.
The children
of those who used to be poor
but were now rich
threw rocks
and pieces of wood
at him, but
the poor boy
paid not the slightest
attention.
He went running along,
kicking up
fierce sprays of sand.

Then we arrived
outside a house,
a little house.
The little boy

put me inside
through the sacred window.
While he did that,
he began to speak.
He told exactly
the story of
what had happened.

From inside the house,
an elderly couple
came walking up,
raising their hands
and lowering their hands
to shade their eyes.
When I looked at them,
although they were
very poor,
both of them had
the facial features
of a well-born man and woman.
When they saw me,
they bowed down low,
bending their waists over double.
The old man
straightened
his girdle
and worshiped me.

    "O Owl God,
    o weighty deity,
    thank you
    for having come
    to our humble house
    in all our poverty!

In the old days,
I used to
count myself
among the well-born,
but now
I have become
poor and despised
as you can see.
It would be presumptuous
for such as me
to give lodging
to the Owl God,
the weighty deity,
but since today
it is now dark already,
we will give lodging
to the weighty deity.
Then tomorrow
we will send
the weighty deity home[3]
even if only with *inau*."

Speaking these words,
he made countless
gestures of worship
again and again.
The old woman
spread out
ornamented sedge mats
underneath
the sacred window
and placed me on them.
After that
they all

---

[3] *Omante*, to send off, to give ritual dismissal (synonymous with *hopunire*).

went to bed, and right away
there were the rumbling
sounds of their snoring.

I remained
sitting
between the ears
of my body. Then,
when midnight came,
I stood up.

    "Silver droplets sprinkle down all around,
    Golden droplets sprinkle down all around"

Singing
this song
very softly,
I went jumping around
that little house
on one side of the fireplace
and on the other side of the fireplace,
making tinkling noises as I went.
When I flapped my wings,
all around me
beautiful treasures,
magnificent treasures
came dropping down,
making tinkling noises.
Within a short while,
I had filled up
that little house
with beautiful treasures,
magnificent treasures.

    "Silver droplets sprinkle down all around,
    Golden droplets sprinkle down all around"

Singing
this song,
within a short while
I had changed
that little house
into a splendid house,
a big house.
Inside the house
I made up
magnificent piles of sacred vessels.
I made quickly
magnificent robes,
beautiful ones,
and decorated the inside
of the house with them.
I decorated
the inside
of that house
more beautifully than
the dwelling of a well-born man.
When I finished,
I pretended that
I had been there all the time
and remained
sitting
between the ears
of my armor.[4]

I showed a dream
to the people of the house:
A well-born human

---

[4] The "armor" or "costume" (*hayokpe*) of a god is the outward form he assumes when he comes on a visit to the humans. Chiri Yukie adds the following note: "Birds and animals, when they are in the mountains, are not visible to human eyes, but they each have houses like those of the humans, and they all live in the same form as humans. When they appear in the human villages, they are said to appear wearing armor. The carcasses of birds and animals are the armor. The real body is not visible, but it is said to be between the ears of the carcass." *Ainu shin'yo shū*, pp. 12–13. See also pp. 62–63.

has bad luck
and becomes poor.
Those who used to be poor
but are now rich
insult him
and treat him badly.
Seeing this,
I take pity on him.
Even though I
am by no means
a low-ranking deity,
I spend the night
in the house of the humans
and prosper them.
This I made known
to them [in the dream].

A little while
after that,
morning came,
and the people of the house
all got up
at once.
Rubbing their eyes again and again,
they looked around them.
Then all of them
fell down [in amazement]
on the floor.
The old woman
wept
loud and long.
The old man
shed
many sparkling teardrops,

countless sparkling teardrops.
After a while,
the old man
stood up,
came up toward me,
and made countless
gestures of worship
again and again.
While he did this,
he spoke these words:

"I thought that
it was a dream,
that I was asleep,
but—amazing thing!—
it has really happened!
We would have been grateful enough
if he had done nothing more
than just come
to our humble house,
in all our poverty
and all our misery.
But the Owl God,
the weighty deity
has taken pity
on us for
our misfortunes
and has given us
the most weighty
of all blessings!"

Saying this,
he worshiped
tearfully.

Then the old man
cut trees
for making *inau*.
He whittled
beautiful *inau*
and decorated me with them.
The old woman
straightened
her girdle
and had the little boy
help her
to gather firewood
and to draw water
in preparation
for brewing the wine.
Within a short while
they put six wine-tubs
at the head of the fireplace.

After that,
I amused myself in conversation
with the Fire Goddess
about different topics
of news among the gods.

When two or three days
had gone by,
the aroma of the wine,
the beloved
beverage of the gods,
wafted about
inside the house.

At that time,

they dressed
the little boy
on purpose
in old clothes
and sent him out
to invite
all the people
throughout the village
who used to be poor
but were now rich.
I looked after him [and saw that]
when the little boy
would go into
each house
and would speak the message,
those who used to be poor
but were now rich
would laugh together [saying]:

    "What in the world
    does it mean?
    The poor people
    are presuming
    to brew
    some kind of wine
    and to invite us
    to some kind of a feast.
    Let's all go
    and see
    what this is all about,
    and have a good laugh at them!"

Saying these things,
a large crowd of them

got together
and came walking this way.
From far away,
when they had merely caught a glimpse
of the house alone,
they were astounded
and ashamed.
Some of them turned back right away.
Others came up
as far as the outside of the house
and fell down [in amazement].

Just then
the lady of the house
came outside
and invited
all of them inside.
When she brought them inside,
all of them
came creeping
and crawling
inside,
and none of them dared
even to raise their faces.

After that,
the master of the house
stood up
and made an oration,
his voice ringing out clear
like the voice of the cuckoo.
He told in detail
the story
of what had happened.

"Being poor,
we were unable
to visit each other
without reserve,
but now
the weighty deity
has taken pity on me.
Since I was
never guilty
of any evil deeds,
I have been blessed
like this. So,
since we
in the village
are all one people,
from now on
let us all
be friendly with each other
and go to visit each other!
This is what
I request of you."

When he had spoken
this oration,
all the people
raised and lowered
their outstretched hands
again and again
and apologized
to the master of the house.
They agreed
that they would be friendly with each other
from then on.
I also

was worshiped by them.

After that, the spirits
of all the people
were softened,
and they held
a peerless drinking feast.
As for me,
I enjoyed conversation
with the Fire Goddess,
the God of the House,[5]
and the Goddess of the Spirit Fence,[6]
while taking delight
in watching
the humans
as they performed *tapkar*
and *rimse*.

When two or three days
had gone by,
the drinking feast came to an end.
Seeing that
the humans
were now friendly with each other,
my heart was at ease.
I bade farewell
to the Fire Goddess,
the God of the House,
and the Goddess of the Spirit Fence.

After that,
I went back
to my own home.
Before I arrived there,

my own home
had been filled
with beautiful *inau*
and delicious wine.
At that time,
I sent out messages
to the gods nearby
and the gods far away,
inviting them,
and I held
a peerless drinking feast.
During the drinking feast,
I told the story
to the assembled gods.
When I recounted in detail
how I had visited
the human village,
and told what had happened
and what had taken place,
the gods
praised me.
When the gods
left for home,
I gave them each
two or three
of the beautiful *inau*.

When I turn my glance
toward that human village,
everything now
is peaceful.
The humans
are all
friendly with each other.

---

[5] *Chise-kor-kamui*. The God of the House, the guardian of the household, is said to reside in the northeast corner of the house, that is, among the treasures at the head of the fireplace. He joins with the Fire Goddess in guarding and protecting the house and is sometimes said to be the husband of the Fire Goddess. The "body" of the god is made at the time when the house is built and consists of an effigy made of lilac or pagoda-tree wood to which curled shavings are attached.

[6] *Nusa-kor-huchi*. The goddess ruling the spirit fence, the place where the gods customarily assemble for conversation. When the goddess appears in visible form, she assumes the form of a serpent.

That old man
now rules the village.
The little boy
has now
grown up
into a man.
He has a wife
and children.
He takes good care of
his father
and his mother,
Whenever
he brews wine,

at the beginning of the feast
he always worships me
with offerings of *inau*
and offerings of wine.

I also
continue forever
to hover behind[7]
the humans
and always watch over
the land of the humans.

Thus recounted the Owl God.

[7] I.e., to give them supernatural protection.

13. Song of the Thunder God

This *kamui yukar* was recorded in writing by Kubodera from the reciter Hiraga Etenoa on August 31, 1932. It was sung with two burdens: first *Rittunna*, then *Humpakpak*. The shift in burdens in the course of the song obviously signals a change in mood. The speaker is the Thunder God (*kanna kamui*). Thunder gods are depicted as dwelling in the Upper Heavens (*rikun kanto*). They assume the form of fiery serpents or dragons.

This song was widely disseminated and has been collected in many variants. The speaker, the Thunder God, flies down to admire the beauties of the human homeland. As he flies upstream along the Shishirmuka river, he comes over the village of one chieftain (sometimes identified as the culture hero Okikurmi, sometimes not specifically identified). The village chieftain commands his kinsfolk to maintain a reverent attitude (*oripak*), for a weighty deity has come. The entire village immediately assumes an attitude of reverence. Then he goes upstream along the Shishirmuka until he comes over the village of another chieftain (sometimes identified as Samai-un-kur). This chieftain gives the identical command, sometimes including an injunction against sharpening knives and weaving mats. Evidently it was taboo for women to weave mats and for men to sharpen knives during a thunderstorm. The command is disobeyed by impious individuals in the village, and the Thunder God, enraged, rains down a shower of sparks and embers. The village of the second chieftain is destroyed by fire.

In a number of mythic epics, the culture hero figure is split up into two antipodal personalities, called Okikurmi and Samai-un-kur in the Saru dialect. In the Saru region, Okikurmi performs heroic feats and is wise and good, while Samai-un-kur is stupid, weak, and destructive. Chiri derives the word Okikurmi from words meaning "he wears a leather robe with a shiny hem," perhaps a shaman's costume, but this derivation is dubious.[1] Somewhat more plausible is Chiri's derivation of Samai-un-kur from a

---

[1] Chiri Mashiho, "Jushi to kawauso," p. 66.

conjectural *saman-ye-kur* > *samai-ye-kur* > *samai-un-kur*, which would mean "shaman-speaking god" or "shamanizing god."[2]

The typical story about Okikurmi and Samai-un-kur, which is repeated with many variations in a large number of mythic epics, can be summarized as follows in skeleton form: A deity visits two villages or two persons. He is insulted in village A (or by person A), and he is greeted worshipfully in village B (or by person B). The deity responds by bringing misfortune on village A (person A) and blessing village or person B. The story is extremely popular in the mythic epics, no doubt because it is short and can be conveniently sung in these short songs with burdens, and also because the content must have appealed to the native sense of ethics.

The text of this selection is Kamui Yukar 76 in Kubodera's *Ainu jojishi: Shin'yō, seiden no kenkyū*, pp. 347–50.

I wanted to see
the human land
and so
I came down to
the human country.
I came down to
the top of the country.
the country of the *repunkur*.[3]
After that
I came down to
the country of the *yaunkur*.[4]
I came shoreward
heading toward
the mouth
of the Shishirmuka.[5]

After that
upstream along

the Shishirmuka river
I moved myself along
with a leisurely traveling,
and I cast my glance
out over the face of the country.
The human country,
the human land,
it was because
I had wanted to see it
that I had come down,
and now my heart leaped
with pleasure at
the beauties of the land,
the beauties of the country
as
I moved on
slowly, leisurely
upstream along

[2] Chiri Mashiho, *Bunrui Aini-go jiten*, vol. 1, p. 89.
[3] "People of the sea," "islanders." The name of the alien race living north of the Ainu. This people has been identified with the people of the Okhotsk culture and were the enemies of the Ainu. See Introduction, pp. 40–44.
[4] "People of the land," "mainlanders." The name applied by the Ainu to themselves in the epics.
[5] A mythical name for the Saru river in Hidaka.

the Shishirmuka river.

The chieftain ruling over
the section midway along
the Shishirmuka river
was Ainurakkur,
the god Okikurmi.
I moved on
slowly, leisurely
over his village.

Just then
the village chieftain
the god Okikurmi,
Ainurakkur,
appeared at the window.
To the head of his village,
to the foot of his village
he called out
saying these words:

> "It sounds
> as if a weighty god
> were traveling by.
> Let both the womenfolk
> and the menfolk as well
> carefully
> maintain an attitude of reverence!"

These words
he called out
to the head of the village,
to the foot of the village.
Oh how very

readily they obeyed!
Both the womenfolk
and the menfolk
remained respectful.

Looking at this,
I moved on
slowly, leisurely
upstream along
the Shishirmuka river until
I moved
slowly, leisurely
over the village of
Samai-un-kur.

Samai-un-kur
the village chieftain,
appeared at the window.
To the head of the village,
to the foot of the village
he called out
saying these words:

> "It sounds
> as if a weighty god
> were traveling by.
> Let my kinsfolk
> carefully
> maintain
> an attitude of reverence!"

He called this out
to the head of the village,
to the foot of the village.

Then
from one of the houses
a woman
came out
in this way:
she came out
carrying
a pot full of dirty water,
and she threw out
that dirty water while
uttering
these words:

> "What if it be a god?
> Does that mean then
> that we are not
> to cook meals?"

Saying this,
she threw out
that dirty water
and went back inside.

From one of the houses
a woman came out
in this way:
she came out
carrying
a handful of rushes.
That handful of rushes
she dipped in the water
and shook it
straight at my face,
saying these words:

> "Suppose it be a god!
> Does this mean that
> one is not allowed
> to weave mats?"

Saying this,
she shook
that handful of rushes
straight at my face.
Then
she went back inside and was gone.

At this[6]
I got angry and so
I hit and hit
the head of my chariot
and hit and hit
the foot of my chariot.
As I did this
its metal cords,
the thin cords
and the thick cords,
tightened up
with a very loud
shrill whistling.
The thin cord tips
whistled shrilly,
and the thick cord tips
hummed and rumbled.

As this went on
from the top of the chariot,
the metal chariot,
a rainbow of sparks

---

[6] Here the burden changes from *Rittunna* to *Humpakpak*.

went flying up.

Then
Samai-un-kur's
village,
from the head of the village
to the foot of the village,
burst into flames.

Where that village,
where the village had been,
only charred sticks of wood
were left jutting up.
Looking back
behind me,
I departed in anger
and went back
toward the Upper Heavens,
toward my home.

After that
I turned around and looked
behind me
and saw this:

I had thought
that no humans,
not a single one,
would remain alive, but
the two women,
the ones I had punished,
were still alive.

I got angry and
wanted
the humans
to know
that such things
are punished by the gods. So
the one I punished more
I stuck a poplar leaf
to her genitals,
and the one I punished less
I stuck an oak leaf
to her genitals.

These things
recounted
the Thunder God.

14. Song of a Dragon God

This *kamui yukar* was recorded in writing by Kubodera from the reciter Hiraga Etenoa on September 28, 1932. It was sung with the burden *Tōkantō*. It does not appear to have any particular meaning, and there are other songs with similar burdens (*Tōkanakana tōkantō, Tōkina tō, Kinatō kantō, Tanne tō*).

The speaker is a dragon god (*sak-somo-ayep*). Dragons are always depicted as living in lakes or swamps and emitting a terrible stench. They are variously called *hoyau* ("snake"), *chatai* (a loan word from the Japanese *jatai* which may mean "snake" or "dragon"), and *sak-somo-ayep*. The latter term means "that which must not be mentioned in the summer." The dragons thrive in heat and abhor the cold, and it is taboo to mention them during the summer or by the fireside. Dragons are sometimes companion spirits of shamanesses. This is one of the very numerous mythic epics in which the culture hero chastises evil deities. A human bids the dragon in the lake to go upstream, promising that he will be treated well and will find a wife. When the dragon follows this advice, he is stung to death by hornets (*shi-soya*). All the time, it was Okikurmi who had deceived him and driven him from his home. There is a didactic ending in which the dragon warns other dragons not to repeat his misdeeds.

The text of this selection is Kamui Yukar 38 in Kubodera's *Ainu jojishi: Shin'yō, seiden no kenkyū*, pp. 189–94.

I lived all alone
in my big lake,
at the head of the lake.
On and on
uneventfully
I lived.

If any gods
or any humans
came close
to my big lake,
they would all die
because of my stench.

This is the way
I lived
on and on.

Then one day
there was the sound of voices
downstream.
I looked
and saw that it was
a young human man
coming this way.

>"When even the gods
>come close
>to my big lake,
>they all die.
>This one who comes
>must surely
>want to die!"

Thinking this,
I waited there.
He kept coming until
he had come down
beside the shore
of my big lake.
He remained
standing there
for a very long time.
Then he said:

>"Greetings,
>o deity dwelling
>in this place!

Listen to
what I have to say!
The truth
of the matter
is this:
When you were sent down
from the Upper Heavens
to this land of the humans,
the gods took counsel together
and decided
that you were to be sent down
to this big lake
and were to dwell
in this big lake.
Since this was
what the gods decided,
you were sent down
to this big lake,
and you have
been dwelling
in this big lake
until now.

>"Nevertheless,
>you have now
>grown tired
>of this place.
>For this reason,
>I have come here
>to teach you
>where to go.

>"Go right away
>up along the river

from here.
When you have gone
far upstream,
there will be a fork in the river.
Go upstream along
the river flowing down from the west.
As you go on and on,
you will finally come
to the headwaters
of the river flowing down from the west.
When you look out
in front of you,
this is what you will see.

''There will be
a populous village,
stretching out peacefully
into the distance.
In the center of the village
there will be
an immense house,[1]
a big house
standing there
majestically.
Outside the house
crowds of young women
and crowds of young men
will be pounding grain
to make dumplings.

''Go on
through the village,
and when you come
to the yard outside

that big house,
without hesitation
go right inside
that big house.
When you go in,
an old man
and an old woman
will be sitting
side by side
on the right-hand side of the fireplace.
When you sit down
by the fireside,
the old man
will say these words:

'My daughter,
listen to
what I have to say.
I am without an heir,
and you are
my only child.
The gods took counsel together
and decided
that I should marry you
to a weighty deity.
If this were done,
he would care for me
for the rest of my life.
Well, it was decided
by the counsel of the gods
that I should marry you
to the Dragon God,
the weighty deity.
Now

[1] Literally, "a house the size of a mountain"

the god my nephew[2]
has come.
Feed him!'

"The old man
will say these words.
At that time,
crowds of young men
and crowds of young women
will gather
until the house is full of them.
They will be
running about busily
this way and that
to cook dumplings.
At that time,
they will bring in
a fish of silver.
It will be placed
on a silver chopping block
and will be laid
at the head of the fireplace.
That fish
will be meant
for you to eat.
You will make
worshipful gestures
toward the fish of silver
and will eat it.
It will be
more delicious than
any other fish.

"After you have

eaten it,
you will marry
that old man's
daughter,
and this will truly
enhance your glory
as a deity.
Therefore,
I have come
to teach you
where to go."

The young human man
spoke
these words.
I laughed inwardly
in amusement,
thinking to myself:

   "Who is he,
   a mere human,
   to teach me
   what I am to do!"

I remained there
thinking this.
That young man
went away.

After he left,
I continued
to live on until
one day
I decided that I wanted to go

---

[2] I.e., my son-in-law

upstream along the river.
Therefore, I began
to go slithering,
creeping up
along the river.
After that,
I went on and on.
When I had come
far upstream,
there was a fork in the river.
I went upstream along
the river flowing down from the west.
I went on and on until
I came to
the headwaters of the river.

When I looked out
in front of me,
true enough,
there was
a populous village
stretching out peacefully
into the distance.
Looking at it,
I went slithering along,
I went creeping along.
As I went on,
in the center of the village
there stood
an immense house,
a big house.
Outside the house
crowds of young men
and crowds of young women

had gathered together
to pound grain
and were pounding grain
to make dumplings.

I went
to the yard outside the house.
At that time,
it was incredible
how very afraid of me
they seemed to be.
Nevertheless,
without hesitation,
I went inside.
I walked along the floor
on the left-hand side of the fireplace
and walked up
by the fireside.
On the right-hand side of the fireplace,
by the fireside
an old man
and an old woman
were sitting
side by side.
Crowds of young men
and crowds of young women
came inside
until the house was full of them.
They went running about busily
this way and that
to cook dumplings.

At that time
the old man

spoke these words:

"My daughter,
the gods took counsel together
and decided
that I was to marry you
to the Dragon God,
my nephew god.
Now at last
he has come."

When he said this,
they brought in
from outside
a fish of silver.
The fish of silver
was laid
on top of
a silver chopping block.
After that,
the old man
spoke these words:

"At any rate,
you have come
now
to dwell here
as my son.
This fish of silver
has been brought in
for you to eat."

The old man
spoke these words.

Therefore,
I drew that chopping block
toward myself.
They gave it to me
along with
a silver carving knife.
Then I began
to eat
that fish.
When I tasted it,
it was incredible
how very
delicious it was.
I ate and ate
until I had finished it all.

Then
quite suddenly
my belly
started to hurt.
After that,
I writhed
and tossed about
lying flat on my back
on the floor
on the left-hand side of the fireplace.

Until that very moment
I had thought
that there was a house there,
and that I
was in it,
but now the house
was gone.

I had thought
that there were
crowds of young men
and crowds of young women.
But the fact of the matter was this:
Actually
I had been sent
to the land of the hornets,
to the country of the hornets.

The old man
spoke these words:

"Listen,
you dragon,
to what I have to say.
I am
the master of the hornets.
I was sent down
from the Upper Heavens
together with my kinsfolk
to dwell
in this place.
Since I dwell
in a desolate country,
even the gods
are afraid
of my fierce disposition.
Thus, I had thought
that no one,
not even any of the gods,
would dare to come near
my abode.
Then the god Okikurmi

found out
somehow or other
where I live.
In order to punish you
for your evil deeds,
for your evil disposition,
the god Okikurmi
deceived you
and sent you
to my place.
Before sending you here,
he sent a message,
saying these things:

'If he were
to dwell
in the human homeland,
in the land of the humans,
neither the gods
nor the humans
would be able
to survive.
O master of the hornets,
o weighty deity,
you and you alone
can I rely on
for your bravery.
I am going to send
the Dragon God,
the utterly evil deity,
to your place.
Punish him
on my behalf,
I pray you.'

"Thus, the god Okikurmi
[said that he would] send you here.
And now,
true enough,
he has sent you here.
This is why
I am now
punishing you.
Now, after this,
you will never
be able to dwell
in the land of the humans."

The old man
spoke these words.
Only then
did I look and see that,
all along,

the god Okikurmi
had been deceiving me
to make me leave
my abode
so as to punish me.
Only then
did I realize it.

After that,
I died
a miserable death,
a terrible death.

You dragons of today,
do not have evil dispositions!

These things recounted a dragon.

15. Song of an Evil Bear

This *kamui yukar* was recorded in writing by Kubodera from the reciter Hirame Karepia on February 19, 1936. It was sung with the burden *Heninuisa.* It does not appear to have any particular meaning.

The speaker is an evil monster bear (*wen arsarush*). He has many racks for drying fish and meat outside his house; this seems to mean that he is a famine god (*kemram kamui*) who withholds the food from the humans and hoards it for himself. As in the previous selection, the culture hero Okikurmi uses deception to banish the evil god.

In a variant obtained by Kindaichi in 1915 from Taukno, Okikurmi enters the home of the famine god and tells him to visit an old man dwelling at Atui-sachsachi ("place where the sea dries up"?) across the sea. After he leaves, Okikurmi scatters all the fish and meat over the mountains and rivers. The famine god decides to remain with the old man across the sea and does not return.

The text of this selection is Kamui Yukar 15 in Kubodera's *Ainu jojishi: Shin'yō, seiden no kenkyū,* pp. 118–19. He gives another version of the same song obtained from the same reciter on a different occasion (September 9, 1935) as Kamui Yukar 14. The only differences are minor ones in wording.

On and on
I lived
uneventfully.
I had outside my house
many racks for drying fish,
many racks for drying meat.
As I lived on,

one day
there was the sound of voices
outside.
I looked and saw
Okikurmi,
the human god.[1]
He came walking inside
and spoke these words:

---

[1] *Ainu pito.* The term is applied to chieftains and epic heroes and is interchangeable with *kamui rametok,* "mighty warrior."

"Listen well
to what I have to say!
Now I am going to tie
this garland of curled shavings[2]
to your neck.
When I do so,
go downstream right away
along the river.
As you go downstream,
the sound of the waves on the beach
will come closer and closer.
Walk down
along
the big promontory.
When you walk out
to the tip of the promontory,
dive right down
into the sea.
Go swimming along,
sending this way and that
many ripples in the water,
countless ripples in the water.
When you have reached
the opposite shore across the sea,
go up on shore.
Then many gods
looking exactly like you
will be there,
rooting around in the seaweed
and rooting around in the kelp.
You also
will do the same,
and you will greatly enhance
your glory as a deity.''

He spoke
these words.
Therefore,
I went outside.
So very angry
was I that
I knocked down
the many racks for drying fish
and the many racks for drying meat,
and scattered them all about.[3]

After that,
I went down along the river.
As I went downstream,
the sound of the waves on the beach
came closer and closer.
Then I came down
to the seashore.
A big promontory
was seen clearly
jutting out in the distance.
I walked out
along
that promontory.
Then, at the tip of the promontory,
I dived down right
into the sea.
I swam along,
sending this way and that
many ripples in the water,
countless ripples in the water.

When I reached
the opposite shore across the sea,

[2] *Inau kike*, curled wood shavings. The shavings are regarded as *inau* and have considerable supernatural potency.
[3] In Taukno's version, the culture hero knocks down the racks for drying the fish and meat after the famine deity's departure.

I went up on shore.
When I looked around,
true enough,
there were many gods
each with a garland of curled shavings
tied
to their necks.
They were rooting around in the seaweed
and rooting around in the kelp.
They all looked as if
they were about to die at any moment.
I walked up to them.

Since this was what
they were doing,
I started
to root around in the seaweed
and to root around in the kelp.
But I still was hungry.
After a while of this,
I starved to death.

Only then

did I look and see
that this was
the place where
all of
the evil bears,
the ones who
are being punished,
are banished.[4]
Only then,
after I had died,
did I see this.

You evil bears of today,
do not, on any account,
steal in the villages,
steal in the countries [of the humans].
If you do not,
it will be well.[5]

These words
were spoken
by an evil bear.

---

[4] In another version by the same reciter recorded in writing about six months previously (on September 9, 1935), there was the statement at this point: "I had been banished by the god Okikurmi because I had stolen [food] from the humans and eaten it."

[5] In the earlier version of September 9, 1935, the final warning is: "You evil bears of today, do not steal from the humans!"

16. Song of a Huri Bird

This *kamui yukar* was recorded in writing by Kubodera from the reciter Hiraga Etenoa on September 6, 1932. It was sung with the burden *Hetuna hetuna*. The meaning of the burden is not clear. It resembles the alternate burden mentioned by Kubodera for selection 1, *Hetuina*.

The *huri* is a huge mythical bird mentioned in legends and epics; we might possibly call it a griffin. In the Saru region there is a cult of a pair of these birds, which are said to live in a place called Chikapohi ("place where there are birds") near Piratori. In the epics there are *huri chikap* ("huri bird"), *huri chikap kamui* ("huri bird deity"), *huri kamui* ("huri deity"), and *huri nitnehi* ("demon huri"). These birds are depicted as being extremely ferocious and are sometimes invoked in battle by evil characters. Munro says that the *huri* was "a huge bird which lived in a cave and devoured human beings."[1]

In this song, the culture hero Okikurmi transforms himself into a little old man to deceive the *huri* bird. There is a didactic ending of the usual type.

The text of this selection is Kamui Yukar 63 in Kubodera's *Ainu jojishi: Shin'yō, seiden no kenkyū*, pp. 298–99.

I roamed about in the mountains.
I roamed about on the beaches.
I would kill
even those gathering
grasses to feed themselves,
and I would feed myself on them.
This is the way
I used to live
on and on.

As time went on,
one day,
no matter how
I roamed about in the mountains,
I was unable to catch
even any [humans] gathering
grasses to feed themselves.
I was quite hard pressed
and went roaming about on the beaches.

[1] Munro, *Ainu Creed and Cult*, p. 22.

Just then,
there was a little old man,
all naked,
holding
a dirty old ax,
cutting firewood
on the grassy downs by the beach.

Therefore,
from the heavenly skies
I swooped down
on him.
Down and down
I went,
heading
straight toward him.
I thought
surely that
I had caught him,
but he had already
run away
before I came down.
I passed
all the way through
six layers of earth,
and my beak
struck the bottom.

Then I tried
to get up,
but I was quite unable
to manage it.
Just then,
the little old man

came running up beside me.
Grasping in his hand
a goodly club,
he beat me mightily.
While doing this,
he uttered these words:

  "You evil *huri*,
  what deeds
  are these
  you are doing!
  Are the humans
  not to be allowed
  to feed themselves?
  You kill
  even those gathering
  grasses to feed themselves,
  and feed yourself on them.
  You do not allow
  the humans
  to make their livelihood,
  nor do you allow
  the gods
  to make their livelihood.
  To punish you
  for doing this,
  I was lying
  in wait for you.
  Then you acted
  as if you wanted to eat
  even me.
  But I have been
  lying in wait for you
  in order to teach you

a good lesson!''

Saying
these words,
he beat me mightily.
After a while,
he gave me a mighty kick,
and I was hurled down
to the sixfold Underworld.

The fact of the matter was
that it had been

the god Okikurmi
lying in wait for me
to punish me.

You *huri* of today,
do not, on any account,
kill the humans!

These things
were recounted
by a *huri* bird god.

17. Song of a North Wind Goddess

This *kamui yukar* was recorded in writing by Kindaichi from the reciter Nabesawa Taukno in 1915. It was sung with the burden *Kenekumaka pētuitui*. The burden appears to mean "Water drips down on the alder drying racks." A variant of the same song obtained by Kindaichi from Utekare uses the burden *Penekumaka penetuitui*; the meaning of this latter burden is less clear.

The speaker is a north wind (*matnau*) goddess who dances atop the mountain, causing a storm at sea. Okikurmi and Samai-un-kur are caught in the storm in their boat, and Samai-un-kur dies. Okikurmi shoots arrows of swallow-wort (*ikema*) and kills the goddess. There is a didactic ending.

The Gilyaks (Nivkhi) of Sakhalin, the northern neighbors of the Ainu, also told of wind goddesses. E. A. Kreinovich, a Russian investigator, was told by a Gilyak informant that winds are produced by a woman. When this woman sits at home and occupies herself with some kind of work, the weather is quiet. But when the woman goes outside and dances, the wind starts to blow. If she dances quietly for a short time, the wind blows weakly. The stronger she dances, the stronger the wind will blow. (E. A. Kreinovich, *Nivkhgu, zagadochnye obitateli Sakhalina i Amura*, p. 61)

I obtained the text directly from Kindaichi's field notes of 1915.

The only work I did
was my needlework.
Casting my glances
ahead of the needle,
following with my eyes
after the needle,
I lived on.

Then, so exceedingly
lonley
was I,
I put aside
my needlework.
Sixfold robes
I fastened under my girdle,
and sixfold robes

I wore hanging loosely.
I put on
a silken cap,
and I wore
silken gloves.

I stepped
outside.
I went down closer and closer
to the edge of the mountain.
Back and forth I tripped
making countless dancing steps.
As I danced,
many calm breezes
blew about
over the sea,
and the calm sea
stretched out
into the distance.

Just then
I noticed
Okikurmi
and Samai-un-kur
sailing out to sea together
to go fishing.
I turned around
and went back.
Going back
inside my house,
I took off
my magnificent robes.
I attired myself
in ragged clothes.

I put on
a ragged cap
and ragged gloves.

I stepped
outside.
I went down closer and closer
to the edge of the mountain.
Back and forth I tripped
making countless dancing steps.
As I danced,
fierce winds
came blowing down
and whirled about
over the sea.
As the winds blew,
it looked
exactly as if
the waters at the top of the sea
went down to the bottom,
and the waters at the bottom of the sea
emerged at the surface.

Okikurmi
and Samai-un-kur
cried out
with youthful shouts
as they continued
to row the boat.
Many bloody blisters
appeared
on the backs of their hands
and on the palms of their hands
as they continued to row the boat.

They went floating about
this way and that in the ocean waters.

Samai-un-kur
first of all
died of exhaustion.
Okikurmi,
even though a mere human,
seemed not to be weary at all.
He showed on his face
an expression
of renewed strength.
As he continued to row the boat,
finally he too,
being a mere human,
showed on his face
an expression
of weariness.

Just then,
he did something
which I would never
have expected him to do.
He felt around
inside his tinder box.
He brought out
a little bow of swallow-wort
and little arrows of swallow-wort.[1]
He spoke these words:

   "O evil north wind over yonder,
   these things that you are doing
are truly
detestable.
You may be doing this
thinking that
I can't see you,
but I'll teach you a lesson!''

Saying these words,
he shot me with an arrow.
He shot with mighty force
one of my legs
and broke it.
As I hopped about
on one leg,
once again
he shot with mighty force
my other leg.
Both of my legs
were broken.
I still went on dancing,
jumping along
on my sides.
Then he shot with mighty force
my big belly.
He also shot arrows
at my arms.
Then finally
he killed me.

You north winds of today,
do not do these things!
Then it will be well.

---

[1] The roots of this plant (*ikema, Cynanchum caudatum* Maxim) were used widely as a medicine and for various magic purposes.

18. Song of a Swordfish

This *kamui yukar* was recorded in writing by Kindaichi from the reciter Nabesawa Wakarpa in 1913. It was sung with the burden *Tusunabanu*.

The song must have been extremely popular, as there are a number of variants. One was obtained by Batchelor in 1880 from Kanturuka; this one by Kindaichi from Wakarpa in 1913; another by Kindaichi from Utomriuk, the elder brother of Wakarpa, in 1915; another by Kubodera from Hiraga Etenoa in 1932; and still another by Kubodera from Nitani Kunimatsu in 1935. All of them coincide except for differences in the wording. Etenoa's version is much more detailed and longer than the other four extant variants.

The story is very simple. A swordfish is harpooned by Okikurmi and Samai-un-kur and flees, pulling their boat after it all over the ocean. Samai-un-kur dies and Okikurmi curses the swordfish. The swordfish meets with a terrible end. All the variants have didactic endings.

The text is from Kindaichi, *Ainu jojishi: Yūkara gaisetsu*, pp. 362–67.

Okikurmi
and Samai-un-kur
came [sailing] along
together.
I emerged
and waited
just in their path.
Grasping in his hand
a goodly little harpoon,[1]
[Okikurmi] speared me with it,
he pierced me with it.
I fled, pulling them after me,
across many ocean waters,
across countless ocean waters.
Time went on, and
day after day
for six days
and night after night
for six nights
I fled, pulling them after me.
Then Samai-un-kur
died of exhaustion.
Nevertheless,
Okikurmi

---

[1] In Etenoa's version of this epic, at this point Okikurmi addresses the swordfish. He asks the swordfish to come to him peacefully and promises to worship it with *inau*, enabling it to enhance its glory as a deity.

seemed not to be
weary at all.
He began anew
to cry out
with youthful shouts,
and once again
I fled pulling him after me
day after day
and night after night.

Time went on, and
many bloody blisters
appeared
on the backs of the hands
and on the palms of the hands
of Okikurmi.
His countenance now
looked withered and wasted.
At that time
Okikurmi
spoke these words:

    "What are these things
    that you are doing,
    you evil swordfish?
    Even though you do these things,
    [this is what will happen to you].
    The harpoon head
    is made of metal,
    and inside your belly
    metals will be heard hitting
    with clanking noises.
    The harpoon tip
    is made of bone,

and inside your belly
bones will be heard
scraping.
The shank
is made of hydrangea wood,[2]
and forests of hydrangeas will grow
on one side of your body.
The shaft
is made of bird cherry,[3]
and forests of bird cherry trees will grow
on one side of your body.
The line
is made of nettle fibers,
and nettle thickets will grow
on one side of your body.
The rope
is made of linden bark fibers,
and forests of lindens will grow
on top of you.
You will be sorely
distressed.

"Since you have done this
because you wanted to do it,
you will be feared everywhere
over the entire expanse
of the ocean.
As you continue to go on,
you will come ashore
at the mouth
of the Shishirmuka.
Then all sorts of dogs,
all sorts of foxes,
all sorts of crows,

[2] *Rashpa-ni* (*Hydrangea paniculata*, Sieb.). The wood is viscous.
[3] *Shiuri* (*Prunus Ssiori* Fr. Schm.). The wood resembles that of the Japanese flowering cherry.

and all sorts of birds
will peck at you from all sides
and bite at you from all sides.
They will defecate on you
and will piss on you.''

Saying this,
he cut the rope
and let me go.

However,
I thought to myself:

    ''What of it?
    It is only human talk!''

and I snickered to myself
deep down in my throat.

After that,
when I went on,
true enough,
inside my belly
metals were heard hitting,
and bones were heard scraping.
My heart
grew dazed from it.
On one side of my body
forests of bird cherry trees grew up.
On the other side of my body
forests of lindens grew up,
and nettle thickets grew up.
My heart
was sorely distressed by it.

I was feared
everywhere
on the ocean.

As I continued to go on,
true enough,
I was carried ashore
at the mouth
of the Shishirmuka.
Just as Okikurmi
had said,
all sorts of dogs,
all sorts of foxes,
all sorts of crows,
and all sorts of birds
bit at me from all sides
and pecked at me from all sides.
They defecated on me
and pissed on me.

Just then
the god Okikurmi
came walking down.
He laughed
gleefully
and said:

    ''There now! What did I say?
    You went right ahead,
    thinking that
    it was nothing
    but human talk,
    but look!
    Just as I said,

all sorts of dogs,
all sorts of birds
are pissing on you
and defecating on you!
Even though you are a god,
now this is your fate—
your spirit
must wander lost

without any *inau*.[4]
This will be
a lesson [for others].''

You swordfish of today,
do not make fun
of the words of the humans![5]

[4] To be deprived of *inau* would be the greatest misfortune for a god, since it would signify complete withdrawal of human favor.

[5] In this version, it seems as if the transgression of the swordfish was to despise Okikurmi's prophecy about the forests of bird cherry trees, lindens, and so forth. However, in Etenoa's version the swordfish is punished for *disobeying* Okikurmi's words (that is, when Okikurmi asked the swordfish to come peacefully). Etenoa's version seems more consistent.

19. Song of an Old Boat Goddess

This *kamui yukar* was recorded in writing by Kubodera from the reciter Hiraga Etenoa on August 31, 1932. It was sung with the burden *Poinashō*. The meaning of the burden is not clear. Kubodera reports that Nitani Kunimatsu informed him that the same *kamui yukar* could also be sung with the burden *Sō wa sō*.

The speaker is an old boat goddess (*onne chip kamui*). The song consists of two parts. In the first part, a tree growing on top of a waterfall on the Soratki river refuses to be cut down by Samai-un-kur but allows Okikurmi to cut her down. Okikurmi makes the tree into a boat and goes trading. In the second part, many years later the son of Okikurmi (*pon Okikurmi*) takes the old boat on another trading expedition. On the way home, the boat is wrecked by a storm. Young Okikurmi dismisses it with many offerings.

Kubodera also collected variants of the same song from the reciter Hirame Karepia. The first part and second part are performed by Karepia as separate songs using different burdens (the first one *Koinawash*, the second one *Tehama tehuri*).

The text of this selection is Kamui Yukar 69 in Kubodera's *Ainu jojishi: Shin'yō, seiden no kenkyū*, pp. 319–26.

I was living
all by myself
on top of the waterfall
on the Soratki river.
On and on
I lived
uneventfully.

Then, one day
there was the sound of voices
downstream.
I looked and saw
that it was
Samai-un-kur
coming this way
carrying on his back

six axes
and six hatchets
all pointing in different directions.
He walked up
to the outside
of my house.
Walking around
and around the house,
he spoke these words:

"You, tree!
Worthless tree!
I will make you into a boat.
Then I will take you
with me
on a trading expedition.
I will decorate
your bosom beautifully
with trade wine,
trade brew,
and with grains as well.
Your will enhance
your glory
as a deity."

Thus did he speak.
However,
so very angry
was I, that
I exposed on the outside
my hard flesh,
and I hid on the inside
my soft flesh.

As I did so,
he broke
the six axes against me,
and he broke
the six hatchets against me.
After that,
he went away,
pouring out
many words of abuse,
countless words of abuse.

After that,
on and on
I lived
uneventfully.

Then, one day
there was the sound of voices
downstream.
I looked and saw
the god Okikurmi
coming this way,
carrying on his back
six axes
and six hatchets
all pointing in different directions.
When he came up
by my side,
he walked around
and around the house,
my house.
Then he spoke
these words:

"Greetings,
o Goddess Ruling the Earth![1]
Listen to
what I have to say!
I will make you into a boat.
Then I will take you
with me
on a trading expedition,
and I will decorate
your bosom beautifully
with wine,
with foods,
and with tobacco.
You will enhance
your glory as a deity,
and you will take
great delight in this."

While saying
these words,
he began to chop me down.
After this,
since he was intending
to make me into a boat,
I hid on the inside
my hard flesh,
and I exposed on the outside
my soft flesh.
Immediately,
large ax-chips
and small ax-chips
went flying in all directions.
As the ax-chips
went flying,

it sounded to me
like these words:

*"Sake-pe tui-tui
inau-pe tui-tui"*[2]

This is what
I seemed to hear
as the ax-chips
went flying.

After that,
he started to make me into a boat.
He finished making the boat.
Then he made carvings
on the boat in this way:
On the side of the boat facing the mountains,
he carved
many pictures,
countless pictures
of the gods dwelling in the mountains.
On the side of the boat facing the beach,
he carved
many pictures,
countless pictures
of the gods dwelling in the sea.

After that,
as he lowered me
over the top of the waterfall
on the Soratki river,
he spoke these words:

"O god ruling

---

[1] *Shir-kor-kamui*, "deity ruling the earth," an archaic expression meaning "tree." The ruler of all the trees is called *Shirampa-kamui*.

[2] Meaning "wine-drops drip-drip, *inau*-drops drip-drip." The sound made by the ax-chips reminds the tree goddess of these auspicious-sounding Ainu words, perhaps the refrain of some song. Wine and *inau* were of central importance in Ainu ritualism.

the top of the waterfall
on the Soratki river!
Grasp firmly
my dear little boat
by her stern
and let her down gradually!
O god ruling
the basin below the waterfall
on the Soratki river!
Support firmly
my dear little boat
under her prow!''

Saying this,
he lowered me
over the top of the waterfall
on the Soratki river.
Just as the god Okikurmi
had said,
the god ruling
the top of the waterfall
on the Soratki river
grasped me firmly
by the stern
and lowered me gently.
He let my stern
down gradually.
The god ruling
the basin below the waterfall
on the Soratki river
supported me firmly
under the prow,
and I was lowered
gently

into the basin below the waterfall
on the Soratki river.

After that,
I went downstream
along the river until
I came down
to the river mouth
of the Soratki river.

After that
I went along with
the god Okikurmi
on a trading expedition.
I went
to the land of the Japanese.[3]
Just as the god Okikurmi
had said,
my bosom was
decorated beautifully
with wine,
with tobacco,
with grains,
with sacred vessels,[4]
and with treasures.[5]
Taking great
delight in this,
I returned homeward.
After that,
I was drawn ashore
midway between
the lower grassy downs
and the upper grassy downs [near the beach].
There I remained,

---

[3] *Tono kotan. Tono* is a Japanese loan word meaning "lord," "master." It was originally applied to the officials and samurai of Matsumae, but in time it came to mean simply "Japanese." The more common word for "Japanese (person)" is *shisam*

[4] *Iyoipe*, eating utensils, especially imported lacquer utensils regarded as treasures by the Ainu.

[5] *Ikor*, household treasures, fancy goods, riches. These treasures include swords with decorated sheaths. They are counted as the person's wealth and can be offered as indemnities in case of quarrels.

living on and on
uneventfully.
Year after year,
year in and year out,
I remained there.

During this while,
when the breeze blew
from the west,
many sprays of sand,
countless sprays of sand
came trickling down
into my bosom.
When the breeze blew
from the east,
many sprays of sand,
countless sprays of sand
came trickling down
into my bosom.
My heart became weary
and sorely distressed.
This is the way
I continued to live
on and on
for a very long time.

Then, one day,
back of me
the sound of crunching footsteps in the sand
came closer and closer.
I looked and saw
the Young Okikurmi[6]
coming down.
He was still a lad,

a youth,
a young boy
lacking as yet
even the shadow of a beard.
He came down
by my side.
He remained for a while
standing by my side,
absorbed in thoughts.
He brushed away the sand
piled up in heaps
in my bosom.
He wiped it off again and again
and cleaned it out again and again.
After a while,
he turned around
and went away again.

Some time passed,
and then he came down
[again] in this way:
He came down
carrying
an armful of *inau*.
Decorating
my bosom beautifully
with those *inau*,
he spoke these words:

"Listen,
o Lady Boat,
to what I have to say!
Long ago,
in days gone by,

---

[6] The son of the culture hero Okikurmi.

when my father
was still alive,
he took you
on a trading expedition
and decorated
your bosom beautifully
with wine,
with tobacco,
and with grains.
You took
great delight in that.
But
my father
departed, leaving me.
After that,
you have been
lonely
until now.

"However,
I will strengthen you
with new power,
with new energy,
and will take you with me
on a trading expedition.
Then I will decorate
your bosom beautifully
with trade wine,
trade brew,
with tobacco,
with grains,
and with sacred vessels.
Then you will take great
delight in this."

While saying this,
he decorated
my bosom beautifully
with splendid *inau*
and then went away.
The night
went by.
The next morning,
he came down again,
bearing on his back
big bundles
of articles traded with the Japanese,
deer furs and hides,
and bear furs and hides.

After that,
he lowered me
onto the face of the ocean.
He filled
my bosom
with those furs and hides.
After that,
he sailed out
to sea,
and this was the way
we went on:
We sailed across
many ocean waters,
countless ocean waters.

We went on and on
until we came
to the land of the Japanese.
The Young Okikurmi

decorated
my bosom beautifully
with those things
he had promised me:
with wine,
with vessels,
with grains,
and with tobacco,
and we set sail
and were sailing homeward.

Just then,
when we had reached
the mid-point in the ocean
between the ocean of the *repunkur*
and the ocean of the *yaunkur*,
this is what happened.
Atop the mountain peaks,
the peaks far in the distance,
many black clouds,
countless black clouds
rose up.
Downstream along the course
of the Soratki river,
storm clouds,
black clouds
came floating
and came out over the ocean.
After that
a fierce storm
broke out
at sea.
It seemed as if
the waters at the bottom of the sea

had come up to the top
and the waters at the top of the sea
had gone down to the bottom.
On the face of the ocean
many fierce mountainous waves,
countless fierce mountainous waves
broke over each other
with a noisy slapping.
In the midst of all this,
I was buffeted about
among many mighty waves,
between countless mighty waves.

After that
the Young Okikurmi
uttered youthful whoops
to drum up
his spirits.
I still continued
to go on.
Then, just when
I had mounted
the crest of the billows
out in the offing,
my backbone
began to shake and shiver.
The Young Okikurmi
still continued
to utter youthful whoops
to drum up
his spirits,
and I kept coming shoreward.
When I had mounted
the crest of the billows

near the shore,
something happened
which I would never
have expected to happen.
My backbone
broke with a crack,
and I lost all consciousness
of what was happening.

When I [awoke and] looked around,
this is what I saw.
The fragments of a wrecked boat
had been washed up
on the sandy beach
and were lying there
piled up in stacks.
Beside them
piles of wine [barrels],
piles of [grain] sacks,
as well as tobacco
and sacred vessels
had been washed up
and were lying there.
The Young Okikurmi
stood beside them,
absorbed in thought
for some time.
Then he walked off
away from the beach.

After a short while,
a large crowd of people
came down to the beach.
They carried away

all of it—
the wine,
the [grain] sacks,
and the tobacco.

After a while,
the Young Okikurmi
came down to the beach.
He came down
carrying
wine
and an armful of *inau*.
He also brought down
tobacco.
He offered
these *inau*
to the fragments of the wrecked boat.
Making offerings
of the wine,
he spoke these words:

    "Listen,
    o Lady Boat,
    to what I have to say!
    You have now
    grown weak with old age
    and decrepit.
    You have become
    too feeble to withstand
    the storm demon.
    At this time
    I am performing
    these rites
    to prepare you

for going [back]
to your abode
as a newborn deity,
as a newborn spirit.

"Take along with you
the splendid *inau*,
as well as the wine,
the tobacco,
and the foods.
Go now
from here!
Go up
along the stream
of the Soratki river.
When you have gone
to the top of the waterfall
on the Soratki river,
at the top of the waterfall
there will be standing
only the stump
of a tree which was felled
long ago.
As soon as
you reach
that stump,
ascend
into the heavenly skies
from atop the stump,
from that stump.
Then you will
be able to arrive
at the abode
of the god your master."[7]

The Young Okikurmi
spoke
these words.

As the Young Okikurmi
had told me,
I took along with me
the wine,
the *inau*,
the grains,
and the tobacco
and went upstream
along the river,
the Soratki river.
When I arrived
at the top of the waterfall
on the Soratki river,
there was standing there
only the stump
of a tree which had been felled
long ago,
in days gone by.
I ascended
into the heavenly skies
from atop the stump,
from that stump.
As I went on and on,
I arrived
in the land of the gods,
bringing along with me
as splendid presents
the wine
and the splendid *inau*
which had been given to me as offerings.

[7] The reciter gave an alternative version of this passage: "Go to the land of the gods from atop the stump, from that stump. Then you will arrive at the place of your ruler, and you will be praised." The "god your master" or "ruler" is the ruler of all the trees, *Shirampa-kamui*.

When I arrived,
all of the gods
praised me.

These things
were recounted
by an old boat goddess.

The Culture Hero and His Work

A central hero in the mythic epics is a character whom we may call the "culture hero." Among the Ainu, this hero is the sacred ancestor of the human race, a demigod who lays the foundations for all human life. This great ancestor figure gives useful knowledge, does battle against harmful demons, and makes it possible for the humans to lead pleasant and comfortable lives. Sometimes he himself descends from the heavens; in other versions, his father descended from the heavens but has since returned, leaving the hero an orphan in the care of an older woman, whom the hero calls his "foster sister" or "elder sister." In any case, the hero is generally a child and an orphan, like the hero of the *yukar* epics. The culture hero myth complex probably is of the greatest antiquity, and there is a wide variety of divergent and sometimes contradictory versions.

In his most archaic form, the culture hero appears in a dual light. At times he seems to be a sublime, lofty, heroic being. But sometimes he may be a mischievous trickster, a foolish, cruel rogue whose deeds are outrageous and at the same time amusing. This combination of heroic and dastardly elements into a single image must have reflected a definite thought pattern among the early hunters and fishers. On the one hand, the culture hero is the ancestor of the human race, the originator of everything of value in human life, and the possessor of powers far superior to those of any of the gods in heaven or on earth. Here we see clearly the archaic concept of the superiority of human beings over gods. However, this same hero is depicted as being stupid, violent, and uncouth. In some accounts he is made to steal someone else's wife. In other cases he is unable to control his fury and, after victory over the harmful demons, proceeds to ravage the human homeland. This contradiction does not seem to strike the native audience as odd. The highest ideal of a hero for them apparently has nothing to do with right or wrong. The hero is great simply because he is great, and ethical considerations do not apply to him. He is the incarnation of wild, ruthless might and is cruel and terrible when enraged. He may also be kind and compassionate. The qualities of compassion and cruelty, of the noble and the ridiculous, seemingly contradictory ones, are here subsumed among the attributes of the culture hero, and no one senses any discrepancy.[1]

Although in the most archaic strata of the mythical traditions the hero seems to be an ambiguous combination of both positive and negative qualities, there is a tendency for these qualities to be separated. With social changes, with changes in the population's attitude toward the cult of the hero, and with the gradual evolution of the folklore tradition itself, there took place a splitting, a polarization of the myths and tales about the culture hero. The heroic element was detached from the comical element and concentrated in an all-good, noble hero, while the comical and ridiculous elements were split off and attached to an antipodal image. Now we have twin heroes. One is the wise, mighty, and creative culture hero. His twin brother or alter ego is stupid, weak, and destructive. The unlucky, ineffective twin becomes the butt of derision and provides an even more pronounced contrast to the positive qualities attributed to the culture hero.[2]

This splitting of the single primeval culture hero into twins, one ridiculous and the other sublime, appears to have been a later development in Ainu folklore. This can be proved easily by pointing to the confusion in the names of the twins. In some areas, the noble hero is called Okikurmi, and his negative counterpart is called Samai-un-kur; but in other areas the names and the roles of the positive and negative heroes are reversed completely.

Another later development is the tendency to detach a certain group of songs about the culture hero, segregate them into a definite folklore genre, and assign a special word to this group of songs. In Hidaka and Iburi, this has been done; in these areas, the word *oina* is sometimes used to refer to a special "sacred tradition" connected with the culture hero.

In the Saru region of Hidaka there are a number of names for the culture hero. One is Oina-kamui. Chiri assumes that the world *oina* must have meant anciently "to go into a trance," "to shamanize." He argues that the word is derived from the verb *oira*, "to forget," and thus concludes that *oina* is a synonym of *tusu*.[3] If we accept this theory, Oina-kamui means "god who shamanizes." It seems more probbale that *oina* means simply "to sing" or "to sing

---

[1] Kindaichi Kyōsuke, *Ainu bungaku*, p. 49.

[2] This process of splitting of the culture hero figure into positive and negative twins has been described on the basis of cross-cultural materials by V. E. Gusev in his *Estetika fol'klora*, pp. 303–4. Even though Gusev probably was not acquainted with the Ainu mythic epics, his theoretical formulation fits the Ainu culture hero myths perfectly and provides us with an excellent key for interpreting them.

[3] Chiri Mashiho, *Bunrui Ainu-go jiten*, vol. 1, pp.88–89.

the sacred tradition." In that case, Oina-kamui would mean "god of the sa-
cred tradition (*oina*)." Another name of the culture hero is Aeoina-kamui,
which means either "god concerning whom we sing the *oina*" or "god about
whom we shamanize," depending upon which interpretation of *oina* we
adopt. Still another name of the culture hero is Ainurakkur, which means
"he who has a human smell" or perhaps "he who is of human descent." This
appellation emphasizes the culture hero's solidarity with the human race.
Another name is Okikurmi, which Chiri interprets as meaning "he wears a
leather robe with a shiny hem." (See introduction to selection 13) In the
Horobetsu dialect of Iburi, this name is Okikirmui.

There being such a wide divergence in local traditions, it is not surprising
to find varying accounts about who exactly the culture hero is. The Ainu
themselves were responsible for some of the confusion, since some of them
were accustomed to telling visitors that their Okikurmi was the Japanese
hero Minamoto no Yoshitsune.[4]

According to the most reliable native accounts from the Saru Ainu obtained
by Kindaichi, the culture hero Okikurmi was a half-divine, half-human
being (*arke ainu arke kamui*) who was the father of the Ainu race. He was the
first ruler of the land of men and laid the groundwork for the Ainu life of
today. All Ainu customs and mores were taught by this god. He himself lived
entirely according to human, i.e., Ainu, patterns, and for this reason he is
called Ainurakkur.[5] In many of the mythic epics of Saru and Iburi, the cul-
ture hero is identified and symbolized by his mystic paraphernalia or trap-
pings which consist of an elm-bark fiber coat with a flaming hem (*o-uhui nikap
attush*) and a sheath with a flaming tip (*o-uhui shirka*). When these trappings
are mentioned in the course of an epic account, the audience automatically
understands that the hero being described is the culture hero. In the Saru and
Iburi regions, the culture hero is said to have dwelt along the Shishirmuka
(Saru) river. His stronghold was at the hill Hayopira near the village of
Piratori in the Saru region.[6]

The culture hero is credited with having given a number of cultural boons
to the humans in his role as the great teacher of mankind. Some of them are:

(1) Ritual techniques: which gods are to be worshiped, and how to pray
to them; how to whittle and erect *inau*; how to offer wine to the gods. These

---

[4] The entire question of the Ainu and the legend of Yoshitsune was dealt with at length by Kindaichi in an essay reprinted
in Kindaichi's *Ainu no kenkyū*, pp. 307–40. The spurious account was accepted at face value by a number of Western
writers, including Chamberlain, Hitchcock, and even Batchelor.

[5] Kindaichi, *Ainu no shinten.*

[6] Kindaichi Kyōsuke, *Ainu bunka shi*, p. 268.

activities are restricted to males, and women are forbidden to perform them.

(2) Handicraft techniques for both sexes. These include the wood carving performed by the men and the needlework and basketwork made by women.

(3) Hunting techniques: how to make poisoned arrows, how to make spring bows, how to make bows and arrows.

(4) Fishing techniques.

(5) Agricultural techniques.

(6) Architectural techniques: how to build houses.

(7) Medicinal techniques: diagnoses of illnesses and methods of praying to cure them; how to identify the grasses and roots which are useful for medicinal purposes.

(8) Methods of reciting ritual salutations and methods of settling disputes.

(9) Folklore: all types of songs, epics, and entertainments.

In short, it would seem that all cultural skills and activities which the Ainu believed to be native to them were originally attributed to the culture hero.[7]

Although the culture hero plays an active role at the beginning of Ainu cultural history, he does not continue to do so. In fact, the culture hero is widely believed to have departed in indignation (*ikesui*) and gone to live in another country, Samor-moshir (see selection 25). According to Wakarpa, during the later years of the culture hero, the Ainu became more and more depraved, in many instances committing sacrilegious acts toward him. Finally, the culture hero forsook the human homeland and went to live in a neighboring country. Hearing about this, the *yukar* hero also departed. Since then, the world has continued to degenerate until finally the Ainu have come into days of irreparable evil.[8] This concept of the departure of the racial heroes and the arrival of evil days reflects the extreme conservatism of the traditionally minded Ainu and their complete dissatisfaction with life under the new conditions resulting from Japanese colonization.

At any rate, the materials from Saru depict the culture hero as the "human god," the head of the human race. There are head gods who rule the bears, the owls, the killer whale, and all the other species. In the case of the human beings, the lord of the species is the culture hero, who represents the humans in their dealings with the gods. When there is famine, the culture hero intercedes for the humans, and he defeats the demons and evil deities who

[7] Kindaichi, *Ainu no kenkyū*, p. 102, pp. 214–15.
[8] Kindaichi, *Ainu no shinten*, p. 162.

plague them. There are no gods anywhere—in the heavens or on the earth— who can compare with him in his might and wisdom. His superiority over orders of beings represents the excellence of mankind, and the mythic songs about the culture hero may be understood in terms of the archaic concept of the superiority of humans over the world of animals and spirits.

The culture hero is the ancestor, benefactor, advocate, and teacher of the human race. It was he who arranged things in the world of men in their present order. To him is attributed everything that is precious and noble in human (i.e., Ainu) culture. In revering and worshiping the culture hero, the humans are paying tribute to their own vision of a glorified humanity. It seems that this is what we find at the core of the Ainu culture hero myths, The primeval mythic act by which man becomes human is perpetuated and recollected in the cult of the culture hero, who founded human culture. The culture hero *is* man, and in worshiping him man glorifies his own species.

This section contains six selections dealing with the exploits and the origins of the culture hero. Five of them are from the reciter Hiraga Etenoa, and one is from Hiraga Tumonte. All were recorded in writing by Kubodera.

20. Song of Aeoina-kamui

This is a mythic epic of the *oina* type recorded in writing by Kubodera from the reciter Hiraga Tumonte of Shin-Piraka village, Saru, on August 14, 1932. It was sung with the burden *Kane-ka-un, ka-un.* The meaning of the burden is not clear. Nitani Kunimatsu informed Kubodera that the same song could also be sung with the burden *Unhu unhu, unhu unhu.*

In this account, the culture hero Aeoina-kamui does battle against a huge char in a lake to save the human race from famine. He uses a twig of mugwort (*noya-nit*) to stab at the char. After his victory, the hero's vigor is so abundant that he grasps the edge of the lake and shakes it, causing mountain floods. He is barely restrained by his elder sister. After he returns home, the hero is worshiped by the humans, who send him offerings of wine and *inau* in thanksgiving, exactly as they would to a cult deity.

It is of interest that the hero appears in a dual light: both as the benevolent hero and as a frenzied destroyer who may possibly ravage his own homeland. The hero is depicted as if he might be a giant.

The text is Oina 2 in Kubodera's *Ainu jojishi: Shin'yō, seiden no kenkyū*, pp. 489–92.

My elder sister
raised me,
and we lived
on and on
uneventfully.
Stacks of sacred vessels
were stretched out
like a low cliff.
Just below the treasures
was a magnificent seat,

a movable seat.
I dwelt
on the seat
and was raised well.

My elder sister—
it was incredible
how she could ever be
so very beautiful,
so very comely.

She transformed herself
into a ball of flashing lightning.
We lived there.
Together with
my younger sister
we lived
on and on until
by this time
I had come to look
like a young man.
The only work
I ever did was
to carve on precious swords,
to carve on treasures.

Then once,
my elder sister
went outside.
Afterward, [she came inside again and]
shed
many sparkling teardrops.
After this had continued for some time,
she huddled her head close
to my younger sister
and whispered these words
into her ear:

"My younger sister,
listen to
what I have to say!
We used to have also
an elder brother
and lived together with him,
but at the headwaters
of our native river

there is a big lake.
In that lake
there dwells
a fiendish monster,
the god of the lake.
He is a famine god,
a huge char.[1]
He brings about famines
in the land of the humans.
For this reason,
the gods who were living
in the land of the humans
gathered
at that lake.
The gods
gathered
to do battle against
the god of the lake,
but they were all killed.
By that time,
it looked as if
all of the gods
were about to be killed,
and our elder brother also
went there.
When he left,
this is what he said:

'If I die,
bloody rain will fall
in the western part of the land.
The sun will shine bright
in the eastern part of the land.'

"These were the words he spoke

---

[1] The Ainu word is *tukushish*. This is the white-spotted char (*Salvelinus leucomaenis leucomaenis* Pallas), a trout-like fish found in the rivers of northern Japan and Hokkaido.

when he went there.
Now, this day,
bloody rain is falling
in the western part of the land.
The sun is shining brightly
in the eastern part of the land.
Thus, our elder brother
must surely have died.
The god we are raising,
our divine nursling,[2]
is still too young,
and it would be dangerous
if he heard of it.
Thus, I have not
told him about it."

When I heard
her say this,
I spoke these words:

    "My elder sister,
    what did you say?
    Say it again!
    I want to hear it!"

Then my elder sister
shed
many sparkling teardrops.
After a while [she said]:

    "It would be dangerous
    if you were to hear
    about these things.
    Since you were still so young,

I was worried
that you might hear,
and this is why
I did not tell you.
But now that you
have already heard,
I will tell you."

When my elder sister
had spoken,
I clad myself
in a magnificent robe.
A metal buckled belt
I wrapped around myself
in a single wrapping.
A god-given sword
I thrust under my belt.
I tied firmly
the dangling cords
of a delicately fashioned helmet.
After that
I stepped
outside.
I went upstream
along the river,
with blasts of wind
whirling in my ears.
Going on and on,
I went
far upstream.
While I ran along,
I broke off
a twig of mugwort[3]
and used it as a staff.

---

[2] This formula (in Ainu *a-reshpa kamui/a-reshpa pito*) is used by the older relatives to refer to a young epic hero. Both of the components mean "god whom I (or we) raise." Both *kamui* and *pito* are loan words from early Japanese. The Japanese words mean "god" and "human," respectively, but in the Ainu language both the words are usually used synonymously to mean "god" or "spirit."

[3] The Ainu name is *noya*. This plant (*Artemisia vulgaris L. var. yezoana* Kudo) is believed to be efficacious for driving away evil spirits. "Mugwort effigies" (*imosh kamui*) are made in extreme emergencies and used to repel powerful evil spirits.

As I went on up
along the river,
there was a big lake.
On the shores of the lake
the lodges [built by]
many gods
were standing.
As I went on,
I looked and saw that,
true enough,
the god of the lake,
the famine god,
a big char,
was waving his fins
at the head of the lake
and was waving his tail
at the foot of the lake.

I stabbed mightily at him
with the twig of mugwort.
The fiendish monster
put forth his strength
and jerked me down into the water
to a depth half-way up my leggings.
Then I, in my turn,
put forth my strength
and tossed him up
onto the shore of the lake.
After we continued doing this
for dozens of times,
the flesh of the fiendish monster's
body was torn,
and I chopped him to pieces
with my sword.

Becoming noxious insects,
[the pieces] went flying up together.

After that,
I kicked
at the dead bodies
of all the many gods
lying piled up
on the shores of the lake
like many pieces
of driftwood washed ashore.
Rubbing their eyes again and again,
the gods all [said]:

> "We thought that
> we were asleep
> for just a short while,
> and now the exalted hero[4]
> has restored us
> to life, it seems!"

Saying these words,
all of them
stood up,
rubbing their eyes again and again.
At that time,
the one who was
my elder brother
stood up,
rubbing his eyes again and again.

> "Thanks to you,
> my dear younger brother,
> I too

---

[4] *Kamui-ne-an-kur*, a title frequently applied to epic heroes. The literal meaning is apparently "he who becomes a god."

have woken up,
it seems!''

Saying these words,
he stood up.
After that
I considered
what I ought to do,
turning over various
things in my mind.
I grasped in my hands
the edge of the lake
and shook it again and again.
Just then
a terrible mountain flood
went flowing down.
My elder sister
appeared at the window [and said]:

    ''What are you doing?
    You were supposed
    to save
    the human homeland.
    And now,
    what is this you are doing?
    Are you trying to ravage
    the land of the humans?
    My younger brother,
    calm yourself,
    calm yourself please!''

Thus did she speak.
At that time

I came to my senses
and went down
to my own home.
As I was going down,
offerings of human *inau*
and of human wine
came to my abode.

    ''O weighty god,
    thanks to you
    the most evil deity
    has been killed,
    and now
    there is nothing
    for us to fear.
    To show our gratitude,
    we send offerings
    of wine
    and of *inau*
    to the weighty god.''

With this message
from the humans,
many *inau*
and much wine
came to my abode,
and I live on
with my glory as a deity
greatly enhanced.

These things
were recounted
by Aeoina-kamui.

21. Song of Aeoina-kamui

This is a mythic epic of the *oina* type recorded in writing by Kubodera from the reciter Hiraga Etenoa on September 4, 1932. It was sung with the burden *Atte panna*. The meaning of the burden is unclear.

In this account, the culture hero Aeoina-kamui does battle against the Earth Crone (Moshir Huchi) dwelling at the bottom of the ocean and destroys her wickerwork fish trap along the Shishirmuka river in order to save the humans from famine. After he has broken down the fish trap, the hero walks along the mountain peak and kicks lumps of snow out from the tips of his snow-shoes. Here again the hero appears to be a giant, for these lumps of snow are transformed into herds of deer and into schools of fish. He uses silver snow-shoes to alleviate the famine; in other epics he accomplishes this by using a silver fish-spear or silver bow and arrows.

The exact nature of Earth Crone is not known clearly. She appears to be a famine goddess. It is interesting that she lives at the bottom of the ocean and has disheveled hair. In the fray with the hero, she uses her hair as a weapon, entangling it with the hero's spear and sword. There is no indication of why she is called Earth Crone, but there appear to be similarities with the Eskimo Sedna.

The text is Oina 7 in Kubodera's *Ainu jojishi: Shin'yō, seiden no kenkyū,* pp. 530–35.

My foster sister
raised me,
and this is the way
we lived on and on
uneventfully:
Stacks of sacred vessels
were stretched out
like a low cliff.
Just below the treasures
was a movable seat,
a magnificent seat.
I was raised

on the seat,
and I lived on and on
uneventfully.
As time went on,
I would do nothing but
carve on scabbards,
carve on treasures,
with my eyes staring fixedly
at a single spot.

As time went on,
this is what
my foster sister
began to do.
At frequent intervals
she would take outside
reed mats full of grain.
As time went on,
gradually
this is what
she then began to do.
Now she would constantly
be taking outside
winnows full of grain.

After some time,
one day
she apparently wished
to say something.
She stared fixedly
down into the fire in the hearth
for a while,
then turned to me
and spoke, her voice

ringing out in sonorous accents.
This is what she said:

"O god I have raised,
o my divine nursling,
Young Offspring,[1]
listen well
to what I have to say.
The Earth Crone,
the most evil deity,
became angry
at the exceeding
prosperity
of the human homeland,
and she stole away
the souls of the food.
Midway along the course
of the Shishirmuka river,
she erected a fish trap
in this way:
She made
stakes of walnut wood
and stakes of pagoda-tree wood.
When she set up
these stakes,
walnut-tainted water
went flowing downstream;
pagoda-tree-tainted water
went flowing downstream.
The fish
were unable
even to drink the water.
As a result,
famine has broken out

[1] *Wariunekur*, an epithet applied to the culture hero in the epics of the Saru Ainu. It seems to be derived from the verb *uwari*, meaning "to multipy," "to propagate the race," or "to give birth." The meaning is not entirely clear, but parallels in the Sakhalin dialect lead us to suppose that *wariunekur* might mean "young child," or perhaps "youngest child."

in the homeland of the gods
and in the human homeland.
Now it appears that
the human homeland
is about to be destroyed.
Intending to assist
the humans,
I have been taking outside
reed mats full of grain,
and have been taking outside
winnows full of grain,
and I have been assisting
the humans with this.
But now,
even I
have become
short of provisions.
I should feel uneasy
if it were anyone
else but you;
only you
can I rely on.
If you do not do battle against her,
the country of the humans,
the human homeland
will be destroyed,
and the populace of your land,
the people of your country
will die out.
Were this to happen,
all your life
you would bear life-long disgrace.
You must do battle
against the Earth Crone!''

These words
were spoken by
my foster sister.

Then
I wrapped in a sedge mat
the carving I had been doing
and put it
on top of the stacks of sacred vessels.
Jumping up,
I attired myself
in a magnificent robe.
I went inside
my suit of metal armor.
In a single wrapping
I wrapped around myself
my metal buckled belt.
Under my belt I thrust
my god-given sword.
Over this I put on
my elm-bark fiber coat with its hem in flames.
Grasping in my hand
my short-hilted spear,
I went outside.
I stepped
outside
my native stockade.

After that
I went
across the ocean.
When I arrived
midway between
the ocean of the *repunkur*

and the ocean of the *yaunkur*,
there,
at the bottom of the sea
was the abode
of the Earth Crone.

I headed toward
the window
of the house
of the Earth Crone.
I darted in
onto the floor at the head of the fireplace.
When I looked at her,
this is what I saw.
The Earth Crone,
the most evil deity,
had her hair hanging
as if she were wearing
a half-woven basket
on her head.
Underneath her hair,
only her evil eyes
were gleaming brightly.
She was staring at me
with her eyes opened wide in amazement.
Then
I swung my spear at her,
and she sprang up.

If I were to fight
against the most evil deity,
the Earth Crone,
on the surface of the earth,
the country would be in danger,

the land would be in danger.
Because of this,
I hurled her down
into the Underworld,
the six-layered country.
After that,
I did battle against her.

The accursed hair
of the Earth Crone
would become entangled
with my spear and with my sword,
and this made it
difficult for me to land
any blows on her.
As this went on,
I reckoned the time,
and it seemed to me
as if by this time
I had been doing battle
against the Earth Crone
for six summers
and six winters.
As time went on,
I succeeded at long last
in slaying
the Earth Crone,
the most evil deity.

At this time,
I emerged
on the surface of the earth.
I came forth
atop the ocean.

After that,
I went shoreward
and came down
to the mouth
of the Shishirmuka river.
After that,
I went upstream
along the river.
When I had arrived
midway along the course
of the Shishirmuka river,
true enough,
the Earth Crone,
the most evil deity,
had erected a fish trap
in this way:
Stakes of walnut wood
and stakes of pagoda-tree wood
had been set up there
mixed together.

I broke and scattered
that fish trap.
Dirty, polluted water
was flowing downstream.
On one side of the river
yellowish water
was flowing down,
and on the other side of the river
blackish water
was flowing down.
Then,
after a while,
clear water

began to flow downstream,
and this is what
came about:
The deities dwelling
in the river
came rushing
to draw water.
The deities
expressed their gratitude,
saying:

"On account of
the miserable fault
of the Earth Crone,
the most evil deity,
until now
we have been quite unable
to drink the water at all,
and as time went on
it seemed as if
we were about to
perish of thirst
at any moment.
But thanks to
the Young Offspring,
the mighty hero,
we can drink the water,
and now our lives
have been saved!"

As I heard
the deities
speak these words
of gratitude,

I went upstream
along the Shishirmuka river
until I arrived
atop the peak,
the mighty mountain peak
at its headwaters.

At that time
I went walking about
here and there on the mountain slopes
in this way:
I jumped from one end
of the mountain peak
to the other end,
sliding along
on silver snowshoes.
As I did this,
from the tips of my snowshoes
small lumps of snow
and large lumps of snow
went flying up
over the mountain slopes.
I kicked them with my snowshoes,
and the lumps of snow
fell scattered here and there
over the mountain slopes.
As they fell,
those lumps of snow
on the mountain slopes
were transformed
into herds of small deer
and into herds of large deer
and went skipping and jumping together
over the mountain slopes.

I went down
to the top
of a divinely made precipice.
I went sliding along,
I went gliding along
on my silver snowshoes,
and this is what
came about:
From the tips of my snowshoes
small lumps of snow
and large lumps of snow
went flying up
and came falling down
over the surface of the river.
As they fell down,
this is what happened:
In the fishing grounds
of the Shishirmuka river,
there were fish so abundant
that the schools of fish on the bottom
would rub against the rocks
and the schools of fish on the top
would be scorched by the sunshine.

Seeing this,
I turned around
and went down again
heading toward
my native stronghold.
Then I returned
to the abode of
my elder sister,
my foster sister.
When she caught sight of me,

she nodded approvingly
at me again and again.

    ''Such deeds
    as those you have done,
    o god I have raised,
    o my divine nursling,
    are exploits which win
    the praise of the gods!''

My elder sister
spoke
these words.

These things
were recounted by
Aeoina-kamui.

22. Song of Aeoina-kamui (Excerpt)

This excerpt is from a mythic epic of the *oina* type recorded in writing by Kubodera from the reciter Hiraga Etenoa on August 29, 1932. It was sung with the burden *Hei inou.* The meaning of the burden is unclear. Similar burdens are used with many other mythic epics.

The excerpt given here is the section where the foster sister, who identifies herself as the goddess watching over mount Optateshke, tells the hero the story of his birth. He is the offspring of a little elm growing at the foot of mount Optateshke and the Pestilence God *(Pa-kor-kamui).*

Other informants also agreed with this account attributing the culture hero's parentage to the elm goddess and the Pestilence God. Nabesawa Taukno of Shumunkot village and Kotanpira of Piratori village told this version to Kindaichi.[1] In other versions, he is the offspring of the elm goddess and a sky god ("the younger of two brothers ruling the Upper Heavens"). In some accounts the hero's foster sister is the Sun Goddess; in others she is the Moon Goddess. All accounts from this area of Hokkaido seem to agree that the culture hero's mother is the elm goddess *(chikisani kamui).* It is odd that his father should be the Pestilence God, feared as the source of smallpox and other infectious diseases.

The text is Oina 3 in Kubodera's *Ainu jojishi: Shin'yō, seiden no kenkyū,* pp. 493–509.

One day
my foster sister
stared fixedly down
at the center of the hearth.
She seemed to have
something she wanted to say.

The ashes in the center of the fireplace
she raked out toward the edges,
and the ashes at the edges of the fireplace
she raked out toward the center.
Here and there in the ashes
she jabbed [with the tongs]

---

[1] Kindaichi, *Ainu jojishi yūkara gaisetsu,* pp. 19–23.

and traced furrows and lines.
But she seemed to have
something she wanted to say.
Again and again she would steal
glances in my direction.
However,
it would be understandable
if she hesitated to speak out
to a moderate degree,
[but her hesitation was extraordinary].
She remained silent,
gulping down many words,
gulping down countless words
which had come to the tip of her tongue.
Finally, she raised up
her eyebrows sharply
and spoke these words:

    "Listen to
    what I have to say!
    Since you were still
    much too young,
    much too helpless,
    I have not
    told you the tale
    until now.
    But now finally
    I will tell you.
    The tale is this:

    "Long ago,
    in days gone by,
    the Land Creator God,
    the Country Creator God

came down
to this land of the humans
to create the land,
to create the country.
He created the land,
he created the country.
Then he finished the land,
he finished the country.
This native mountain of ours
is called
the divine mountain
Optateshke.[2]
After he had finished,
the Land Creator God
ascended
into the heavenly skies
from atop the peak of
that mountain.
He had made
a mattock handle of elm,[3]
had fitted it onto his mattock,
and had used it
to create the country,
to create the land.
Then, when he
had finished,
he forgot
that mattock handle
atop the peak
of the divine mountain
Optateshke.
Since it would be a great pity
if something made by hand
by the most weighty god

---

[2] A mountain in Hokkaido at the headwaters of the Tokapchi (Tokachi) river in Daisetsuzan National Park.

[3] The *chikisani* elm (*Ulmus davidiana* Planch. *var. japonica* Nakai). The bark of this type of elm was made into fibers which used to be woven into garments by the Ainu. The word *chikisani* means "fire-drilling tree." According to Batchelor, the dried roots were formerly used to make fire drills.

were left to rot in the ground,
it sprouted forth
and became a little elm.

''During this while,
the gods
would descend
from the heavenly skies
to view the land.
Then they would return
to the heavenly skies
and would speak
admiringly in praise
of the beauties of the country,
the beauties of the land.
The Pestilence God[4]
heard this.
For this reason,
he descended
to view the country,
to view the land.
Nevertheless,
there was not
a single of blade grass,
and there was not
a single tree.
There was not any place
for him to rest on
while viewing the land,
while viewing the country.
After that,
he made his way
through the country
and finally came

to the peak
of the divine mountain
Optateshke.
He looked and saw that,
at the foot
of the divine mountain
Optateshke,
a little elm
was growing.
Since this was
the only tree,
he rested on it.
After that,
he viewed the land.
Delighting in
the beauties of the country,
the beauties of the land,
he viewed the land,
he viewed the country.
This is what
he thought to himself:

'Truly, it is no wonder
that the gods
spoke admiringly
in praise of
the beauties of the land.
What a beautiful
land this is!'

''Thinking this thought,
he continued to view the land.
Then he ascended
into the heavenly skies.

---

[4] *Pa-kor-kamui*, the god who controls infectious diseases and epidemics, especially smallpox. He is the chieftain of a band of pestilence gods who travel around the land spreading diseases. He is sometimes called the Smallpox God.

"After that,
it would have been a great pity
if the fact that
the most weighty deity
had rested on
that little elm
were allowed to fall [fruitlessly] to the
    ground.
[The little elm] became pregnant
and gave birth to a child.

"After that,
the little elm
was blown about together with her child.
When the wind blew
from the west,
it blew her and her child
to the east
of the divine mountain
Optateshke.
When the wind blew
from the east,
it blew her and her child
to the west
of the divine mountain
Optateshke.
Both night
and day
she continued
to be blown about with her child
all the time.
Then finally, one time
the little elm
threw

the baby she had been holding
up to the peak
of the divine mountain
Optateshke.
As she did so,
she uttered
these words:

'My heart is tired
and sorely distressed!
When the wind blows
from the west,
it blows me and my child
to the east
of the divine mountain
Optateshke.
When the wind blows
from the east,
it blows me and my child
to the west
of the divine mountain.
My heart is tired
and sorely distressed!
Surely there must be
some deity sent down
from the Upper Heavens
to watch over
the divine mountain
Optateshke.
Whoever you may be,
look after
my baby for me,
I pray!'

"Saying these words,
she threw you,
she cast you
to the peak of the mountain.

"As for me,
I am
the deity sent down
from the heavenly skies
to watch over
the divine mountain
Optateshke.
At that time
you were cast away.
Therefore,
I took you in
and have until now
been raising you
with a splendid upbringing,
a magnificent upbringing.

"In the meanwhile,
Big Demon
was seeking out lands,
was seeking out countries.[5]
On account of this,
the gods gathered,
and you have heard
them doing battle against
Big Demon.
For a very long time,
many rumbling and thudding noises,
countless rumbling and thudding noises
have been rising up,

and you have
been hearing them.
However,
you were still much too young,
you were still much too helpless,
and I gave up the idea
of telling you the tale of it.
Thus, I have not
told you the tale
until now.
But now at last
I have told you the tale.

"You must go to assist
in the battle,
the battle against
Big Demon.
If you do not,
it looks as if
your land,
your country
will be stolen away from you.
So you must
go to assist
in the battle,
the battle against
Big Demon,
and these are the preparations
I have made for you:

"Since you had
your origins in
the little elm,
I wanted you

[5] He was roaming about seeking lands and countries to steal and make his own.

to have this as your emblem,
and I made with my own hands
an elm-bark fiber coat with a flaming
   hem,[6]
and a sheath with a flaming tip
as your divine armor.[7]
I have prepared
them for you.
Wearing them,
you must go
to assist
in the battle,
the battle against
Big Demon!''

While she said
these words,
my foster sister
brought out
the divine armor:
an elm-bark fiber coat with a flaming hem
and a sheath with a flaming tip
and held them out toward me.

Overjoyed,
I sprang up
on the bed.
I clad myself
in a magnificent robe.
A metal buckled belt
I wrapped around myself
in a single wrapping.
After that,
I stepped
inside
the divine armor:
the elm-bark fiber coat with the flaming hem
and the sheath with the flaming tip.
I describe in detail
how I dressed myself,
how I arrayed myelf.

After that
I headed
toward the doorway.
I stepped
outside.

Here is a prose synopsis of the rest of the story of this mythic epic:
   I went into battle, shedding tears of grief at the thought that I was the off-spring of a little elm. I arrived at the place where the battle against Big Demon was taking place. I engaged Big Demon in battle, and we fought on and on for year after year. Finally my sword broke, and I lost consciousness.
   When I awoke, I was atop the branch of a tree at the foot of the volcano at the source of the Shikot river. I looked down and saw the corpse of a young boy lying under me. I managed with difficulty to tear myself away from the

[6] *O-uhui nikap attush.* This is the distinctive emblem of the culture hero.
[7] *Kamui hayokpe*, the divine armor or costume distinctive of the culture hero.

corpse and went down to the mouth of the Shikot river. The god ruling over the mouth of the river brought out treasures to induce me to turn back, accusing me of fleeing after only a single battle. I jumped over the treasures and went on. When I had come to the mouth of the Iput river, the god ruling over the mouth of the river also brought out treasures and asked me to turn back. I ignored him and went on to the mouth of the Muka river. Here again the god of the river mouth urged me to go back, offering to pay me treasures as inducement. I leaped over them and went on. When I reached the mouth of the Shishirmuka river, the god of the river rapids once again urged me to turn back, offering me treasures. I jumped over them and went upstream along the Shishirmuka river.

I went upstream until I reached a fork in the river. There was a bridge of mist rising up into the sky. I climbed up higher and higher on this bridge. When I had climbed up into the highest heaven, a sort of dog-like creature came toward me. It had jutting fangs and continued to snap at me. I turned around and fled back.

I fled past the god of the mouth of the Shishirmuka river, the god of the mouth of the Muka river, the god of the mouth of the Iput river, and the god of the mouth of the Shikot river. Each one of them laughed at me, but the dog still continued to chase and snap at me.

When I finally arrived at the foot of the volcano at the source of the Shikot river, I jumped down onto the corpse. This was the last thing I remember.

After a period of unconsciousness, I awoke to see a young woman of amazing beauty. She was wearing white robes and was singing a song while blowing puffs of breath on my body. My wounds healed up, and I was revived. The young woman said:

"I am the younger sister of the Wolf God of the Upper Heavens. Both you and Big Demon perished in battle: you were making your way toward the land of the gods. I was asked by my elder brother to cause you to turn back and to restore you to life. He also asked me to go home with you and cook your meals for you. I transformed myself into my shape of a dog and went to meet you, causing you to flee. Now I have restored you to life."

I ignored the young woman completely and returned to the stronghold where I was raised. The young woman trailed along after me.

23. Song of the Young God Okikurmi (Dream Song)

This is a mythic epic of the *oina* type recorded in writing by Kubodera from the reciter Hiraga Etenoa in August, 1932. The burden is not recorded; the reciter said that she had "forgotten" the burden.

This is a parody of the *oina* type mythic epic in which the speaker is the "young Okikurmi" (*pon Okikurmi*), the son of the culture hero Okikurmi. The action is atypical throughout. The young hero is raised by a cannibal foster sister (*ainu ep sapo*) who has previously killed his father. The hero goes into the mountains with her, sings her to sleep, and sets fire to the hut. Just then the hero awakes. The action is presented as if it happened in a dream.

Atypical narratives of this type, containing grotesque departures from the normal order of things, are usually called "dream songs." (This one is called *wentarap kamui yukar*, "dream god-epic.")

The text is Oina 6 in Kubodera's *Ainu jojishi: Shin'yō, seiden no kenkyū*, pp. 527–29

A cannibal elder sister
raised me,
and we lived on.
When she went hunting in the mountains,
she would [come back] carrying on her back
equal amounts of
human flesh and deer flesh.
She would cook
the deer flesh for me,
and she would cook
the human flesh for herself.
This was the way
we lived
on and on.

Then one day
this is what she said:

    "O Young Offspring,
    come along with me!
    Let us go into the mountains!"

She spoke
these words.
Therefore,
I dressed myself.
After that,
we went on and on
somewhere or other.

Finally, we came
to a certain place.
It was incredible
what an amazing
divinely made ravine
it was!
Spanning the ravine,
a needle-thin bridge
was stretched.
Now
this is what
my cannibal elder sister said:

    "I am going
    to go across on
    the needle-thin bridge.
    You must do
    exactly the same as I do!"

Saying this,
she leaped
onto the bridge,
the needle-thin bridge,
and started across.
After that,
at times
the needle-thin bridge
would go swinging up
to the skies.
At other times
it would go swinging down
to the bottom of the ravine.
My cannibal elder sister
would cling tight

to the top of the bridge
and to the bottom of the bridge.
After doing this for some time,
she finally arrived across
at the opposite side.

After that,
this is what she said:

    "Come across, doing
    exactly the same as I did!"

Thus did she say.
After that,
I stripped off my clothes
and leaped
onto the bridge,
the needle-thin bridge.

Then
the needle-thin bridge
at times
would go swinging up
to the skies.
At other times
it would go swinging down
to the bottom of the ravine.
I strove to my utmost,
I did my very utmost
so that I would not
be bested by
my cannibal elder sister.
I clung tight
to the bottom of the bridge

and to the top of the bridge.

After that
my cannibal elder sister
bent backward
and bent forward
with laughter [saying]:

> "It is no wonder
> the Young Offspring
> does such feats,
> for he is the offspring
> of illustrious forebears!"

As she laughed,
human flesh appeared
from between her teeth
and dangled down
when she spoke these words.

I continued to go on
and finally arrived across
at the opposite side.
My cannibal elder sister
spoke these words:

> "Long ago,
> I brought
> your father there
> and killed him
> by doing just that.
> Now once again,
> I have brought you,
> but it is no wonder

that you have done this feat
because you are the offspring
of illustrious forebears.
Your father's
armor
is tied to
the top of [that] spruce.
Remember this well!"

These words
were spoken by
my cannibal elder sister.
When she said this,
I turned aside
for a moment [and thought]:

> "What is this thing
> called father,
> that mine
> should have been killed?"[1]

As I thought this,
I shed
many sparkling teardrops,
countless sparkling teardrops.

After that,
I considered
what I ought to do
with my cannibal elder sister,
turning over various
things in my mind.
This is what
I said:

---

[1] The meaning is: "I did not even know that I had a father, and now it appears that I had a father and that he was killed."

"Look here,
cannibal elder sister,
let us spend this night
here in the mountains.
You have raised me
well, and
I would like to sing epics[2] for you,
so that at least
you might hear them."

When I said this,
she nodded approvingly
at me again and again.

"Are you telling
me the truth,
o Young Offspring?"

I replied
that it was true.
After that
I made
a little grass hut.
I kindled
a blazing bonfire.

Then
I said:

"Listen carefully,
cannibal elder sister!"

and started to sing epics.

One of the eyes
of my cannibal elder sister
went to sleep.
One of her ears
went to sleep.
She was listening
with one eye
and with one ear.
After that
I continued to sing epics
until at long last
I noticed that
both of her eyes
and both of her ears
had gone to sleep.

The window
and the door
of that grass hut
I tied shut
with leather thongs.
I set fire
to the upper thatch layers
and the lower thatch layers [on the roof].
That grass hut
burst into flames
with a tremendous roar.

Now
my cannibal elder sister
went running around inside the hut [crying]:

"O Young Offspring,

---

[2] *Yukar*, the heroic epics. The hero wants to recite epics for his elder sister to recompense her for having given him such a good upbringing.

where are you?
Come quickly
and rescue me!''

I thought I heard
her crying out these words.
Just then there was the sound

of dogs barking,
and at that moment I awoke.

These things
were recounted
by the Young Okikurmi.

24. Song of the Younger Sister of the Owl God

This is a mythic epic of the *pon oina* type recorded in writing by Kubodera from the reciter Hiraga Etenoa on September 9, 1932. The burden is not recorded. Probably it was recited without a burden in the manner of the heroic epics.

This selection is one of a whole cluster of mythic epics dealing with how the culture hero courts a maiden and fights against a rival god for her hand. In this case, the maiden is the younger sister of the Owl God (*Kotan-kor-kamui kot tureshi*), and the rival is the god of mount Poroshir.

The speaker is the younger sister of the Owl God. She is betrothed to the god of Poroshir. One day, the God of the Western Seaboard (*Anrur-un-kamui*) from the opposite coast of Hokkaido comes to visit, and the Owl God gives a drinking feast in his honor. During the feast, the god of Poroshir comes in and accuses the Owl God of having given his younger sister to the God of the Western Seaboard rather than to him, the god of Poroshir. He threatens warfare against the Owl God. The God of the Western Seaboard takes up the challenge and does battle against Poroshir. The younger sister of the Owl God is transformed into a "female sword rivet" (*matne shik*) and accompanies the hero into battle. During the battle she catches brief glimpses of an elm-bark fiber coat with a flaming hem and a sheath with a flaming tip, and this makes it clear that the hero is really Ainurakkur, the culture heroe. After the battles are over, the hero takes the young goddess home with him, and they live together as man and wife.

There are very many variants of this epic, which must have been extremely popular. The most remarkable variant is that of Kannari Matsu (Imekanu) of Horobetsu (called the *pon aina*). Her version has nearly seven thousand lines. The story is closely similar to the version of Etenoa given here. (Imekanu's version is given in Kindaichi's *Ainu jojishi: Yukara shū*, vol. 1)

The text is Kamui Yukar 62 in Kubodera's *Ainu jojishi: Shin'yō, seiden no kenkyū*, pp. 285–97.

My elder brother
raised me,
and we lived
on and on
uneventfully.
Doing nothing but needlework,
I remained with my eyes
focused on a single spot,
and we lived
on and on
uneventfully.

Then, one day,
all of a sudden,
the door opened,
and someone came inside.
When I looked,
this is what I saw:
A young boy
of amazing beauty
came in.
So beautiful was he
that I could not tell
whether he was a human
or whether he was a god.
He was dressed
with his garments hanging loose,
as if he had just come
from quite nearby.
He came in
and sat down
at the head of the fireplace.

My elder brother

remained for some time
with his eyelids
shut tight over each other.
Then he popped his eyes open.
The young boy
made salutations.
After that,
[my elder brother] made inquiries
of the young boy.
In reply,
the young boy
said these words:

> "I am
> the God of the Western Seaboard.[1]
> I have come
> because I was
> so exceedingly
> lonely."

He spoke
these words.
Then
my elder brother
spoke these words:

> "If the weighty god
> has come
> to pay me a visit,
> then it would be
> most unfitting
> for us to meet
> without wine.
> Let me brew

[1] *Anrur-un-kamui*, god from the opposite coast of Hokkaido. This god is said to be from the Ishikari region. The young boy is really the culture hero Ainurakkur, who is merely assuming the identity of the God of the Western Seaboard.

a little wine,
and let us enjoy
our conversation over it!''

Saying these things,
he raced his hands
nimbly
to brew a little wine.
When two or three days
had gone by,
the wine was now
finally ready,
and the odor of the wine
hovered about
inside the house.
After that,
those of the servants
who were whittling *inau*
plied their whittling knives
together this way and that,
and those who were straining the wine
darted their wicker baskets
together this way and that.
The sounds of the wine being strained,
and the creaking sounds of the *inau* being
   whittled
were quite delightful,
and my heart leaped with pleasure.
During the time
while this was being done,
I took great
delight in the voices
of the [two] gods in their conversation.
After some time had gone by,

now the preparations
were finally completed
for holding the drinking feast,
for holding the banquet.
My foster brother
sent out
the messages of invitation.
The first messenger
to be sent out
was the one inviting
the god of Poroshir.[2]
After that,
my foster brother
dispatched messages
to all the gods living nearby
and all the gods living far away.

After a short while,
the invited deities
were shown in with much ceremony.
After that,
my foster brother
stood up and,
leading
the God of the Western Seaboard
by the hand,
seated him
in back of
the big wine-tub.[3]
He himself sat down
facing him.
Then all the guests
at the divine drinking feast
were arranged at their positions

---

[2] Poroshir ("big mountain") is a common name for mountains in Hokkaido. The one referred to here is the peak known today as Horoshiri-dake, on the border between the provinces of Hidaka and Tokachi.
[3] In the position of the chief guest.

from the head of the festal mats
to the foot of the festal mats.
Then I began
to wind my way about
among the guests,
holding
the wine flagon
close by my side,
to pour the wine to them.

Just then,
when the drinking feast,
the banquet
had reached its height,
there was a loud booming
somewhere over the land—
I didn't know exactly where,
I wasn't sure at what place
it might be.
A most weighty god
was heard coming this way
with a loud rumbling.

At that time,
my foster brother
stood up
and seated himself
by the fireside.
While doing so,
he uttered these words:

"This sounds
as if the god of Poroshir
were coming.

Let me alone
speak to him.
No matter what happens,
let no one
beside me
speak to
the god of Poroshir!"

While speaking
these words,
my foster brother
seated himself
by the fireside.

After a short while,
someone dropped down
onto the clearing outside the house
with a mighty thud.
Without any hesitation,
he stepped inside
the entrance porch.[4]
Some sort of being
pushed open
the door hangings
up to the very rafters,
and someone came in.
When I looked,
this is what I saw.
One who looked like
a stout tree
growing in a wood by the river
which has been broken
at the middle of its trunk
came walking in.

---

[4] *Mosem*, the earthen-floored antechamber or entrance shed.

He came darting
into the vestibule,
the earthen-floored vestibule.[5]
He was [so angry that he was]
scarcely able to stand.
When I looked at him,
this is what I saw.
On the back of his head
it looked as if
he had
a reddish bald spot.
He was [so angry that he was]
scarcely able to stand.

Just then
my elder brother,
my foster brother
spoke these words:

>   "The god of Poroshir
>   was the very first
>   I invited,
>   but for some reason
>   he was late
>   in coming.
>   It is good
>   that he has now
>   arrived
>   during the course
>   of our wine feast,
>   our drinking feast."

When my elder brother
spoke these words,

the god of Poroshir
poured out
biting words,
harsh words,
exactly as if
my foster brother
had said something evil.
This is what he said:

>   "Yes, indeed,
>   the Owl God
>   has a beautiful younger sister,
>   and this is why
>   he has deceived me!
>   He told me that
>   he would give her
>   to me in marriage,
>   but he was
>   deceiving me most basely!
>   All along, it appears,
>   he was intending
>   to marry her
>   to the God of the Western Seaboard.
>   This encounter
>   will be your last
>   in the land of the living.[6]
>   I will go back
>   and return once
>   to my own homeland.
>   After that
>   I will launch
>   a war of annihilation,
>   a war of extirpation
>   against your homeland!"

[5] *Aun chiketoi*, the earthen-floored part just inside the entrance of the main part of the house.

[6] The original phrase means literally: "This encounter will be for you a present to take with you into the land of the dead."

After saying this,
he turned around
and went outside.
After that,
he went off
with a loud roaring.
What could ever
have caused him
to be so terribly angry?
As he went off,
the rumbling was so loud
that it seemed as if
the land would collapse.
After it was over,
my elder brother
spoke these words:

 "The truth of the matter
 is this:
 the gods took counsel together
 and decided
 that I should marry
 my younger sister
 to the god of Poroshir.
 When ever
 did I say
 that I would marry
 my younger sister
 to the God of the Western Seaboard?
 Why did he say
 such a thing?"

Thus spoke
my foster brother.

After that
I describe in detail[7]
how the drinking feast went on.
Taking great
delight in the voices
of the conversations of the guests,
the conversations of the gods,
I wound my way about
among the guests
to pour the wine to them.
I continued
to do this until
by now
the peerless drinking feast
progressed majestically
and the drinking feast,
the banquet
came to an end.

After that
the gods
expressed
their gratitude
and left for home.
Only one,
the God of the Western Seaboard,
remained behind.

He stared fixedly
down into the center of the hearth
and remained for some time
saying nothing.
Then he spoke these words:

[7] The verb meaning "to describe in detail," "to relate fully" is *omommomo*. It is used when the reciter wishes to abbreviate a lengthy passage of description which is already familiar to the audience. Even when this convention is used, the first-person narration is adhered to, since the speaker (in this case the Young Sister of the Owl God) is narrating the story about himself or herself. See above, Introduction, pp. 38–39.

"Listen,
o Owl God,
to what I have to say!
So exceedingly
lonely
was I, that
I came
to enjoy
a peaceful visit.
I did not
come here
in the least
for any mischief,
for any lewdness.
But if
such things
are said,
I would rather
take up the challenge myself.
The god of Poroshir
was surely
not speaking
any empty words.
It would be bad
if I were to stay here,
and a war of annihilation,
a war of extirpation
were to be launched.
against the homeland
of the Owl God.
This being the case,
I have decided
to take up the challenge myself.

"If I were to go
and do battle against
the god of Poroshir
and his kinsfolk,
that would be
like play for me.
Nevertheless,
to the west
of mount Poroshir,
the mountain ruled
by the god of Poroshir,
there dwell
these beings:
ordinary wolves,
altogether threescore in number;
poisonous wolves,
altogether threescore in number;
poisonous *huri*,
altogether threescore in number;
ordinary *huri*,
altogether threescore in number;
ordinary *kuruise*,[8]
altogether threescore in number;
and poisonous *kuruise*,
altogether threescore in number.
These creatures
dwell
to the west of the mountain.

"At whatever cost,
I will do battle against
the homeland
of the god of Poroshir.
Then, when the battle,

---

[8] *Kuruise* are man-eating devils said to assume the form of huge predatory insects resembling grasshoppers.

when the war is
half finished,
in the midst of the fighting
battles of the demons
will be launched against me.
This is what it will be like
when the battles of the demons
are launched against me:
For six summers
and for six winters,
the battles of the demons
will rage against me.
If I manage
to come through them alive,
you will hear
a most weighty god
traveling [through the sky]
across the land
with a single roar.
If I die,
bloody rain will fall
on half of the land,
and the sun will shine bright
on half of the land.
These [will be the signs];
be sure to note them carefully,
o Owl God!''

When the God of the Western Seaboard
had spoken
these words,
he stood up.
At first
I thought that

he meant
to leave me behind,
but he picked me up,
rubbed me again and again between his
    hands,
and blew his breath on me.
At this, I was transformed
into a female sword rivet.[9]
He attached me
onto the sheath
of his sword.
After that,
he united himself with
the rising smoke,
the smoke ascending
from the hearth,
and headed up
toward the smokehole.

After that,
he carried me away,
and we went off
somewhere or other.
Where ever
could he be going?
Both night
and day
we traveled on,
with blasts of wind
whirling in my ears.

We came to
a place which seemed to be
the homeland

---

[9] Some of the rivets on the sword hilt are called male and others female.

of the god of Poroshir.
It was amazing
how many were his kinsfolk,
how many were his relatives!
The populous villages
stretched out peacefully
into the distance,
filling up the entire
foot of the mountain,
the divine mountain.

We arrived [in the air]
over the villages.
Just then,
the villages were thrown
into an uproar.
Throughout the villages,
these populous villages,
people were milling about
like swarming insects.
They donned their armor hastily,
they donned their armor quickly,
and there was a noisy
creaking and grating of armor.

After that
the God of the Western Seaboard
plunged head first
into the midst
of this mass of people.
When he drew his sword,
this was the way it was:
How ever could he
possibly wield his sword

in such a way!
Wherever he passed
the corpses mowed down like grass
lay stretched out in the distance.
How ever could he
wield his sword
in such a way,
perform such feats!
All that could be seen
was the flashing of his sword.
In the meantime,
the god of Poroshir
was stamping a war dance
behind his armies.
He cried out these words:

"Come, be quick,
my kinsmen!
Wield your swords fiercely!
Struggle mightily!
Who will be the one to kill
the God of the Western Seaboard?
When we bring
to our homeland
the sacred vessels,
the treasures which are
in the divinely made stronghold
of the God of the Western Seaboard,
even those who are poor
will be made rich.
Wield your swords fiercely,
struggle mightily,
my kinsmen!"

These commands
he cried out
to the least ones of his kinsfolk
and to the chief ones of his kinsfolk.
By this time
the battle had reached
its mid-point, the war
was half finished.
Now what was this
that happened?
From the west of the mountain,
the mountain ruled
by the god of Poroshir,
dense clouds,
black clouds
arose.
They moved swiftly
like an arrow in flight.
They came speeding
in this direction,
heading straight
toward the battle
being fought by
the God of the Western Seaboard.

Within a short while
the dense clouds,
the black clouds
came down and enveloped
the battle.
I felt exactly as if
I had been thrust down
into a black abyss,
and I couldn't tell

when it was daytime
and when it was nighttime.
Within the clouds,
the dense clouds,
the black clouds,
wild shrieks of alarm,
loud screaming voices
went soaring upward.
As I listened
to these voices,
I also heard
other sounds:
Within the clouds,
the dense clouds,
the black clouds,
the sounds of dogs barking,
the sounds of birds flapping their wings
I heard also
within the clouds.
When I would look
from time to time,
I would be able to see
by the light,
the light of sharp blades flashing,
the one who had said
that he was
the God of the Western Seaboard.
I would see him
by the light of sharp blades flashing.
There would be a little mound of mist,
and within the mist
I would see
faintly
an elm-bark fiber coat with a flaming hem,

and a sheath with a flaming tip.
Wondering at this,
I would look again
carefully,
and the God of the Western Seaboard
would be there
exactly as he was before,
and all that could be seen
was the flashing of his sword.
When I saw this,
this is what
I thought to myself:

"It is all for my sake,
my miserable sake,
my contemptible sake,
that the God of the Western Seaboard
is now being harassed
so very sorely!
Let me come out
and do something to help,
even though I may be able to serve no
    better
than an old worn-out mat
which merely gets in the way."

Thinking this,
I tried to
lift up my head
on the sheath where I was.
Then he pressed me down firmly
with his left hand,
and in this way
he did not even let me

raise up my head.

After this,
it seemed to me
as if the battles of the demons
raged on
for six summers
and six winters.
At long last,
he finally emerged alive
from the battles of the demons.
After that
we went
along the land.
Then when we had come
to a certain place,
this is what I saw.
A magnificent house,[10]
a big house
was standing there,
sparkling brilliantly
from the ground up.
He went
inside it.
When I looked,
this is what I saw.
The surface of the floor,
the magnificent floor,[11]
stretched out smooth and flat.
The magnificent hearth frame[12]
extended out far,
gleaming brilliantly.
As I was looking at these things,
the God of the Western Seaboard

[10] Literally, "a metal house."
[11] Literally, "the metal floor."
[12] Literally, "the metal hearth frame."

walked up
onto the floor at the head of the fireplace.
He picked me up
off the sheath
and cast me down onto the floor.

It looked as if
the fire had not been burning
for a very long time,
for there was a hollowed depression
in the place where the fire had been burning.
All around the fireplace
a number of round bright objects,
bright objects which moved about,
were lined up in a row
on the hearth frame.
He stamped his feet
on those bright objects
all around the fireplace.
While doing so,
he spoke these words:

"You low-born servants,
what sleepy-heads you are!
What a long time
you have been asleep!"

While saying this,
he stamped his feet
on those bright objects
all around the fireplace.
When he did that,
men servants
and women servants

got up,
rubbing their eyes again and again.
This is what they said:

"We were going
to stay asleep
for a little while longer,
but now we have
been awakened, it seems!"

Saying this,
they all got up.
Then
the women servants
began to dust
the floor.
The men servants
brought in
many armfuls of firewood,
countless armfuls of firewood
and worked busily together
to kindle the fire.

The stacks of sacred vessels
were stretched out
like a low cliff.
Above them
huṇg noble swords,
with their many sword handles,
their countless sword handles
overhanging each other.
The brightness of the vessels
and the brightness of the treasures
were glittering brightly

and casting shadows
on the walls.
Below the stacks,
the stacks of sacred vessels,
there stood
a movable seat,
a magnificent seat.
He took his place
on the seat.

After that
we lived
on and on
uneventfully.
He carved on scabbards
and carved on treasures,
with his eyes focused
on a single spot.
While we lived on,
this is what
I thought to myself:

    "O for my foster brother,
    who raised me
    so very well!
    What must he
    be thinking of me?
    To what land,
    to what country
    must he be thinking
    that I have gone?"

Thinking this,
I shed

many sparkling teardrops,
countless sparkling teardrops.
As I continued
to live on in this way,
the servants,
the men servants,
day after day,
day in and day out,
would go hunting in the mountains
and would bring home
deer
and bears.
They fed me
well with them,
and we lived on.

Then, one day,
the exalted hero
spoke these words:

    "Just across the river from here
    is the abode
    of your elder brother.
    You may go
    and see him
    if you wish."

When he said this,
I was overjoyed.
Therefore
I piled up many
of the best pieces
of my embroidered handiwork.
Carrying them in my hands,

I stepped
outside.
When I went
across the river,
true enough,
just across the river
was the abode
of my foster brother.
When I went
inside it,
my foster brother
was sitting there
with his eyelids
shut tightly over each other.
I rushed toward him,
crying out
"Brother dear!"
Then
he popped his eyes open.
When he saw me,
he cried out
"Dear little sister!"
We rejoiced
greatly together.
After that
I spoke these words:

     "Sometimes during the fighting
     I would catch glimpses
     of the one who took me along with him,
     the one who called himself
     the God of the Western Seaboard.
     There would be a little mound of mist,
     and I would seem to see

faintly
an elm-bark fiber coat with a flaming hem
and a sheath with a flaming tip
within the mist.
Then when I would look carefully,
the God of the Western Seaboard
would be there
exactly as he was before.
This continued
through all the fighting.
Then, after great effort,
he finally emerged alive
from the battles of the demons.
After that,
we came
along the land,
and he came back
to the place which
was his abode.
After that
I thought to myself:

'O, what land is this,
what country is this,
where I have been
[brought and] abandoned?'

     "And I was shedding
     many sparkling teardrops,
     countless sparkling teardrops.
     Then, only this very day,
     he told me that,
     all the time,
     he had brought me

just across the river
from my elder brother,
my foster brother,
and only today
he told me
where my elder
brother was.
It is thanks to this
that I have come!''

When I said this,
my elder brother,
my foster brother
covered his nose
and covered his mouth [in amazement]
and said this:

"Can this be true?
O to think that
Ainurakkur,
my divine nephew,
my revered nephew
deceived me!
When he said
that he was
the God of the Western Seaboard,
I believed
him to be
the God of the Western Seaboard,
and all the time
I did not know
that Ainurakkur,
my revered nephew,
my divine nephew

was living there
just across the river from me!
To think that
he deceived me!''

These words
were spoken by
my foster brother.

After that,
the best pieces
of my embroidered handiwork
which I had brought
I left with
my elder brother,
my foster brother.
After that,
I came back.
I came back
to the place of
the exalted hero.

Since then,
I have done nothing but needlework,
with my eyes focused
on a single spot.
We have lived
on and on
uneventfully.
We lead
a magnificent married life,
a glorious married life.
I lack nothing
that I want to eat

or that I want to possess,
and I live on.

These things

were recounted
by the younger sister
of the Owl God.

25. Song of the Younger Sister of Okikurmi

This is a mythic epic recorded in writing by Kubodera from the reciter Hiraga Etenoa on December 18, 1932. It was sung with the burden *Anna hōre hore hōre*. The meaning of the burden is unclear.

The speaker is the younger sister of Okikurmi (*Okikurmi kot tureshi*). The word *tureshi* may mean either "younger sister" or "beloved." It is not clear whether the woman is the sister or the wife of Okikurmi. The woman is pining away in longing for her native homeland, the area around the Shishirmuka river. Okikurmi magically shows her pictures of their homeland and tells her why they have left the land of the Ainu and are now living in an adjacent country, Samor-moshir.

A variant of the same song, using the burden *Hōre hōure*, was recorded in writing by Kindaichi in 1915 from Nabesawa Taukno.

In his *Ainu seiten*, Kindaichi notes that various legends were current among the Saru Ainu of his day concerning Oina-kamui's departure. They have various compositions, but in general they describe how Oina-kamui, who had been dwelling at Hayopira and teaching the Ainu, became incensed at them when they grew depraved and refused to obey him. The life of the pious elderly Ainu in Kindaichi's day was imbued with a melancholic sense of forlornness and regret on account of the departure of Oina-kamui. Kindaichi says that this was no doubt an understandable result of the tragic conditions in which the Ainu people found themselves. However, the Ainu were unable to accept this separation from Oina-kamui as being irreversible. The elderly Ainu told Kindaichi that they believed that even at the present day Oina-kamui sometimes came to visit the Ainu villages. For instance, when the first rumblings of thunder were heard in the spring far away at sea off the mouth of the Saru river, and the rumblings would then move up along the river, the pious elders would go outside and worship. They would say that the thunder indicated that Oina-kamui had come to visit. Taking their sense of yearning one step further, the Ainu attributed their own feelings to the younger sister

of Oina-kamui. They came to believe that she, too, yearned for the Ainu
homeland and had become homesick in her place of exile. The Ainu ex-
plained to Kindaichi that this song was transmitted in a dream to an elderly
Ainu in the old days, who would frequently obtain dream revelations of this
type. That is, an upright Ainu elder in the old days once dreamed that he was
rowing a boat at sea in a thick mist. Out of the mist he heard the burden of a
song being repeated sadly: *Hōre hōure*. Then the younger sister of Oina-
kamui, alone, came rowing up to him in a boat. She sang this song to him
and then vanished, leaving behind her the melancholic sounds of the burden:
Hōre hōure. When the Ainu awoke, he sang this song to others (pp. 319–20).

The text is Kamui Yukar 86 in Kubodera's *Ainu jojishi: Shin'yō, seiden no
kenkyū*, pp. 385–89.

In my longing
for my native homeland,
I turned aside
from all food,
both the foods which were not tasty
and the tasty foods.
For a very long time
I remained
without eating anything
and lying in bed all the time.
Black mold
appeared
on the food served to me before,
and white mold
appeared
on the food served to me lately.

During this while,
my foster brother,

my elder brother
did nothing but
carve on scabbards
and carve on treasures,
with his eyes focused
on a single spot.
We continued to live
on and on,
and by this time
I thought that
I was about to die,
I was on the verge of dying
on any moment.
I remained conscious
only deep within my heart,
and this is the way
I continued to live.

Then one day,

my foster brother
wrapped in a sedge mat
the carving he had been doing
and laid it aside.
After that
he stepped
outside
and went away.
After that
he was gone for a while
and then came inside again.
He sat down
by the fireside
on the right-hand side of the fireplace.
After that
he began to stare fixedly
down into the center of the hearth.
After a while,
he turned toward me
and spoke these words:

  "Look here,
  my younger sister,
  get up!
  Since you have been behaving like this
  because you wanted to see
  our native homeland,
  I have made pictures of it.
  Wanting to show them to you,
  I have finished making
  pictures of the country,
  pictures of the land.[1]
  Get up
  and come outside

  to see how
  our native homeland
  looks!''

Thus spoke
my foster brother.
Therefore,
with the utmost effort
I raised myself up
from where I had been lying.
Feeling as if
I would fall over
in this direction
and in that direction,
I crawled along
on all fours
and went
outside.
I sat down
by the outer doorway
and looked.
This is what I saw.

Exactly as it used to be,
the Shishirmuka
could be seen clearly
as it flowed along.
There were many small meadows
and big meadows by the river
spread out one after another.
There were many small woods
and big woods by the river
spread out one after another.
Reed thickets

---

[1] In Taukno's version of this mythic epic, written down by Kindaichi in 1915, the elder brother draws pictures of the native homeland in the ashes in the fireplace. In this version, it is not clear how he has produced the pictures.

grew densely in the background,
and rush thickets
grew densely in the foreground.
It was a delightful sight,
and my heart leaped with pleasure.
The forests
by the riverside
looked like this.
Groves of willows
grew densely in the foreground,
and groves of alders
grew densely in the background.
In the river fishing grounds,
[the fish were so abundant that]
the schools of fish on the bottom
would rub against the rocks,
and the schools of fish on the top
would be scorched by the sunshine.

Groups of young men,
going out to catch fish,
darted their harpoons
this way and that way.
Plying their spear shafts,
they jumped around in every direction.

In the mountain hunting grounds,
the small deer
were running in their own herds,
the stags
were running in their own herds,
and the does
were running in their own herds.
They were all skipping and leaping about

over the mountain hunting grounds.

Groups of young men,
going out to hunt the deer,
tipped their quivers
back [to take out the arrows]
and were all skipping and leaping about.
Loud laughing voices
and loud singing voices
could be heard
rising up all at once
as they jumped around in every direction.

In the woods by the river
small lily-bulb beds
and large lily-bulb beds
spread out one after another.

Groups of young women,
going out to dig up the lily bulbs,
threw down here and there
their small baskets
and raced with each other to fill
their big baskets.
In the woods by the river
the groups of young women
rushed about busily here and there
to dig up the lily bulbs.
Loud laughing voices
and loud singing voices
rose up all at once.

When I saw this,
it was a delightful sight,

and my heart leaped with pleasure.
Since I had been behaving like that
because I longed for
my native homeland,
because I wanted to see it,
I continued to take
great delight in
its beauty.
Then, after a while,
the vision vanished
from before my eyes
as if a light had been put out.

After that
I went inside
and sat down
by the fireside.
At that time,
my foster brother
spoke these words:

    "My younger sister,
    listen to
    what I have to say!
    I was so
    exceedingly
    angry at
    the humans
    that I departed in anger
    and came here.
    The name of
    this country
    is Samor-moshir.[2]
    I was so

exceedingly
delighted by
the beauty of the country
that I departed in anger
and came here
to the eastern tip of the land of
Samor-moshir,
and we have been
living here.
Now
I continue
to live here,
intending
never to go back
to the land of the *yaunkur*.
But since you
have been longing
so very much
for our native homeland,
and your behavior
distressed my heart
so sorely,
I fashioned with my hands
pictures
of our native homeland,
of our native river
the Shishirmuka,
and I have
shown them to you.
From now on,
stop doing
what you have been doing!"

Thus spoke

---

[2] Said to mean "adjacent country." A mythical country where epic heroes go to live when they leave the land of the Ainu. Samor may be an old name for the northern provinces of Honshū, once inhabited by Ainu.

my foster brother.
Only then did I begin
to do nothing but needlework,
with my eyes focused
on a single spot.
This is the way we live
on and on
uneventfully.
My foster brother
does nothing but

carve on scabbards
and carve on treasures,
with his eyes focused
on a single spot,
and we live on.

These things
were recounted
by the younger sister
of the god Okikurmi.

Part II
Songs of Humans

Introduction to Part II

The eight selections in this part are all songs sung by human men or women. Three of them are from the repertory of Hirame Karepia, two from the repertory of Shikata Shimukani of Chikabumi (Ishikari province), and two from the repertory of Hiraga Etenoa. The last one (33) is from an unknown reciter recorded by Batchelor during the 1880s.

The songs in this section belong to different epic genres. The first five selections are shorter epic songs sung with burdens in exactly the same way as the *kamui yukar*. The sixth selection, "Song of the Woman of Shinutapka" (31), is an example of a "woman's epic" (*menoko yukar*). The seventh selection, "The Woman of Poi-Soya" (32), is an example of a *hau*. The hero is Otasam-un-kur, and there are frequent changes of speaker during the course of the epic. The final selection, "The Epic of Kotan Utunnai" (33), is an example of a *yukar* heroic epic. The hero and speaker is Poiyaunpe of Shinutapka.

26. Lullaby

This is an epic in the form of a lullaby (*ihumke*) recorded in writing by Kubodera from the reciter Shikata Shimukani of Chikabumi (Ishikari province) on January 5, 1936. It was sung with the burden *O ō hum peyārā hum*. The words have no particular meaning but were probably used by women when trying to put babies to sleep.

The speaker is an unidentified human woman. The chief of the Traveling Gods (pestilence gods, *payekai kamui*) appears to the woman in a dream and promises her that there will never be sickness in her village, although smallpox will break out to the east.

The text is Kamui Yukar 95 in Kubodera's *Ainu jojishi: Shinyō, seiden no kenkyū*, pp. 423–24.

My little baby,
what could be bothering him
that both night
and day
he screamed
so that I could get
no sleep at all?
Night after night,
day after day,
altogether six full days,
I was unable
to get any sleep at all
as I turned over
to one side
and then turned over

to the other side.

I never would
have thought that
I had dropped off to sleep,
but I found myself to be asleep.
At the head of my pillow
a magnificent personage
with a god-like appearance,
who surely was a god,
was sitting.
This is what he said:

"O woman,
listen to

what I have to say!
I am
the chief god
of the Traveling Gods.
I have come
at the head of the flock,
the numerous flock
of all of my kinsfolk,
and we have come
on our way
to the eastern part of the land
to do business.[1]
When I looked,
I found that
there was no woman
as noble-hearted
as you. Thus,
we took our lodging
on the upper thatching
and the lower thatching
on the roof of your house.
This bothered
your little baby, and
this is why he has been screaming
and crying so loudly.
In the morning,
go outside the house
and look around.
Then you will see
a numerous flock [of birds]
go flying up in the air
from the upper thatching on the roof
and the lower thatching on the roof.
They will go flying off

toward the eastern part of the land.
You will hear [later]
that smallpox has broken out
in the eastern part of the land.
But in your settlement,
there will never be
so much as a cold or a cough
as long as you live.''

I thought that
the god
spoke these words,
but it turned out
to be a dream.
I got up,
went outside the house,
and looked around.
I had thought
that it had been
merely a dream, but
true enough,
I saw
a numerous flock [of birds]
fly up in the air
from the upper thatching on the roof
and the lower thatching on the roof
and go flying off
toward the eastern part of the land.
Afterward, I listened to the news
and heard rumors
that smallpox had broken out
in the eastern part of the land.

We will live on

---

[1] The Ainu word is *irauketupa*. The "business" of the Traveling Gods is to spread smallpox and other infectious diseases among the humans in order to increase the number of their flocks. The souls of the humans who die of the diseases assume the form of little birds and join the flock of the pestilence gods. For *irauketupa*, see p. 62.

all our lives,
until old age
without so much as
a cold or a cough.
Since my [goodness of] heart
has won the approval
of the gods,

we will live on
without so much as
a cold or a cough
as long as we live.

Now stop your crying,
my little baby!

27. Song of a Blood-Red Bird (A Woman of Menash)

This is a woman's epic in the form of a *kamui yukar* recorded in writing by Kubodera from the reciter Hirame Karepia on January 26, 1936. It was sung with the burden *Heinou.* The meaning of the burden is unclear. A similar burden (*Hei inou*) was used with selection 22, and similar burdens are found frequently in the mythic epics.

The speaker is an anonymous woman of Menash. Her lover, Poi-sar-un-kur, commits suicide, evidently on account of her. The woman of Menash also commits suicide to follow him, but when she arrives at his abode in the land of the dead, he curses her and drives her away, blaming her for his untimely death. The woman of Menash is transformed into a blood-red bird (*kem chikappo*) which is fated to roam and wander over the earth and cannot receive offerings of the dead. The way in which the story is handled is rather unusual. There is no preamble of any kind, and we are plunged into the midst of the events immediately. The song ends with a didactic warning of the usual type, addressed to humans.

The text is Kamui Yukar 52 in Kubodera's *Ainu jojishi: Shin'yō, seiden no kenkyū,* pp. 241–43.

I spoke to
Poi-sar-un-kur,[1]
saying these words:

   "The women of Menash
   put
   peerless little daggers
   at the bottom of their treasure bags.[2]
   In the middle of their treasure bags
   they put
   peerless dagger-quiver amulets.[3]
   At the top of their treasure bags
   they put
   peerless long swords.
   Even if strong voices
   are raised up against you,
   I myself
   will win

[1] The woman's lover, a native of a place called Poi-sar ("Little Sar"). Characters in epics are usually identified by their native places.

[2] *Shut ketushi,* a bag or trunk made of sedge matting handed down matrilinealy. When a girl married, she would pack her belongings (inherited in the female line) in one of these bags and take it with her to her husband's house. The bag contained treasured heirlooms and garments, including sometimes the woman's funeral garments.

[3] *Chi-ukoseshkep,* a set consisting of a little treasure quiver (*ikayop-ikor*) tied to a little dagger (*emushpo*). The set is regarded as an amulet.

the argument.''[4]

When I said this,
fierce anger
flared up
on the face
of Poi-sar-un-kur,
as if I had spoken
some evil words.
He sprang up.
Then he went and
unsheathed
a sharp-bladed sword
hanging on the wall.
He turned the blade toward himself
on the floor at the head of the fireplace
and sank down lifeless.

At that time,
I sprang up.
I drew out
that sword [from his body].
After that
I brought out
my woman's treasure bag.
Thrusting my hand
into the bottom of the treasure bag,
I took out
a magnificent silken cloth.
Then I spoke
these words:

"O Fire Goddess whom I serve,
listen well to

what I have to say!
I will put this piece of silk
into the hearth.
If Poi-sar-un-kur
is to remain
dead,
let this piece of silk
burn up.''[5]

Saying this,
I put that piece of silk
into the hearth.
Then
the piece of silk
burned up.

After that
I clung to
the corpse
of Poi-sar-un-kur
and wept and wept.
After that
I brought out
my woman's treasure bag.
I thrust my hand
into the bottom of the treasure bag.
I took out
my ancestral bead necklace
and my ancestral earrings.[6]
I arrayed myself
in my death garments,
my funeral garments.
After that
I grasped in my hand

[4] "Even if you are criticized for marrying me, never mind. I will argue against them and will win the argument." An unheard-of statement for a woman to make.

[5] If the silk burns, he cannot be resuscitated. If it does not burn, it will be possible to restore him to life.

[6] Inherited from mother and grandmother.

that same sword.
I stood it up firmly
in the floor
by its hilt
and threw myself down
on its blade.
I lost all consciousness
of what was happening.

After a while
I [awoke and] saw
that I was sitting
on top of the rafters
with my hands and legs
hanging down limply.[7]

After that
I went out
through the smokehole.
A thin path of light
could be seen clearly
going upstream
along the course of the river.
I rushed forward
along it.
As I went on, [I came to]
a very large house
which was standing there
majestically.
Inside the house,
the voice of Poi-sar-un-kur
was raised loud
in regretful complaints.
As I stood

outside the house,
Poi-sar-un-kur
spoke these words:

"That evil woman,
that contemptible woman—
it was her fault
that I died
in the midst of my youth
and came here!
For what reason
has she followed me here?
Don't let her come inside!
Drive her away!"

Thus did he speak.
And true enough,
they did not let me come inside.

After that,
I could do nothing about it,
and I have since then
been roaming
and wandering about
over the earth.
My elder sister,
even though you make offerings to my soul,
I am unable to receive them.
Do not make
offerings to my soul!

Saying these words,
a blood-red bird
kept pecking

[7] The soul is sitting on the rafters above the corpse. See note 5, selection 9.

and scratching
at the charred posts.
Since then,
I have continued
to cry on and on.

All you humans,
listen to me!
O humans of today,
do not kill yourselves!

28. Song of a Human Woman

This is a woman's epic in the form of *kamui yukar* recorded in writing by Kubodera from the reciter Hirame Karepia on February 25, 1936. It was sung with the burden *Rukaninka huō, rukaninka*. The meaning of the burden is unclear.

The speaker is an Ainu woman (*ainu menoko*). The woman goes with her brothers on a trading expedition. The brothers are poisoned by a wicked Japanese interpreter (*wen tono tunchi*), but the woman is saved and taken home by a huge bird. The spirit of one of her brothers appears as a bird and bids her to continue their line.

The story illustrates well the ambiguous feelings of the Ainu of previous centuries about the Japanese. The Ainu relied heavily on the Japanese for trade, obtaining a large variety of luxury goods from them. On the other hand, they distrusted them and suspected them of treachery.

The text is Kamui Yukar 92 in Kubodera's *Ainu jojishi : Shin'yō, seiden no kenkyū*, pp. 412–16.

My little elder brother
and my big elder brother
raised me,
and we lived
on and on
uneventfully.
Then
one day
my big elder brother
said this:

"Listen well
to what I have to say!
I have gone through
many hardships
in raising both of you.
Even though
we often used to go
trading with the Japanese,[1]
we have not done so
until now.
Now at last

---

[1] *Tono-ko-uimam.* For *tono*, see note 3, selection 19.

I want to go trading.
Let us make a boat
in preparation for it!''

Thus did he speak
After that,
every day
my elder brothers
made a boat
with very loud
cracking and crashing noises.
After a while,
they finally
finished making the boat.
After that,
my big elder brother
picked up
a whittling knife
and stepped
outside with it.[2]
After that,
he came back
and said this:

    ''Now finally
    the boat is finished.
    Let us load the cargo!''

He spoke
these words.
After that,
he carried out the trade articles.
Finally
the big boat decorated with fancy carvings

was filled with them.
After that,
my big elder brother
said this:

    ''If those who have younger sisters
    take their sisters with them,
    they are given both
    women's presents
    and men's presents.[3]
    Since these also
    we long to have,
    let us take
    our younger sister
    along with us.''

These words
were spoken by
my big elder brother.
Therefore,
I picked up
a little treasure bag.
I also picked up
two or three
of the best garments
which I had embroidered.
I went down
along the path,
the path down to the beach.
When I looked,
this is what I saw.
O how could
my big elder brother
ever be so skillful!

---

[2] To make carvings on the boat. The boat was a big one decorated with fancy carvings.

[3] The Ainu did not receive money in exchange for their products at Matsumae. Instead they were given "presents" (*muyanki*, from the Japanese word *miyage*) consisting of rice, *sake*, tobacco, clothing, lacquerware, and other articles of Japanese manufacture.

On the side of the boat,
that big boat,
he had carved
many pictures,
countless pictures
of the gods dwelling in the mountains,
both the good ones
and the evil ones.
On the other side of the boat
he had carved
many pictures,
countless pictures
of the gods dwelling in the sea,
both the evil ones
and the good ones.
It was a delightful sight,
and my heart leaped with pleasure.

After that,
underneath
a little cabin[4]
on the boat's deck,
I did needlework
while my elder brothers
were skillfully
working their arms together
to row the boat.

As we sailed on and on,
when we came
to the middle of the ocean,
a large flock of birds
came along.
At the forefront of the flock of birds

was a big bird,
a white bird.
It was flying along in front
of the flock of birds.
When they passed
over us,
the bird flying in front
of the flock of birds
circled around
over our heads.
Although it was a bird,
the teardrops it shed
came raining down
on us
like large raindrops.
The flapping of its wings
came to my ears
sounding like many words being spoken,
like countless words being spoken.
This is what
I seemed to hear:

  "I also
  went off
  to go trading,
  but a wicked Japanese interpreter
  gave me poisoned wine
  to drink.
  After a while,
  I died and this
  is my dead soul
  which is now going homeward.
  Do not go on!
  Turn back at once!

[4] A cabin, called *shukush-chise* or *shukush-pon-chise*, was built on the deck for younger travelers. The cabin was perhaps a lean-to on the deck which was open to the sunshine (*shukush*).

Go back quickly!''

These are the words
I seemed to hear
as the flapping of its wings
came to my ears
like many words being spoken,
like countless words being spoken.

After that,
my little elder brother
wished to turn back,
and my big elder brother
wanted to go ahead.
Therefore,
they contended fiercely,
each rowing in the opposite direction.
After a while,
my big elder brother
won out.

After that,
we went on until
we came
to the land of the Japanese.
After that,
my elder brothers
landed the boat
and built
a large hut of matting.
After that,
they unloaded the trade goods.
After a while,
they finished the unloading.

After they were finished,
my elder brothers
attired themselves
in the best garments
which I had embroidered
in order to have an audience
with the Japanese lord.
I also
dressed myself
in the best garments
which I had embroidered.
Then we set out.

The Japanese town,
of which I had heard,
went stretching out
far in the distance.
As we walked on,
a large wooden house
stood there
majestically.
We went inside it.
Then
the wicked Japanese interpreter,
of whom we had heard,
came out.
After my elder brothers
had finished their audience
with the Japanese lord,
my elder brothers
were seated
on the entrance porch,
where a single mat
had been spread out.

The wicked Japanese interpreter
got wine and brought it out
from an inner chamber.
He poured out the wine
for my elder brothers.
When I sniffed
the odor,
there was a whiff
of the smell of poison.
When my elder brothers
drank the wine,
their bones broke
and they dropped down.

Right away
I let out
a piercing shriek of alarm
and went running outside.
I ran
screaming
to our boat
and threw myself down
on the sandy beach.
Crying, I writhed and twisted,
wailing, I writhed and twisted
again and again.
I continued to
roll and writhe while weeping.
Then after a while
I opened my eyes a mere slit
and looked about.
Then I saw
a big bird
coming this way

from the direction of the land.
It circled around
over my head for a while.
Then it seized me in its claws
and flew up in the air with me.

After that,
we went homeward,
with blasts of wind
whirling in my ears.
After a while,
I was thrown down
on the sandy beach
at the entrance of the path
to my native place.
A god's voice
rang out sonorously:

> "O evil woman,
> contemptible woman,
> for what reason
> has only your life
> been spared!"

After speaking
these words,
the weighty deity
darted up with a loud rumbling.
The soles of his feet
were whitish, I saw
as I looked after him.

After that,
crying, I writhed and twisted,

25

wailing, I writhed and twisted
again and again
on the sandy beach.
As I continued to cry,
from the direction of the sea
a bird larger than
any [ordinary] bird
came flying this way
and circled around
over my head.
Although it was a bird,
the teardrops it shed
came raining down
on me
like large raindrops.
The flapping of its wings
came to my ears
sounding like many words being spoken,
like countless words being spoken.
This is what
I seemed to hear:

    "My younger sister!
    True enough,
    we were given
    poisoned wine
    to drink,
    and we died.
    Now this is
    my dead spirit
    which has come.
    If you can do it
    somehow or other,
    dwell with some people,

it matters not even if they are lowly.[5]
If you manage to do this,
the first child born to you,
make him my child!
The next child born to you,
make him the child
of my younger brother!
If you do this,
then at least
my ancestral line
will be continued."

These words
I seemed to hear
in the flapping of its wings.
[The bird] could scarcely bring itself
to leave me.
Underneath it,
I screamed out
"Brother dear!"
As I continued to
roll and writhe while weeping,
it went flying up
along the river and was gone.

After that,
I came back
to my own home.
Crying, I writhed and twisted,
wailing, I writhed and twisted
again and again as
I grieved.
As I grieved,
I have been growing fainter and fainter,

---

[5] *Wenkur*, persons of low social status. See Introduction, p. 12–14.

I have been growing weaker and weaker.
Thus I tell
the story of it.

These words
were told
by that woman
about herself.

29. Song of a Human Woman

This is a woman's epic in the form of a *kamui yukar* recorded in writing by Kubodera from the reciter Shikata Shimukani of Chikabumi (Ishikari province) on August 19, 1940. It was sung with the burden *Hunna ō*. The meaning of the burden is not immediately clear, but Kubodera suggested that it might be the cry of a woman seeking help in an emergency.

The speaker is an anonymous Ainu woman who marries the youngest of six Thunder Gods (*kanna kamui*). His older brothers find out his whereabouts and summon him back to heaven. She remarries and has many children. She always remembers her divine husband and prefers him to her second husband, who is a human.

The text is Kamui Yukar 90 in Kubodera's *Ainu jojishi: Shin'yō, seiden no kenkyū*, pp. 404–9.

I did not know
what sort of creature
I was;
as time went on
I gradually became aware.

Then each day,
day after day,
I remained staring
after the many needle paths,
after the countless needle paths,
and in the paths of my needle
there would take form
many swirling patterns,

countless swirling patterns.
The upper clothing racks
and the lower clothing racks
would bend down under the weight
of the beautiful robes
which I had embroidered.
There was a brilliant glittering
over the clothing racks
where hung the beautiful robes
which I had embroidered.

One day
a young man
came.

I married him.
and we lived on.

Every day
he would go into the mountains
and would bring home
bear
and deer.
I lived in plenty,
lacking nothing
that I wished to eat,
and lacking nothing
that I desired to have.

Then one day
from the heavens
a cuckoo with a beautiful voice,
a cuckoo which sang very skillfully
came down
and lighted atop the spirit fence.
Raising its tail,
bobbing its tail
in this direction
and in that direction,
that cuckoo
sang on and on
both night
and day.

My wedded husband
remained
with his face turned away
before
the food which was tasty

and the food which was not tasty.
I would cook
and serve the food
to my wedded husband,
but he
remained
without eating anything.
The foods I had served him first
were covered
with black mold,
and the foods I had served him later
were covered
with white mold.
Day after day,
for six full days,
and night after night,
for six full nights
the cuckoo sang on.
Then the sound of the cuckoo ceased.

One day
my wedded husband
got up.
The ashes at the edges of the fireplace
he raked out toward the center,
and the ashes in the center of the fireplace
he raked out toward the edges.
Here and there
he traced furrows and lines.
As he did this,
he spoke these words:

    "My wedded wife,
    listen well

to what I have to say!
I am not
a human at all
whom you have married.
Who I am is this:

"In the heavens
are six brothers,
Thunder Gods,
and the youngest of them
am I.
When I looked
among the gods,
there was not a single one
who was to my liking.
When I looked
among the humans,
you alone
were to my liking
on account of your disposition,
your skill at needlework,
and your beauty.
For this reason
I came down
in secret
and married you.
My elder brothers
have now found me,
and the lord of the cuckoos
was sent down
from the heavens
to harangue me.
You probably
thought that this

was nothing but
an ordinary cuckoo
singing,
but the lord of the cuckoos
was saying that
if I do not return home
I will be banished
to the Country-without-birds,
to the Land-without-birds.
By all means
I must return home.

"Even though I return home,
I bid you not to weep.
Make for yourself
silken hoods,
sixfold hoods.[1]
Each year
wear one of them
and discard them one by one.
In the meantime
there will be gods traveling [overhead].
First of all
a quiet rumbling
will come along.
At the very last
will come thunder
with a crunching, crashing rumbling.
When there comes a god
thundering like that,
it will be me.

"Since I am a god indignant
at being separated from his wife,

---

[1] The six silken hoods (*sarampe konchi*) which the divine husband commands the woman to wear are "widow's hoods" (*chish konchi*). Ainu widows would customarily wear these hoods for a considerable period (one, two, or three years). The heroine of this song was commanded to wear widow's hoods for six years, after which she was to remarry.

I will be
the god who thunders
with a crunching, crashing rumbling.
Go outside,
and make as if
you are doing something or other.
If you do this,
you yourself
will not be able to see me,
but I, being a god,
will be able to see you.
This is what you must do
from now on.

"One more thing—
after you have worn
and discarded
all six of the hoods,
you will marry
another young man
who will be like me.
Rather than
your marrying me,
who am a god,
it will be better
for both of you
to be humans
married to each other.

"Now I want to eat
of your goodly cooking.
Cook food quickly!"

At these words of his,

I hung over the fire
a pretty little pot.
Into the pot
I poured with a splash
the treasured grains.
Stirring with a wooden spoon,
I finished cooking
the goodly cereal.
Stacking
delicate bowls
on a delicate tray,
I served the meal
to my wedded husband.
Receiving it,
he ate several mouthfuls
as if to taste the flavor;
then the remainder of the bowl
he proffered to me.
Receiving it,
I lifted it up high
and lowered it down low,
and ate the food.

Though I had thought
that it would happen later,
my wedded husband
stood up.
I clung to both hems
of his robe.
Crying out
"My dear husband!"
I screamed out
loud and long,
clinging to both hems

of his robe.
My wedded husband
seemed to make
a flapping motion.
Then he turned
into a bird larger
than any bird
and flew out through the window.

I caught a glimpse
of him sitting
atop the spirit fence.
I went outside
and threw myself down
on the sandy beach.
As I continued
to weep,
that bird
raised its tail
and bobbed its tail
in this direction
and in that direction
and the teardrops it shed
rained down
like a summer cloudburst.

That bird
went flying up
and circled over me,
the teardrops it shed
raining down
like a summer cloudburst.
It swooped down
and grazed me with its wings,

then it flew up again
and withdrew
into the skies.
Though it seemed to me
that it had gone far off yonder,
six more times
it flew back toward me,
circled over me,
and grazed me with its wings,
the teardrops it shed
raining down
like a summer cloudburst.
After that
it ascended toward the skies
and withdrew
into the highest heavens.

> "What was it
> my wedded husband
> said?"
> I thought to myself.

Weeping,
I went back
into the house.
Then I made for myself
silken hoods,
sixfold hoods,
and wore one of them.

As time went on,
when thunder would come rumbling,
first of all
a quiet rumbling

would come along.
At the very last
there would come thunder
with a crunching, crashing rumbling.
Knowing that
this was the sound
of my divine husband coming,
I would go outside
and would make as if
I were doing something or other.
I myself
would not be able
to see
my divine husband,
but I thought that
he could see me,
and I lived on
with this
as my only pleasure.

When I had discarded
all six hoods,
one day
a young man
came, and
I married him.

Every day
he would go into the mountains
and would bring home
bear
and deer.
I lived in plenty,
lacking nothing

that I wished to eat,
and lacking nothing
that I desired to have,
but I never
was able to like
my human husband,
and I was unable
to forget
my divine husband
even for a single day.

As time went on,
children were born to us,
both boys
and girls.
But
always
whenever thunder would come rumbling,
I would go outside
and would make as if
I were doing something or other.
I would think that
my divine husband
could see me,
and I lived on
with this
as my only pleasure.

As for the children,
the boys
have grown up,
and they go with their father
to do different kinds of hunting.
And the girls

who are older
help me.
They help me to gather
different food plants.

Now I am old and heavy of foot,
and as my death approaches,
I tell the story of it
to you, my children:
about how, long ago,
when I was young
the youngest one
of the six brothers,

Thunder Gods,
came down
in secret
to marry me.
I married him,
and we lived on together
until his elder brothers
found him out,
and he returned home,
a god indignant
at being separated from his wife,
a god whose thunder
has a crunching, crashing rumbling.

30. Song of the Woman of Shinutapka

This is a woman's epic in the form of a *kamui yukar* recorded in writing by Kubodera from the reciter Hirame Karepia on February 21, 1936. It was sung with the burden *Penkuratō penkuratō*. The meaning of the burden is not clear.

A young woman of Shinutapka has been killed by her wicked elder sister, who herself desired to marry the younger sister's betrothed, Otasam-un-kur. The young woman was restored to life and raised to young womanhood by the Chestnut-tree Grandmother (*yamni huchi*). Now the Chestnut-tree Grandmother sends the young woman to visit her betrothed, Otasam-un-kur. She tells him the story, and they marry. After he has killed her wicked elder sister, they move to the stronghold of Shinutapka. The hero Otasam-un-kur always worships the Chestnut-tree Grandmother.

The text is Kamui Yukar 104 in Kubodera's *Ainu jojishi: Shin'yō, seiden no kenkyū*, pp. 456–62.

My grandmother
raised me,
and we lived
on and on
uneventfully.
Finally
I came to look
like a woman.[1]
As we lived
on and on
uneventfully,
my grandmother

provided well
for me, feeding
me with nothing
but delicious
cooked chestnuts—
where could she
ever have gotten them?

Then, one day
my grandmother
cooked some chestnuts
and put them into

[1] "I grew to womanhood." This refers to the tattooing around the lips given to Ainu women. The woman had grown to womanhood when this tattooing was completed.

a little silver pot.
This is what she said:

    "Take
this little pot
and go down along
this big plain by the river.
Go on down
until you come
to the lower edge of the plain.
Then a big house
will be standing there.
Go inside it.
Inside the house,
in front of the stacks of sacred vessels
there will be someone
who has been lying in bed
for a long time.
You will set down
this little pot
by his pillow,
and these are the words
that you will speak:

    'Eat
the good food cooked
by the Woman on the Plain!'[2]

    "Speaking these words,
set down
the little pot.
Then quickly
run outside
and come home!"

When my grandmother
said this,
I picked up
the little pot
and stepped
outside.
Swinging
my one free arm,
I walked
down along
the big plain by the river.
When I had gone down
to the lower edge of the plain,
there was a big house
standing there
majestically.

I stepped
inside the house.
I looked around and saw
big stacks of sacred vessels
stretched out
like a low cliff.
Above them
hung noble swords,
with their many sword handles,
their countless sword handles
overhanging each other.
Underneath the stacks
was a magnificent seat,
a seat raised above the floor.
On the seat
there was someone,
I could not tell who,

---

[2] Nupka-ush-mat, "Woman-Growing-On-the-Plain-by-the-River." This is the name of the Chestnut-tree Grandmother (*Yamni huchi*), the "grandmother" of the heroine of this epic.

lying there
with many robes
pulled up over his head.
By his pillow
stood row and rows of [servings of] food.
Black mold
had appeared
on the food served to him long before,
and white mold
had appeared
on the food served to him recently.

I set down
the little pot
by the pillow
of the person lying in bed,
and these are the words
I spoke:

    "Eat
    the good food cooked
    by the Woman on the Plain!"

As soon as I had said this,
I ran outside
and came back.
I came back
to my grandmother's place.

After a while,
one day
my grandmother
spoke these words:

"Listen,
my little girl,
to what I have to say!
Your elder sister
at Shinutapka
was raising you.
According to
the instructions left behind
by your mother,
when you grew up
you were to be
given in marriage
to Otasam-un-kur.
the exalted hero.
But your evil elder sister
thought to herself:

'If my worthless younger sister
is alive,
she alone
will be married
to a well-born husband.
I will kill
her quickly. Then
after she is gone
I myself will marry
Otasam-un-kur,
the exalted hero.'

"This is what she thought.

"I am
the Chestnut-tree Grandmother,
who was sent down

from the Upper Heavens
to the upper edge
of this big plain by the river.
Your evil elder sister
came here carrying you on her back.
She knocked you against the trees
and killed you.
Feeling sorry for you,
I restored you to life,
and I have been
raising you
until now.
But now
I have grown old,
and I am about
to ascend
to the heavenly skies.
Otasam-un-kur,
grieving over you,
has remained
lying in bed despondently
his whole life long.
By now
you have grown old enough,
and you can now
cook his food for him.
Go down
and tell him:

'The Chestnut-tree Grandmother
raised me.
Such-and-such is
what she told me.'

"After that,
even if you come
here again,
there will be
no house here.
Don't come back,
but cook food
for the exalted hero.
Since I
long to have
human *inau*,
worship me with [offerings of] them.
I will take them along with me
and will ascend
to the heavenly skies.
In this way
I will exalt
my glory as a deity."

These words
were spoken
by my grandmother.
Thinking about
how well
she had raised me,
I shed
many sparkling teardrops,
countless sparkling teardrops.
As I was crying,
my grandmother [said]:

"Go down quickly now!"

She spoke

these words.
I stepped
outside.
I walked down
in tears
and went inside
that big house.

After that
I kindled
a blazing fire [in the fireplace].
I swept
the floor.
After a while,
the exalted hero
got up
and sat down
by the fireside.
[I lowered my head so that] the tips of my
    locks of hair
were resting on the floor.
I did not
raise my eyes
at all.
After a while
he spoke,
his voice ringing out
in sonorous accents.
This is what he said:

    "Where have you
    come from?
    By the names of each other's homelands
    are we able

to know each other.
Tell me
the name of your homeland.''

These words
did he speak.
When he said this,
my forehead
began to quake in fear,
since I
had never
even heard
a man's speech
until that time.
Repeating the words again and again,
repeating the words over and over,
he questioned me.
I was quite overawed
and terrified.
I told him
all the things
that the Chestnut-tree Grandmother
had told me.

After that,
he seized me,
he held me tight.

    "It was just for you
    that I was grieving
    and have been lying
    in bed despondently
    until now.
    Truly the

gods are powerful,
for you have
until now
been raised by the gods!''

While saying
these words,
he shed
many sparkling teardrops,
countless sparkling teardrops
over me.
After that
he spoke these words:

"I had thought that,
if your evil elder sister
was raising you,
she would follow
the words of your mother,
the instructions of your parents
and would be giving you
a good upbringing.
But one day,
she came here
and said this:

'My younger sister
fell ill
to some sickness,
some ailment,
and died.
Since I would not dare
leave the exalted hero
unaware of this,

I have now come
to tell you about it.'

''She said
these things
and came here.
I was so angry that
I began to
turn aside
from all food,
both the tasty foods
and the foods which were not tasty.
Both night
and day,
she would
bring food to me,
but I loathed to eat
the foods cooked
by your evil elder sister.
All around me
the small bowlfuls of food
and the big bowlfuls of food
have been standing in rows,
and this is the way
I have continued to live on
until now.
And all the time
you were alive!''

He spoke
these words.
After that
I began to cook
the food

for the exalted hero.
After a while [he said]:

> "You owe your life
> to the Chestnut-tree Grandmother,
> for your life was spared
> because she raised you.
> Let us go
> and worship her!"

He spoke these words.
Then he whittled *inau*,
and we went there,
with him carrying
a big bundle of *inau*.
I had thought
that my grandmother
had raised me
inside
a big house,
but there was no house at all.
Where it used to be,
there was only a big chestnut tree,
a very old chestnut tree,
which was lying there fallen over.
I went down again
in tears.
The exalted hero
made offerings of *inau*
to that chestnut tree.
Then we went down again.
The exalted hero
spoke these words:

> "I want to go and attack
> your evil elder sister.
> I am going to
> hack her to pieces!"

Saying this,
he rushed outside
and could be heard going off
with a loud roaring.
Right after this,
the dying spirit
of my evil elder sister
could be heard going off
with a loud roaring
and an intense rumbling.
I thought to myself that,
if only my evil elder sister
had been skilled
at correct behavior,
at good manners,
she would not
have been killed.
I shed
many sparkling teardrops,
countless sparkling teardrops.
After a while
the exalted hero
spoke these words:

> "It would be an inexcusable [offense]
> against the ancestors
> and against the gods
> if the divinely built stronghold
> of Shinutapka

were left to be neglected
by nothing but lowly servants.
Let us go there!''

These words
were spoken
by the exalted hero.
After that
I made my preparations,
and we went to
my native stronghold
at Shinutapka,
of which I had heard.
I describe in detail[3]
the beauties
of the divinely built stronghold.

Since that time,
we have led

a magnificent married life,
a glorious married life,
and we live
on and on
uneventfully.

Since then,
whenever we brew wine,
the exalted hero
always worships elaborately
the Chestnut-tree Grandmother
with his own hands,
and this is the way
we live on,
and I tell the story of it.

These things
recounted about herself
the Woman of Shinutapka.

[3] See note 7, selection 24.

31. Woman's Epic: Repunnot-un-kur

This is a full-length woman's epic recorded in writing by Kubodera from the reciter Hiraga Etenoa from December 26 to 28, 1932. The epic is sung without a burden.

The speaker is a *yaunkur* woman who is being raised at a place called Repunnot by a man whom she calls Repunnot-un-kur and believes to be her elder brother. He is a *repunkur*. A bear-cub appears to her in a dream and reveals that she is a *yaunkur* woman from Shinutapka who has been stolen away and raised by Repunnot-un-kur, who intends to marry her when she has grown up. The bear-cub saves her life and returns her to her native stronghold, where her two elder brothers are living. Later, they give the bear-cub a magnificent ritual dismissal. In the end, the bear-cub returns in human form and marries the woman.

A much shorter version of the same woman's epic was recorded by Nevskii and is published, together with Nevskii's Russian translation, in his *Ainskii fol'klor*, pp. 53–66. The name of Nevskii's informant is not recorded.

I obtained the text from Dr. Kubodera's typed manuscript. It is in volume 14 of the Ainu epic typescripts at the Institute for Japanese Culture and Classics, Kokugakuin University, Tokyo. Except for the short version translated into Russian by Nevskii, this epic has never been translated into any language.

At Repunnot,
my elder brother
Repunnot-un-kur[1]
raised me,
and we lived
on and on

uneventfully.
He raised me
with a magnificent upbringing,
with a splendid upbringing.
As time went on,
I finally

---

[1] The "elder brother" is a native of Repunnot and is therefore called Repunnot-un-kur. Repunnot is located somewhere in *repunkur* territory.

came to look
like a woman.
After that time,
I did nothing but needlework,
with my eyes focused
on a single spot.
While I was doing this,
my foster brother
for his part
did nothing but
carve on scabbards,
carve on treasures.
As we lived on
in this way,
he brought down
a bear-cub [from the mountains],
and we were
raising it.
As time went on,
the bear-cub we were raising
had by now
spent three years
with us.

Then one day
my foster brother
spoke these words:

    "Our bear-cub
    has been
    among the humans
    for quite a long time.
    After such a long time,
    I would not dare

to send him back
with only Ainu wine.[2]
Thus, I want to go
trading with the Japanese.
Then I will bring home
trade wine,
trade brew.
I wish to
send him back with this,
adding it to
the Ainu wine."

Saying this,
he made preparations
to go trading.
After a while,
they said that
he was now about
to set sail,
and the servants
carried outside
the best ones of
the goods traded with the Japanese.[3]
After this,
my foster brother,
before going outside,
spoke these words:

    "Even when I am gone,
    be sure
    to cook the food
    nicely
    for my god[4]
    in my absence!"

---

[2] It would be unfitting to use only native millet beer (*ainu sake*) in the bear ceremony. The elder brother will obtain trade wine (*uimam sake*) from the Japanese and hold the bear ceremony using both Japanese and native liquors.

[3] *Tono chihoki*, chiefly hides and furs of bear and deer.

[4] *A-kor kamui*, "my god," "my bear."

Saying these words,
he went out and was gone.

After he went away,
I did nothing but needlework,
remaining with my eyes
focused on a single spot.
Every once in a while
I would wash my hands
from the shoulders on down,
would cook
good food,
and would feed it to
our bear-cub.
This is the way
I lived
on and on.
By now,
I began to think
that it was almost time
for my foster brother
to return home.

Then one day,
the outdoor servants
came bustling inside,
and the indoor servants
went bustling outside.
They whispered
to each other, saying
that a boat
had been sighted.
This is what they
whispered to each other.

Then after a while,
they said that [the boat]
was heading toward
the harbor entrance,
that a boat bearing
the boat's emblem
of my foster brother
was coming shoreward.
These things
the servants
were whispering
to each other.

After a while,
the boat finally
came ashore, it seemed,
for the servants
went outside
to unload the cargo,
throwing down
the shorter carrying slings
and racing each other to get
the longer carrying slings.[5]

After a while,
this is what I heard:
For some reason,
I didn't understand why,
the cargo was
being unloaded
to the house of
Kotanra-un-kur.[6]
This is what
I heard.

---

[5] The servants want to have the longer slings and discard the shorter ones. The carrying slings (*tar*) are carrying cords worn over the forehead for carrying bundles on the back.

[6] "The man living below the village," a relative of Repunnot-un-kur living in village below the the latter's village.

As time went on,
little by little,
this is what I heard:
From the house of
Kotanra-un-kur,
both night
and day,
the sounds of drinking,
the sounds of feasting
came soaring upward.
While I continued
to hear these sounds,
our bear-cub
both night
and day
would growl angrily,
his voice resounding out
over the village.

While this was
going on,
I would cook
good food
and feed it to him,
but he would not eat it.
He would act angrily,
as if he wanted to break out
of the bear cage.
At that time
I thought to myself:

    "Perhaps it is because
    you have been
    cooking badly

that your bear-cub
is so angry."

Thinking this,
I threw away
the food I had cooked before.
Then once again
I cooked
a good meal
and fed it to him,
but he would not eat it,
and night
and day
would act angrily
as if he wanted to break out
of his cage.
By this time,
the sounds of drinking,
the sounds of feasting
at the house of
Kotanra-un-kur
had continued to
soar upward
night after night
for six full nights
and day after day
for six full days.

Then, one night
I lay down
in tears
by the fireside,
resting my head on my sleeve
as a pillow.

I would never
have expected
that I would go to sleep,
but I was asleep,
and I saw a dream.
This is what I dreamt.

By the east side of the house
there was the sound of someone
coming this way in a hurry.
When he came
under the sacred window,
the hangings on the window
were flipped upward,
and someone appeared
at the window.
I looked,
and this is what I saw.
He was a god
and had a god-like appearance,
but he was quite a young boy.
Wrapped in
layer upon layer
of black robes,
he appeared at the window.
This is what he said:

  "Listen well,
  human woman,
  to what I have to say!
  It is not because
  you are a descendant of *repunkur*
  that you are being raised
  among the *repunkur*.

Long ago,
in days gone by,
your mother
and your father
once lived.
They had between them
two sons
and one daughter.
[Your father] was
the ruler of Shinutapka,[7]
the exalted hero.
Your mother
carried you on her back
in order to give you
the most protection.
Your father
and your mother
together
set out to sea
to go trading,
leaving
your elder brothers
in the stronghold
at Shinutapka.
As they sailed on,
they passed off the shore
of mainland Karapto.[8]
They were beckoned
shoreward
with wine
and with *inau*.

The husband
wanted to go ashore,

---

[7] The father's name is Shinutapka-un-kur, "native of Shinutapka" or "ruler of Shinutapka." Therefore, the heroine of this epic is known as Shinutapka-un-mat, "woman of Shinutapka."

[8] *Yanke Karapto*. Karapto is the island of Sakhalin (Karafuto in Japanese). "Mainland Karapto" is probably that part of the island nearest to Hokkaido, or perhaps a part of Hokkaido inhabited by *yaunkur*.

and the woman
refused to go ashore.
They contended fiercely,
each rowing in opposite directions.
Then he gave up,
and they sailed out to sea.
After that,
they sailed on.
When they sailed by
the shore of
offshore Karapto,[9]
they were beckoned
shoreward
with wine
and with *inau*.
But the woman refused
to go ashore,
and they turned the boat
out toward the sea.
But two hundred boats
came out to sea.
Shinutapka-un-kur,
your father,
was forced to
bring his boat ashore.
After that,
both night
and day,
he was given
poisoned wine to drink.
After a while,
the drunken man,
speaking under the wine's influence,
speaking under the liquor's influence,[10]

said these things:
He offered to buy
together with his kinsfolk
the principal treasure of the land
of offshore Karapto.
In their turn
they wanted to see
the guardian spirit of his boat.
Both sides became enraged,
and as a result of this
fierce fighting,
fierce battles
broke out on all sides.[11]

"After that,
offshore Karapto
was completely
laid to waste.
Then the fighting
came ashore.
The fighting came ashore
to mainland Karapto,
and mainland Karapto
was completely
laid to waste.
After that,
the fighting
went offshore.
The fighting
extended to
many lands of the *repunkur*,
countless lands of the *repunkur*.
After some time,
your father,

[9] *Repun Karapto*. Probably that part of Sakhalin which is farthest away from Hokkaido.
[10] Literally, "the wine caused him to speak, the liquor caused him to speak"
[11] This account is the same as that given in "The Epic of Kotan Utunnai," p. 368.

since he had
been made drunk,
was killed
in the midst of the fighting,
in the midst of the battles.
After that,
your mother,
carrying you on her back,
continued to fight.
Though she moved through
many lands of the *repunkur*,
countless lands of the *repunkur*,
she was never
overtaken.
As this continued,
at the last,
your mother
moved on
to the land of Santa.[12]
Now, there is no place
which has as many people
as the land of Santa.
At that time,
since there are
many wizardesses,
many shamanesses[13]
among the *repunkur* women,
your mother
was captured.

"At that time,
Repunnot-un-kur,
your foster brother,
had gone to join

in the battles,
the battles against
your mother.
When he saw
your mother
being captured,
he stole you
off her back.
After that
he ran off with you
and came home.
He brought you here,
to Repunnot,
and after that
he raised you
secretly.
While he was raising you,
this is what
he thought to himself.
He would raise you
until you were grown up,
and after that
he would marry you.
He raised you
with this thought in his mind.
This is what he thought
until now.
But now,
after you came to look
like a woman,
this is what
he thought to himself:

'I will go

---

[12] Japanese Santan. The old name for Manchuria and the Amur estuary.

[13] *Nupur hikehe, tusu hikehe.* The enemy shamanesses discovered her whereabouts, and she was taken captive because of this.

to trade with the Japanese.
Then I will bring home
trade wine,
trade brew.
Adding it to
the Ainu wine,
I will send off [the bear-cub].
Then after that
is finished,
I will then
marry her.'

"Thinking this,
he left us here together
and went off
to trade with the Japanese.
And now
he has finally
come back.
As he was coming home,
Kotanpa-un-mat[14]
came down
on the path,
the path down to the beach,
and called out
to your foster brother.
She called out these words:

'O Repunnot-un-kur,
my little elder brother,
listen to
what I have to say!
You said that

Shinutapka-un-mat
was the only woman,
the only lady,
and you raised her
with a magnificent upbringing,
with a splendid upbringing.
But indeed,
she is the offspring of our murderers,
she is a descendant of our enemies,
and it is no wonder
that in your absence,
after you set sail
to go trading,
the ones that you were raising
lay together like dogs,
did wicked things together.[15]
Therefore,
I was worried
lest you,
being a great chieftain,
might arrive
at your own home
without knowing
what awaited you there,
and this is why
I am telling you
the things which
your nurslings have done.'

"Kotanpa-un-mat
called out these words.
Repunnot-un-kur,
your foster brother,

---

[14] "Woman living at the head of the village," a high-ranking *repunkur* woman living in the village of Repunnot. She is evidently jealous of the captive Ainu woman whom Repunnot-un-kur intends to marry.
[15] The two nurslings, Shinutapka-un-mat and the bear-cub, transgressed together.

was angry about this,
and he unloaded
the trade wine,
the trade brew
at the house of
Kotanra-un-kur,
and after that
both night
and day
you have been
hearing the sounds
of noisy reveling.
When the drinking,
when the feasting
comes to an end,
after that
they are going
to kill us both.
These things
they have been plotting together
while they drank
night after night
for six full nights
and day after day
for six full days.
Tomorrow morning
they will come
to kill us,
to slay us.
When they come,
I will break out of my cage
and come out.
Don't cry!
Get up now

and cook the meal.
After we have
finished eating,
dress yourself
and wait.
When it seems to you
as if I have come out,
then you must go outside
and stick closely
behind me.
No matter
what I do,
do not
be afraid of me.
Stick closely
behind me,
closely by my side.
Only if you do this
will your life
be saved!''

I dreamt
that the young man
spoke
these words.
After that
I got up
in tears.
Washing my hands
from the shoulders on down,
I cooked
good food
and fed it
to my bear-cub.

After the meal
was finished,
I put on
the best garments
which I had embroidered.
After I had
finished dressing,
by this time
the first faint signs
of dawn began
to appear.
Just then
many people
could be heard running
up the road
with a noisy tumult.
Just then,
the angry growling
of my bear-cub
could be heard faintly.
At the same time,
there was a crash
as he broke out of his cage.
As soon as I thought
that he had come out,
I stepped
outside.
I looked around.
and this is what I saw.

On the road
crowds of people
were running around.
The companies of armored men
were running around.
There were companies
of spearmen,
and there were companies
of archers.
These crowds of people
were running around.

Then
this is what
my bear-cub
did.
My bear-cub
dived head first
into the midst of
these crowds of people.
After that
he wound and twisted himself
like a soft hoop [made of vines]
in the very midst
of these crowds of people.
Whenever he would seize one
in the crowds of people,
he would slash him
in two
and cast him away.
He would break
their necks
and would scatter them about
all around him.
He raged fiercely
all around me.
Just then,
Repunnot-un-kur,

my foster brother,
was standing
in back of the crowds.
He cried out these words
to exhort
his own forces:

"Up with you now,
my kinsfolk!
Struggle mightily!
Kill them,
the evil-doers."

These commands
he cried out
to his kinsfolk.
As he cried this,
the companies of archers
twanged on the grips of their bows
with buzzing sounds.
The companies of spearmen
aimed
their spear tips
at my bear-cub.
The companies of archers
aimed
the points of their arrows at him.
But
my bear-cub
darted about
between the spears
and between the arrows.
Wherever he passed
the corpses mowed down like grass

lay stretched out in the distance.
The companies of spearmen
he beat and broke their spears.
The companies of archers
he beat and broke their arrows.
As he did this,
the broken corpses
of the enemies he struck
he scattered about
all around him.
As he continued to do this,
within a short while,
he had completely
laid to waste
the village of Repunnot.

After that
my bear-cub
seemed to be
very tired.
He threw himself down
and was trying
to catch his breath.
During this while
I was shedding
many sparkling teardrops,
countless sparkling teardrops.

After a while,
the sound of
my bear-cub's breathing
came to my ears
sounding like many words being spoken,
like countless words being spoken.

This is what I heard:

   "O woman,
   listen to what
   I have to say!
   I am going
   to take you back
   to your native land,
   Shinutapka.
   You must do
   exactly as I do.
   Only then
   will your life
   be saved!"

I heard
these words
in the sound of
my bear-cub's breathing
like many words being spoken,
like countless words being spoken.

After that
he got up
and went walking off
toward somewhere or other.
I went along with him
wherever he went.
After that
we went on
toward somewhere or other.
Finally we came out
beside the sea.
He lay down

on the sandy beach
and stayed there for a while.
Then he got up,
and the sound of his breathing
came into my ears
sounding like many words being spoken,
like countless words being spoken.
This is what I heard:

   "After this
   we are going
   to go across
   the sea.
   Hold on
   to my back.
   If you keep hold of me
   and do not
   let go of me,
   only then, when we come ashore,
   will your life
   be saved!
   Whatever may happen,
   do not let go of me!"

These words
I heard
in the sound of his breathing.
After that
my bear-cub
dived into the sea.
Therefore,
just as I had heard
him say,
I held on

to his back.
After that
we went
across the sea.
Both night
and day
we went across.
Finally, after great effort,
when we came ashore
on the mainland,
this is what I saw.
There was
a big river
emptying into
the ocean,
its rapids swirling
out seaward.
We came ashore
by the river mouth.
My bear-cub
came ashore
on the sandy beach
and remained there
resting.
I sat down
by his side
and was shedding
many sparkling teardrops,
countless sparkling teardrops.
After a while,
once again
I seemed to hear
these words
in the sound

of my bear-cub's breathing:

"We will go
upstream along the course
of this big river.
Then there will be
a populous village.
Then, as we pass
on the outskirts of the village
a cry will go up
in the village.
They will cry out:

'Look, these ones
coming along must be
the ones we heard about—
the ones who were raised together
by Repunnot-un-kur,
the exalted hero,
who did wicked things together
and lay together like dogs!
As if that were not enough,
they completely
laid to waste
the village of Repunnot.
Kill them!'

"This cry
will go up
in the village.
After that
there will be
companies of archers,
and there will be

companies of spearmen.
Crowds of people
will attack us.
What ever may happen
do not run
even so much as
a single step
away from me!
If you do,
your life
will not be saved.
No matter what
I may seem
to be doing,
do not be afraid of me.
Stick closely
behind me!
Only if you do this
will your life
be saved.''

I heard
these words
in the sound of
my bear-cub's breathing
like many words being spoken,
like countless words being spoken.
After that
my bear-cub
stood up
and went walking
along the river.
I went along with him
wherever he went.

We walked on until
we had come to a place
far up along the river's course.
I looked out
in front of me,
and this is what I saw:
A populous village[16]
stood there.
In the center of the village
a divinely made stronghold
was seen standing
majestically.
I saw this
in front of me
as we walked on.
Then, as we came
to the outskirts
of the settlement of the common folk,
the sounds of dogs barking noisily
rang out.
Just then
a cry went up
in the village.
This is what they cried:

  ''Look, these ones
  coming along must be
  the ones we heard about—
  the ones who were raised together
  by Repunnot-un-kur,
  the exalted hero,
  who lay together like dogs
  and did wicked things together!
  As if that were not enough,

---

[16] It is stated later on that this village is Ishikar.

they devastated
the village of Repunnot.
They completely laid
to waste
the village of Repunnot
so that where the village once stood
it looked like a stony field.
Kill them both!''

This cry
went up
in the village.
Then, after that
within the village,
the populous village,
crowds of people
went running around.
There were companies
of archers,
and there were companies
of spearmen
running around.
Then
this is what
my bear-cub
did:
In the midst of
these crowds of people,
he wound and twisted himself
like a soft hoop [made of vines]
and went raging fiercely
all around me.
The companies of spearmen
he beat and broke their spears.

The companies of archers
he beat and broke their arrows.
Their broken corpses
he scattered about
all around him.
As he continued to do this,
within a short while,
the populous village
was reduced to nothing but
charred, bare sticks of wood,
and not a single one
of the crowds of people
was left alive.

After that
we went on
toward somewhere or other.
When we arrived
at a certain place,
we came out
by the seashore.
After that
we walked along
by the seacoast.
When we arrived
at a certain place,
a pretty little river
could be seen clearly
flowing down.
We came to
the river mouth.
Midway along the course
of the pretty little river
a majestic steep crag

was standing.
This is the way it looked:
The steep crag
was enveloped half-way
in twisting billows of mist.

My bear-cub
walked up
along the little river,
and I went along with him.
As we walked along,
up along the crag,
the majestic steep crag
a path had been made.
The path twisted again and again
in many bendings,
in countless bendings.
The traces of the mattock
looked dark,
and the traces of the scythe
looked bright.[17]
When we went up
along the path,
this is what we saw:
On both sides of the path
stone Buddhas[18]
were standing
like living spirits,
like living gods.
Looking at all this,
I finally arrived
at the top of the crag,
the majestic steep crag.
I looked around,

and this is what I saw:
The entire top of the crag
was filled by
a divinely made stockade,
which stood there
majestically.
I looked at
the beauties
of the stockade-god,[19]
which was exactly
what I would expect
to find only in
the abode of a god.
I stepped
inside the stockade.
The entire area inside the stockade
was filled by
a big house
which stood there
majestically.

Just then,
my bear-cub
made his way
along the side of the house.
He went up to
the spirit fence[20]
and seated himself
leaning against
the spirit fence.
At the same time
I also
seated myself
on the rubbish heap in the yard

[17] When viewed from a distance, the places where the path had been cleared with mattocks looked black, and the places where it had been cleared with scythes showed up brightly.

[18] The Ainu word for Buddha is *potoki*, a loan word from Old Japanese. The contemporary Japanese is *hotoke*. Many of the Japanese loan words in Ainu reflect an early historical stage of Japanese phonology. See Introduction, p. 11.

[19] The stockade is spoken of eulogistically as being a god (*chashi kamui*). *Chashi* may mean either "stockade," "stronghold," or "house."

[20] *Inau-chipa*. The fence of clustered *inau* located outside the sacred window.

and waited there
shedding
many sparkling teardrops,
countless sparkling teardrops.

In the meantime,
there were noises
inside the house,
and someone come outside.
Before
whoever it was
came out,
many flashes of light,
countless flashes of light
came streaming out.
Above the flashing lights
a human face
appeared.
I looked at it,
and this is what I saw:
It was a human man
of such majestic beauty
as I had never before seen.
His hair was
curly hair,
magnificent hair[21]
stretching out
over his head.
Many streams of glistening water.
countless streams of glistening water[22]
went trickling down
amidst his hairs.
The tips of his hairs
went out into curls,

went out into ringlets.[23]
His beard
was like sedge
and covered
his entire chest.
His beard hung down
in plaits on its sides.
On account of it
he looked all the more beautiful,
all the more imposing.
This human man
came outside
and saw me.
He turned toward
the spirit fence
and saw
my bear-cub
sitting there.
After that,
without saying a word,
he went back inside.

After a while,
he came back
outside.
He came out
holding
a beautiful
swordguard treasure
with curled shavings tied to it.
He walked up
to the spirit fence
and tied
the swordguard treasure

---

[21] *Kane otop*, literally "metal hair"
[22] *Kane wakka*, literally "metal water"
[23] This personage, the elder brother of Poiyaunpe, is named Kamui-otopush on account of his remarkable hair. The name means "He-has-divine-hair." Curly hair was highly prized and was called *kamui otop*, "divine hair," "magnificent hair."

onto the neck
of my bear-cub
While he did so
he uttered these words:

    "I give this
    to the weighty god
    as payment
    for his coming inside."

Saying
these words,
he tied
the swordguard treasure
onto the neck
of my bear-cub.
Then
he went back inside.
After that
my bear-cub
walked up beside me.
It seemed that
he wanted me
to go inside.
So I stood up
and walked
to the doorway.
My bear-cub
cast fierce
glances at me,
and it seemed that
he wanted me
to go inside
first.

Then I went inside
first,
stepped inside the doorway,
and sat down.
Only then
did my bear-cub
come inside after me.
He walked
up along the floor
on the left-hand side of the fireplace
and sat down
leaning against
the sacred window.

In the meanwhile,
I looked around,
and this is what I saw:
Stacks of sacred vessels
were stretched out
like a low cliff.
Above them
hung noble swords,
with their many sword handles,
their countless sword handles
overhanging each other,
their dangling tassels
swaying together.
The brightness of the treasures,
the brightness of the vessels
glittered brightly
and cast shadows
on the walls.
The surface of the floor,
the magnificent floor[24]

---

[24] *Kane amso*, literally "metal floor."

gleamed brightly
Below the stacks,
the stacks of sacred vessels,
there stood
a movable seat,
a magnificent seat.
What sort of being
was sitting
on the seat?
The upper part of his body
was enveloped in
twisting billows of mist,
and it was impossible
to see him
in his human form.
He remained
seated there
on the seat.

On the right-hand side of the fireplace
next to the fire
there was sitting
the human man
whom I had seen
come outside.
He stared fixedly
down into the center of the hearth.
After a while,
he turned toward
my bear-cub.
Raising his hands
up high [in worship],
he said:

"Listen,
o weighty god,
to what I have to say!
It is from you,
o weighty god,
that we ought to hear
the explanation,
and we question you.
We want to hear
for what reason
are you, the weighty god,
traveling about,
but we are
unable to hear
the explanation
from you, the weighty god.
Since you brought along with you
a woman who is
a human like us,
let us humans
converse with each other.
Only then
can we hear
for what reason
you, the weighty god,
are traveling about.
By all means,
o weighty god,
do not be angry with us!"

While saying
these things,
the human man
made gestures of worship

toward my bear-cub.
After he was finished,
he turned to me
and said:

"O divine lady,
please seat yourself
beside the fire!"

Thus, I went up
beside the fire
on the left-hand side of the fireplace.
Then [he said]:

"Listen,
o divine lady,
to what I have to say!
What is the reason
that you have come,
and from what place
did you come?
Only if you tell us
the causes behind
both of your coming here,
will we be able
to know each other."

These words
were spoken by
the lord of the house,
the master of the house.
Therefore,
I spoke these words:

"I did not know
who I was,
or how it was
that I was being raised.
Repunnot-un-kur
raised me,
and this is what
I thought:
I thought only
that my real elder brother
was raising me.
He raised me,
and we lived
on and on.
But all the time . . .[25]
. . . .
Within a short while
he had completely
laid to waste
the populous village.
Then once again
I went along with him
as he went off
toward somewhere or other,
and we came along
and arrived here
at the stronghold."

When I said this,
the one who
was sitting
on the seat,
the magnificent seat
which was placed

[25] I omit here an extremely long passage (over 500 lines) which recapitulates the whole story up to this point.

below the stacks,
the stacks of sacred vessels,
he too
came down
by the fireside.
The one who
was sitting
at the head of the fireplace,
and the one who
was sitting
by the fireside,
on the right-hand side of the fireplace
both of these
human men
said:

    "Our younger sister!"

Saying this,
all at once
they grabbed me,
and one after another
we wept over each other.
When that was finished,
the elder one of them
spoke these words:

    "My younger sister,
    listen well to
    what I have to say!
    Even though
    I am
    the eldest,
    the first born,

I was entirely
too faint-hearted,
too weak.
I had decided
to forget completely
that our mother,
carrying on her back
our younger sister,
had gone trading
together with
our father,
and to remain
at the very least
together with
my younger brother,
my divine nursling.
This was the only thing
that I ever thought about
as I was raising
my divine nursling
until this time.
But as time went by,
this is what
I began to think.
Once the god I am raising,
my divine nursling,
grows up,
after that
I will follow
in the footsteps
of my father
and my mother
and will carry on their battles.
Just as I was

thinking this,
thanks to
the weighty god,
our younger sister
has come back to us!''

While he spoke
these words,
Kamui-otopush,
my elder brother,
turned around toward
my bear-cub
and worshiped him.
bowing his head
down to the ground.

After that
the one who was
my little elder brother
also continued to sit
right by the fireside.
It was incredible
how he could ever
rejoice over me so greatly.

While we were
engaged in this,
Kamui-otopush,
my elder brother,
took the servants
with him
and stepped
outside
to make

a cage
for my bear-cub.
After a while
had gone by,
the cage was finished,
and they put
my bear-cub
into the cage.

After that
we raised
my bear-cub
with a magnificent upbringing,
a splendid upbringing,
and this is how we lived
on and on,
uneventfully,
with me doing nothing but needlework,
my eyes focused
on a single spot.

After we had lived on
in this way for some time,
on one occasion
Kamui-otopush,
my elder brother,
remained for a while
without saying anything.
Then this is what he said:

"O god whom we are raising,
o our divine nursling,
and you also,
our younger sister,

listen well to
what I have to say.
Although we are
reluctant to part with
our bear-cub,
he was kept,
it seems,
for quite a long time
at Repunnot.
Besides that,
since he arrived here
at our native Shinutapka,
he has now
been here
for two years, for three years.
Since it would be
an indignity
to make a weighty god
remain
for a very long time
among the humans,
I want to go
to trade with the Japanese
in preparation
for sending him home,
for giving him ritual dismissal.
Then I will bring back
trade wine,
trade brew,
will add it to
the Ainu wine,
and will give dismissal
with it
to our bear-cub."

Kamui-otopush,
my elder brother,
spoke these words
and set out to sea
to go trading.
After he was gone,
I remained
together with
my little elder brother.
I continued to raise
my bear-cub
with a splendid upbringing.
After a time,
Kamui-otopush,
my elder brother,
came back
from trading.
He brought ashore
trade wine,
trade brew,
as well as sacks [of rice].

After that
he prepared
to give dismissal
to my bear-cub,
getting the servants
to help him.
Time continued
to pass in this way
until finally
the wine was ready,
and those who were straining the wine
darted their wicker baskets

together this way and that,
while those who were whittling *inau*
plied their whittling knives
together this way and that.
The sounds of the *inau* being whittled
and the sounds of the wine being strained
made a very loud
creaking and squeaking.

After this went on
for some time,
now they said that
the preparations were completed,
and the drinking would begin,
the feasting would start.
At that time,
Kamui-otopush,
my elder brother,
whispered these words
to himself:

    "Ishikar-un-kur,
    my evil younger brother,[26]
    what on earth
    ever made him decide
    to go to the assistance of
    Repunnot-un-kur?
    He came very close,
    it seems, to killing
    both of them—
    my little sister
    and the weighty god.
    That is why
    his village

was devastated.
Even though we
give ritual dismissal to
the weighty god,
we ought to
give up all thought of
inviting him,
Ishikar-un-kur.''

Kamui-otopush,
my elder brother,
whispered these words
to himself
and sent out word to
all the relatives nearby
and all the relatives far away.
After that,
the invited guests,
both the women
and the men,
were shown in with much ceremony.

After that
the time finally came
for them to let
my bear-cub play,[27]
and my elder brothers
went outside for this.
Right after that,
I also went outside.
I walked up
next to the spirit fence
just east of the house
and remained there.

[26] The chieftain of Ishikar was evidently a relative of the family of heroes of Shinutapka. Ishikar was the second place where the bear-cub had to fight a battle on the way to Shinutapka.

[27] *Shinotte*, to allow the bear-cub to play. Part of the bear ceremony consists in leading the bear-cub around on a rope among the assembled crowd just before killing it.

During this while,
a large crowd of people
had gathered so thick that
the ground under them
looked black.
Kamui-otopush,
my elder brother,
was at the head of the crowd.
He came outside,
holding my bear-cub
by a rope.
After that
my bear-cub
played
peacefully
by the side of
the spirit fence.
After a while,
when this was finished,
I heard
them say that
now it was time
for them to put
my bear-cub to sleep.
This is what
I thought to myself:

"It was thanks to him,
your bear-cub,
that your life
was saved.
And now
they say that
you will never see him again!"

Thinking this,
I threw myself down
and wept
by the spirit fence.
After that
I shed
many fierce, sobbing tears,
countless fierce, sobbing tears.
After I continued
to do this
for some time,
I looked,
and this is what I saw:
Over the spirit fence
was one who was a god
and had a god-like appearance.
He was quite a young boy,
who lacked
even the shadow of a beard,
and he was wrapped in
layer upon layer
of black robes.
He transformed himself
into a ball of flashing light
and remained
standing
over the spirit fence.
He said this:

"Woman, listen to me!
If you are really doing this
with sincere thoughts,
with true emotions,
then this is what

you must do.
As you celebrate the feast,
do not even do so much
as to lick the bits [of food]
sticking to your fingers.
Celebrate the feast in this way,
and all will be well.''

After saying this,
he vanished
and was gone.
After that
the women
all took me
by the hands
and spoke these words:

"Shinutapka-un-mat,
our little sister,
listen well to
what we have to say!
You are grieving
for your bear-cub.
All the more reason
for you to celebrate
a good feast.
Wash your hands
carefully
and cook a meal
for your bear-cub.
Then exalt yourself
tranquilly
with a good feast!''

The women
spoke
these words
as they took me
by the hands
and brought me inside.
In the meanwhile
my bear-cub
had been brought inside.[28]

After that,
I washed my hands
from the shoulders on down.
In the meanwhile
the women
went running about
this way and that
while cooking the food.
After they had cooked for a while,
I removed the pot from the fire,
and the women
commanded me
to serve the food.
Although I served the food
to my bear-cub,
just as the weighty god
had told me to do,
I did not so much as
lick my fingers.
Though I received portions of food
and served food,
through the entire feast
I did not eat
anything at all.

[28] The head of the bear is brought inside the house and laid in state by the sacred window. During the final feast, food is set in front of it.

The feast went on
and finally came
to an end.
It seemed to me
that my elder brothers
gave ritual dismissal[29]
to my bear-cub
more splendidly
than any other god ascending.
When the feast was over,
when the drinking feast
had come to an end,
all the guests
praised me
and went home.

After that,
doing nothing
but needlework,
I lived on
with my elder brothers.
We lived
on and on
uneventfully.
During this time,
my little elder brother
would remain
on the seat,
the magnificent seat,
and would do nothing
but carve on scabbards,
carve on treasures,
with his eyes focused
on a single spot.

This is the way
we lived on.

By now,
some time had gone by.
Then one day,
by the side of the house,
there was the sound of someone
coming this way in a hurry.
Without hesitation,
he headed straight
toward the doorway.
He opened wide
the door hangings.
Before
whoever it was
came in,
many flashes of light,
countless flashes of light
came streaming in.
Above the flashing lights
a human face
suddenly appeared.

When I looked at him,
this is what I saw:
The exalted hero,
the one whom I had seen
before
standing
on the spirit fence,
came inside.
His appearance now,
his beauty now

[29] The verb used here is *hopumpare*, meaning "to cause to ascend."

was even more imposing than before.
He transformed himself
into a ball of flashing light
and came inside.
He walked along the floor
on the left-hand side of the fireplace
and sat down
at the head of the fireplace.
He remained for a while
staring fixedly
down into the middle of the hearth.
Then he spoke these words:

"O human men,
listen well to
what I have to say!
Unless I myself
say the reason
why I have come down,
we will not be able
to know each other.
This is the reason
why I have come down:

"I am the bear-cub
that you sent off.[30]
I went
to the place of
the god my father
with bundles of wine,
bundles of millet cakes,
and big piles
of both *inau*
and food.

After that
we invited
all the gods,
and we held
an excellent feast,
an excellent drinking feast.
After it was finished,
all of the gods
thanked me
and praised me
and left for home.
After that,
this is what
I said
to my father:

'I want to marry
the human woman.'

"When I said this,
this is what
my father said:

'If you want
to marry
the human woman,
then you may
go down
among the humans
and then marry
the human woman.[31]

"Thus spoke
my father.

---

[30] *Arpare*, to send off, to give ritual dismissal to

[31] In the version recorded by N. A. Nevskii, the father says at this point: "I am a weighty god, and if you were to take a human woman and marry her in the land of the gods, I would be censured by the weighty gods. If you want to marry a human woman, then go down there and marry her!" Nevskii, *Ainskii fol'klor*, p. 66.

Therefore,
because
I feel sorry for
your younger sister,
who grieves for me
so excessively,
even though I am
a god, the child
of a most weighty god,
I have raised
myself up
and have come down.
If you think
it would be well
for us to dwell together
as a single family
from now on,
then I would like
to live
together with
your younger sister.
This was what I thought
as I came down.''

When the most weighty god
said this,
my little elder brother
came down
beside the fire
and sat down
in the position above[32]
Kamui-otopush,
my elder brother.
Both my elder brothers

made again and again
many gestures of profound worship,
countless gestures of profound worship.
As they did so,
my little elder brother
spoke these words:

  ''This comes at an auspicious time,
  for we were
  without relatives,
  without brothers.
  Our younger sister,
  though she is unattractive,
  though she lacks beauty,
  has come back to us
  thanks to
  the weighty god.
  If only on account
  of our younger sister alone,
  we must thank
  and show gratitude
  to the weighty god,
  but now
  he has raised
  himself up
  and has come to us!
  We are most grateful
  and worship you
  most reverently for this.
  Were such a thing
  to take place,
  we would greatly enhance
  our standing among the gods
  and our position among men.''

---

[32] The younger brother Poiyaunpe sat in the more honored position nearer the head of the fireplace. The younger brother is treated as being of a higher rank than the elder brother Kamui-otopush.

These words
were spoken by
my little elder brother.
After that
we lived
on and on,
and I lived
together with
the exalted hero.
After a while
Kamui-otopush,
my elder brother,
spoke these words:

> "It would be an indignity
> to make the weighty god
> take his lodging with us
> forever.
> Therefore,
> let us build him
> a separate house,
> and let the weighty god
> dwell in it!"

These words
were spoken by
Kamui-otopush,
my elder brother.
After that,
every day
east of the stronghold
there were very loud
crashing, cracking sounds
of wood being carved,

of wood being cut,
which they said were
sounds of building
the separate house.

After a while
they finally said
that the separate house
had been finished.
Then Kamui-otopush,
my elder brother
took things outside.
He chose some
of the vessels and
some of the treasures.
Some of these
he took out
through the window,
and there was a tinkling
as they went out
by the window.
Some of them
he took out
through the door,
and there was
a loud tinkling
as they went out
by the door.

After a while,
Kamui-otopush,
my elder brother,
said these words:

"Now at last
the building of the house
is finished."

Since then,
I have been living
together with
the exalted hero
inside
the separate house
east of the stronghold.
We are living
on and on
uneventfully.
Since I am married
to a most weighty god,
I have nothing
to worry about,
and I am leading
a magnificent married life.
My wedded husband
does nothing but
carve on scabbards,
carve on treasures,
with his eyes focused
on a single spot,
and this is the way
we live
on and on
uneventfully.

32. The Woman of Poi-Soya

This is a full-length heroic epic of the *hau* type recorded in writing by Kubodera from the reciter Hiraga Etenoa from October 3 to 11, 1932. The epic is sung without a burden.

Like all *hau* epics of the Saru area of Hidaka, the hero is Otasam-un-kur. The story is an interesting and involved one, revolving around the outrageous indignities committed by the woman of Poi-Soya (Poi-Soya-un-mat), who breaks taboo after taboo by dressing up like a man and hunting in the mountains, or by sailing around trading with the *repunkur* and provoking them into fights.

The Ainu title is *Poi-Soya-un-mat shipitonere shikamuinere*, meaning something like "The Woman of Poi-Soya Exalts Herself and Behaves with Outrageous Arrogance." The sense is that she has exalted herself above the gods (both the word *shipitonere* and the word *shikamuinere* are synonymous and mean "to make oneself into a god") and has deviated from all norms of respectable human life. Her outrageous conduct enrages Otasam-un-kur, who learns that he is betrothed to her. In the end, after many vicissitudes, the hero marries the woman of Kunnepet (Kunnepet-un-mat), who has restored him to life by her wizardry.

The structure of the epic is complex. There are the following five sections, each one with a shift in speaker: (1) Otasam-un-kur is the speaker; (2) Poi-Soya-un-mat is the speaker; (3) Otasam-un-kur is the speaker again; (4) Kunnepet-un-mat is the speaker; (5) Otasam-un-kur is the speaker again. I have not labeled the speakers in each of the sections.

The frequent shift in speakers in the epic adds a very interesting, multidimensional depth to the telling of the story. Some of the incidents overlap, and the same incidents are viewed from the points of view of more than one character, each speaking in the first person. This gives the narration a much greater psychological depth than would be possible if the entire story were narrated by a single character. One can only marvel at the symmetry, the economy of detail, and the thorough consistency with which Etenoa sings the story, weaving all the strands together into a harmonious whole.

I obtained the text from Dr. Kubodera's typed manuscript. It is in volume 10 of the Ainu epic typescripts at the Institute for Japanese Culture and Classics, Kokugakuin University, Tokyo. This epic has never been translated into any language.

I

My elder sister
raised me,
and we lived
on and on.
The stacks of sacred vessels
were stretched out
like a low cliff.
Above them
hung noble swords,
with their many sword handles,
their countless sword handles
overhanging each other,
their dangling tassels
swaying together.
Below the stacks
there stood
a movable seat,
a magnificent seat.
I was raised
on the seat.
My foster sister—
it was utterly amazing
how she could ever

be so imposing in appearance,
so beautiful.
The brightness of her face
was like the rising sun,
sending out
dazzling rays of light.
She and my younger sister,
the two of them together,
would send out
brilliant flashes of light.
It was amazing
how very lovingly
my foster sister
treated me.
She raised me
with a splendid upbringing,
with a magnificent upbringing,
and this is the way
we lived
on and on
uneventfully.
During this while,
I did nothing but
carve on scabbards,
carve on treasures,

with my eyes focused
on a single spot.
We continued to live
on and on
uneventfully.

Then, beginning not long ago,
I started to hear
rumors.
This is what they said:
Poi-Soya-un-mat[1]
has been behaving
in this manner:
She would disguise herself
in men's garments,
in men's clothing.
She would outfit herself
with a quiver with a sling attached
and a bow wound with cherry bark,
would take six
servants with her,
and would go hunting
in the mountains.
Then, when she would see
someone who had killed a deer,
she would extract
as indemnity[2]
their hunting swords,
along with the deer.
When anyone had caught fish,
she would beat them and take away the fish;
and when anyone had killed a deer,
she would beat them and take away the deer.
These rumors

I continued to hear
all the time.

   "Even if a man
   had done such things,
   I would be terribly angry,
   but for a woman to do it
   means self-exaltation,
   outrageous arrogance!"

Thinking this,
I would feel shock
as if cold water
had been splashed
onto my flesh.
I continued to be
haunted in my sleep,
haunted in my dreams
by Poi-Soya-un-mat,
and this is the way
I continued to live
on and on
uneventfully.

As this went on,
one day
I wrapped in a sedge mat
the carving I had been doing
and laid it
on the stacks of sacred vessels.
After that
I came down
by the fireside
and spoke these words:

[1] The woman of Poi-Soya. Poi-Soya means "Little Soya" and is evidently a subsidiary settlement of the Soya Ainu. Soya is the northernmost part of Hokkaido, separated by the Sōya Kaikyō (La Perouse Strait) from Sakhalin.
[2] Her acts amounted to brigandage.

"My foster sister,
listen to me!
Bring out
some garments,
that I may put them on.
I want to go hunting
in the mountains
and kill a nice deer.
Then since you,
my foster sister,
have gone through
so many hardships
in raising me,
I want to
provide food
for you to eat.''

When I said this,
she spoke in a hushed voice,
saying these words:

"How astonishing
are the words
you speak,
o god whom I have raised,
o my divine nursling.
Deer is not
something which we can eat
only if it is killed
by my divine nursling![3]
The area near the mountains
behind our village
is infested by droves
of robber birds,

of stealing birds.
If anyone resembling
a human
goes hunting in the mountains,
they steal him away.
I am afraid of this,
and now you,
o god whom I have raised,
o my divine nursling,
say that you want
to go hunting in the mountains!''

These words
were spoken by
my foster sister,
but I insisted
again and again.
After a while,
she looked as if
she were very frightened.
She ran to the back of the house
and brought out
a woman's treasure bag.
She thrust her hands
to the bottom of the bag.
She took out
a pair of
grass leggings
and held them out toward me.
Overjoyed,
I took them
and wrapped them
around my legs.
After that

---

[3] "It is not necessary for you to kill deer so that we can have venison to eat. The servants go hunting for us.'' The foster sister tries to dissuade the hero from going hunting in the mountains.

I wrapped around myself
a thin garment.
I tossed up
onto my back
a quiver with a sling attached.
I grasped
a bow wound with cherry bark
at the center of its handgrip.
After that
I went outside.
I stepped
outside.

Only now, for the first time
did I acquaint myself
with the outside
of my native stronghold.
It was amazing
how very beautiful
was my native stronghold.[4]
The older stockade posts
stood bending
up backward,
and the newly erected posts
stood bending
up forward.
On account of this,
this is what
was happening
above them.
Over the posts,
the newly erected posts,
clouds went soaring
up high into

the heavenly skies
like white mist.
Over
the older posts
clouds went soaring
up high into
the heavenly skies
like black mist.
On account of this,
black clouds
and white clouds
were hovering
in thick billows there.
The upper boards [of the stockade]
curved upward into the clouds.
The lower boards
went curving deep down
into countless layers of the earth.
On account of this,
the upper spear holes
had turned into nests
of little birds
and stood out brightly.
The lower spear holes
had turned into nests
of rats
and looked like black spots.
The wind beating against the spear holes
rang out sonorously
like the chirpings of little birds.
It was a delightful sight,
and my heart leaped with pleasure.

The trail followed

---

[4] The Ainu word *chashi* may mean "stockade," "stronghold," or "house." What follows is a stereotyped description of the beauties of a stockade. Compare this description with that in "The Epic of Kotan Utunnai," p. 387.

by the servants
when they went into the mountains
could be seen clearly.
I started up
along the trail,
and as I went along
some spirits,
some gods
must have attached themselves to me,[5]
for my companion spirits
sent forth rumblings
above me.
Just then
a divine wind came blowing down,
and I was swept up
lightly
in the forefront of the wind.
After that
I continued
to go on.
When I had come
to a certain place,
there was a big stag
bending his head down low
as he ate.
When he took grass nearby
he drew his antlers
back over his body,
and when he took grass far away
he raised his antlers
up high.
When I saw this,
this is what
I thought to myself:

I have heard
it said
that he who approaches
the game too closely
is an unlucky hunter.
Thus, I aimed my arrow
at the tops of the leaves
of the low-growing trees.
I aimed my arrow
at the middle of the trunks
of the tall trees.
I shot
my pretty little arrow.
The pretty little arrow
went speeding
along swiftly.
The pretty little arrow
lodged itself with a thump
on the torso
of the big stag.
The white arrow feathers
were swallowed up,
and the black arrow feathers
were quivering there.
After that
the big stag
went stumbling
along swiftly
away from me.
He spread out the grass
like a mat underneath himself,
toppled down and lay
outstretched majestically.

---

[5] *I-turen*, attached themselves to me as my companion spirits. The Ainu word for "my companion spirit" (a person's spirit helper) is *i-turen kamui*.

When I walked up
to where he was,
his eyes were focused
on me from afar,
as if he had heard
some rumor about me.[6]
Enraged at this,
I grasped in my hands
his fore limbs
and his rear limbs,
and I knocked him against
the slender trees
and the stout trees,
making cracking noises
and thudding noises.
After a while,
I threw him down on the ground
in the woods by the river.
Then I thought
things over
carefully,
and I realized
that this must be
the usual manner
of game animals.
After that
I broke with a snap
his fore legs
and his hind legs
and busily set about
the work of skinning the animal.

While I was
continuing to do this,

just then
there was a loud boom
over the land,
I didn't know where.
A large number
of gods were coming this way
making a loud roaring
and an intense rumbling.
After a short while,
a short distance from me,
something the size of a grove of trees
was soaring upward,
and a large number of them
came dropping down.
When I looked at them,
this is what I saw:
One who appeared to be
the much-rumored
Poi-Soya-un-mat,
dressed exactly like a man
in men's garments,
in men's clothing,
with a quiver with a sling attached
together with
a bow wound with cherry bark,
was carrying
on her back
the quiver with the sling attached,
and was holding
the bow wound with cherry bark
at the center of its handgrip.
She had brought along with her
six servants
and was holding

[6] The hero, who knows nothing about hunting, is angered at first when the eyes of the dead deer stare at him fixedly. Later he realizes that this is, of course, the way with game animals when they are killed.

a short-hilted spear.
She came dropping down
a short distance away from me.
Nevertheless,
I pretended that
I had not seen them
and turned my back
toward them.
I continued to
busy myself with
the work of skinning the animal.
After a while
Poi-Soya-un-mat
sent one of her servants
to speak this message:

"We have been roaming about
intending to kill,
intending to slay
a deer,
and you, a stranger
have gone ahead of us
and spoiled our hunting.
No matter who you may be,
give us as indemnity
your hunting sword
along with the deer
as well.
If you refuse,
we will hack you
to pieces!"

The servant
came and spoke

this message.
Enraged at this,
I struck
the servant
with a club
and threw his mangled corpse
down to the ground.
Then
once again
another servant
came with a message.
I killed
this servant too.
Once again
she sent a servant
with a message.
Each time they came
I would kill them.
As this went on,
I finally killed
all six servants.
After that
the evil woman
poured out
many words of abuse,
countless words of abuse.
She spoke these words:

"A stranger
from an unknown land,
were he to commit
such unforgivable
indignities
in the mountains,

this alone
would enrage me.
But not stopping at that,
you have annihilated
all my kinsmen,
you have massacred
the chief ones of my kinsmen.
Do not delude yourself
that you will
save your life,
that you will
survive at all,
for you have committed
unforgivable
indignities.
No matter
that I may be
a woman,
there are no warriors
comparable to me,
no warriors like me,
even among men,
in any land,
in any country.
Whoever you may be,
you stranger
from an unknown land,
you have exalted yourself
and behaved with
outrageous arrogance!
Nevertheless,
do not delude yourself
that your life will be saved,
that you will survive!''

While speaking
these words,
she came stamping
fiercely toward me.
However,
I paid no attention
and busied myself
with the work of skinning the animal.
During this while,
I exerted
many utmost efforts,
countless utmost efforts
to prevent her from seeing me
in my human form.
For this reason
I scattered
all around me
many billowy clouds of mist,
countless billowy clouds of mist
in the forms of men.
Just then
she came up
beside me.
The evil woman's
eyes
stood there
side by side
like little stars.
She could scarcely
remain standing.
She spewed out at me
biting words,
harsh words.
This is what she said:

"Look here, stranger,
no matter who
you may be
who are behaving
in this way,
I loathe
concealing
one's own identity.
The name
of my native land
is Poi-Soya,
and I who am
doing this here
am Poi-Soya-un-mat.
If you who are
doing this here
have a native land,
if you have a country,
state your native land,
state your country,
that I may hear it!
I am a warrior
who slashes down
slow speakers
before they start to speak.
I am a warrior
who slashes down
fast speakers
after they finish speaking.
If you speak slowly,
I will slash you down
before you start to speak.
If you speak quickly,.
I will slash you down

after you finish speaking.
Speak quickly!
Come, speak up!''

The evil woman
spoke
these words.
Just then
I sprang up suddenly
and lunged toward
the evil woman.
I pulled mightily
at her hair
and wound in my hands
her locks of hair.
After that
I beat her violently,
I struck her mightily,
and at the ends of my arms
there were thudding noises
and cracking noises.
Like many dead fish,
like countless dead fish,
I dragged her along
after myself.
I avoided
the slender
trees growing on the ground.
I knocked her against
the stout trees,
and at the ends of my arms
there were thudding noises.
After a while
I threw her mangled corpse

down onto the ground.

After that
I hurled her down
onto the surface of the ground.
I went running around
among the clumps of trees
growing on the ground
and busily set about
cutting vines.
After that
I tied
Poi-Soya-un-mat
with the vines
onto the trunk
of a stout
tree growing on the ground.
After that
I laid out
her servants
side by side
facing in the direction
of the land of Poi-Soya.
After that
I made
the big stag
into a large bundle.
After that
I returned home.

I came down
to my native stronghold
and put the meat in
through the window.[7]

At that time
my foster sister
came walking up
to the window
clapping her hands
together
to greet me.
Her voice resounded faintly
as she rejoiced over me.

After that
I went inside
and sliced
the parts eaten raw.[8]
I served
my foster sister
heaping trayfuls
of food.[9]

Afterward
my foster sister
rejoiced
and spoke these words:

"I would rejoice
when eating this
even if the common servants
served it to me,
but now the god I have raised,
my divine nursling
serves me
with his own hands,
and this makes
the deer

---

[7] Gods and spirits enter and leave the house through the sacred window. This is why the meat of game animals is put in through this window.

[8] The organ meats of fish and game, called *huipe*, were eaten raw and considered to be the greatest delicacies.

[9] Literally, "I served my foster sister food so that it was impossible to grasp the trays." The food was served on wooden platters.

all the more
delicious!''

My foster sister
spoke
these words
while she ate.

After that
I did nothing but
carve on scabbards
and carve on treasures,
with my eyes focused
on a single spot,
and this is the way
I continued to live
on and on
uneventfully.

Then, beginning not long ago,
slight rumors
began to come to my ears.
This is what they said:

Poi-Soya-un-mat
one day
went hunting
in the mountains,
but she did not
come home
all night long.
When she went hunting
into the mountains
she had taken with her

servants
six in number,
but none of them,
neither she
nor the servants
came home.
Then this is the way
they finally came home:
Poi-Soya-un-mat
was entirely without
any signs of life,
and the servants
came back carrying
the lifeless corpse
of Poi-Soya-un-mat.
Since then
Poi-Soya-un-mat
has been nursing herself
back to health.
Poi-Soya-un-mat
did not know [who it was],
and they all consulted
together about it,
but Poi-Soya-un-mat
has never been able
to find out who it was
who had struck her down.

This was the rumor
that came to my ears.
When I heard it,
I laughed to myself
in amusement.
While doing so,

I did nothing but
carve on scabbards
and carve on treasures,
with my eyes focused
on a single spot,
and this is the way
I continued to live
on and on
uneventfully.

Then on one occasion
my foster sister
stared fixedly down
at the center of the hearth.
She seemed to have
something she wanted to say.
The ashes in the center of the fireplace
she raked out toward the edges,
and the ashes at the edges of the fireplace
she raked out toward the center.
Here and there in the ashes
she jabbed [with the tongs]
and traced furrows and lines.
After some time
she turned toward me
and spoke these words:

    "O god whom I have raised,
    o my divine nursling,
    listen to
    what I have to say!
    I had been intending
    to tell you the story,
    but since you were

still much too young,
I have remained
silent about it
until this time.
In the meanwhile,
quite suddenly,
you said that you wanted
to go hunting
in the mountains.
But never in the world
did I expect
that you would do
such a thing.
I never thought
that it was you,
of all persons,
who had struck down
Poi-Soya-un-mat.
The fact of the matter
is this:
The story
does not have to do
with any
stranger.
The words of your parents
are these:

'When you have grown up,
you are to marry
Poi-Soya-un-mat,
the divine lady,
and you are to be together
a well-matched couple.'

"These are
the words of your parents,
the instructions they left behind.
However,
before I had
even told you,
you have, they say,
[killed] your own betrothed,
mistaking her for someone else.
Nevertheless,
my divine nursling,
you must never
even think
of disobeying
the words of your parents,
the instructions they left behind.
This was why
I have raised you
with such a splendid upbringing,
such a magnificent upbringing.
You must
agree to
my well-meaning request!"

My foster sister
spoke
these words.
Nevertheless,
this is what
I thought to myself:

    "Even if it had been
    a complete stranger
    who had done this,

I would have been
terribly angry,
but now, it turns out,
it was none other than a relative,
someone called my betrothed,
who has, they say,
exalted herself
and behaved with such
outrageous arrogance!"

Thinking this,
I continued
to be overcome
with feelings of anger,
and this is the way
I continued to live
on and on.

Then, little by little,
I began to hear
these rumors:

Ever since
Poi-Soya-un-mat
recovered her health,
this is what
she has been doing:
She takes aboard with her
six servants
and sets sail
for the lands of the *repunkur*
to go trading.
While she travels
about trading,

those who fall in love with her
because she is such
an exceedingly beautiful woman
propose to Poi-Soya-un-mat,
asking her hand in marriage.
Then Poi-Soya-un-mat
is enraged at them
and says these words:

"I am not
by any means
an unbetrothed woman.
I was raised
in a portion
of the swaddling clothes
in which was raised
Otasam-un-kur,
the exalted hero.[10]
In saying that,
you evil-doing
criminals
are behaving
disrespectfully to him
behind his back."

Saying
these things,
she has been going around
fighting battles
of revenge.

These things
I continued to hear,
and this is the way

I continued to live
on and on,
overcome
with feelings of fury
and feelings of anger.
In this way
I continued to live
on and on.

Then, one year,
I decided that I wanted
to go trading.
I commanded
the servants
to make a boat.
After that
day after day,
day in and day out,
the servants
could be heard
building the boat,
carving away at the boat
with loud cracking and crashing noises.
While I heard
them making these noises,
I continued to
carve on scabbards
and carve on treasures.
After a while
had gone by,
the servants finally
finished
building the boat.
Therefore,

---

[10] This means that she and the hero Otasam-un-kur were betrothed to each other from the cradle by their parents.

I took up
my whittling knives
and stepped
outside.
I went down to the beach
and made carvings
on the boat.
This was what I carved:
On the side of the boat facing the sea,
I carved
many pictures,
countless pictures
of the gods dwelling in the sea.
On the side of the boat facing the mountains,
I carved
many pictures,
countless pictures
of the gods dwelling in the mountains.
Now finally
I finished
carving the boat.
After that
I came back
to the stronghold
and commanded
the servants,
saying these words:

    "Come now,
    load
    onto the boat
    the best ones
    of the articles traded with the Japanese!"

I said these words.
In the meanwhile
I made my preparations
for going trading.
While I was doing this,
the servants
worked together busily
in loading
the articles traded with the Japanese.
After a while,
everything was finally
ready for me
to set sail.

After that
I came down
bringing along with me
the servants.
I came down
along the path,
the path leading down to the beach.
I came down to the beach.
We lowered the boat,
the big boat decorated with carvings,
onto the face of the sea.
After that
I got into the boat.
Then
the servants
watched out ahead of the boat
and sang
rowing songs,
which passed along
from mouth to mouth.

On the stern of the boat,
I skillfully handled
the rudder.
After that
we sailed on and on
until we arrived
at the land of the Japanese.

After that
I traded
the articles traded with the Japanese,
and this is what I obtained in exchange:
I got in exchange
nothing but wine,
as well as tobacco
and also grains.
After that
I sailed homeward
in this way:
At every village
on the way home
I would stop overnight,
and would bring out
wine,
as well as tobacco,
and also grains
and would take them ashore.
Continuing to do this,
I sailed homeward.

Ahead of me
I began to hear
these sounds:
Many thudding, rumbling sounds,

countless thudding, rumbling sounds
were rising up somewhere in the distance.
Listening to them,
I came sailing onward.
Then I sailed shoreward,
heading
in their direction.
I looked out,
and this is what I saw.
A huge steep crag
could be seen standing up
majestically.
Atop the steep crag
a stronghold
seemed to be
standing.
Underneath the steep crag
there stood
settlements of the common people,
populous settlements.
Where the settlements
of the common people were,
fierce battles,
fierce fighting
had broken out on all sides,
so it appeared.
As I sailed shoreward,
looking out
in front of me,
someone—
I didn't know who—
called out,
and these words
came flowing

from his lips:

"Listen well,
yaunkun nishpa,[11]
to what I have to say!
I have seen
that your boat's emblem
is that of
Otasam-un-kur,
the exalted hero,
whose god-like
fame I have heard.
I will tell you
what has happened.
I loathe
those who conceal
their own identity.
The name
of this my native land
is Repui-shir,[12]
and I have two
elder brothers.
Poi-Soya-un-mat
was traveling
about trading
and came ashore
to our land.
At that time,
my younger elder brother
became infatuated
with Poi-Soya-un-mat
for her exceeding
beauty
and her skill at needlework.

For this reason,
my eldest brother
proposed to
Poi-Soya-un-mat
that she marry
my younger elder brother.
Poi-Soya-un-mat
became furious at that
and said:

'I am not
by any means
an unbetrothed woman.
Otasam-un-kur,
the exalted hero,
is half human
and half god,
and thus for the most part
he eats among the gods
and for the lesser part
he eats among the humans.
He is half god
and half human,
and the words of our parents,
the instructions they left behind
were that
I should marry him.
For the sake of this,
I have kept myself unsullied,
I have maintained myself unblemished
in the absence
of Otasam-un-kur,
the exalted hero.
But you have behaved

[11] *Yaunkur* gentleman, mainlander gentleman. A term of respect applied to the Ainu (the *yaunkur*) by the *repunkur*.
[12] Repui-shir or Repunshir is no doubt the island known today as Rebun-tō. It is located just off the coast of Hokkaido near the Sōya Kaikyō.

disrespectfully to him
behind his back,
in his absence,
although only in words.
Now that these words
have been uttered,
your land
will by no means
be safe!'

"Saying
these words,
she has been
fighting battles
of revenge.
Just at this time,
a boat bearing
the boat's emblems
of Otasam-un-kur
came shoreward.
The evil woman
is acting in this way
not because of any
mischief,
any lewdness
done by my younger elder brother.
I implore you,
yaunkun nishpa,
do not hold
any grudge
against us!''

These cries
came dropping down

over me.
At the mere
hearing of it,
a frenzied rage
burst over me.
For this reason
I turned the boat
toward the shore
and moved shoreward.
When I had come
onto the crest of the billows,
the billows out in the offing,
I sprang up
from inside the boat.
Holding in my hands
a silver club,
I went flying up
from inside the ship.
I darted down
onto the sandy beach.
I walked on.
The settlements of the common people,
the populous settlements,
were spread out,
filling up
all the lower cliff
and filling up
all the higher cliff.
But
in the midst of the settlement,
the settlement on
the lower cliff,
large crowds of people
were milling about

like swarming insects.
In the middle of the crowds
Poi-Soya-un-mat
was whirling about
like a bird.
Wherever she passed
the corpses mowed down like grass
lay stretched out in the distance.

Just then
I dived head first
into the midst of the crowds,
the large crowds of people.
I followed right after
Poi-Soya-un-mat
as she whirled about.
I ran right up
next to
Poi-Soya-un-mat.
Just as she jumped,
just as she flew,
I slashed at the nape of her neck.
On the nape of
Poi-Soya-un-mat's neck
the silver club
struck home
with a thud.
Poi-Soya-un-mat
turned around
like a fish thrashing about.
I trailed immediately
behind her.
As I struck her
with the silver club,

at the ends of my arms
there were thudding noises,
there were cracking noises.

After that
I tied ropes
around the legs
of Poi-Soya-un-mat's
mangled corpse.
After that
I tied her
to my ankles
and went down to the beach.
The servants
of Poi-Soya-un-mat
were in
their hut of matting.
I beat them soundly
and commanded them
to move quickly
and start for home.
They went scattering
all at once,
got into their boat,
and set sail.
After that
I went running
to my own boat.
Then
I set out
heading toward
my native land.

After that

I sailed homeward.
After a while
I arrived
exactly
off the shore of
the land of Poi-Soya.
Just then
I untied
Poi-Soya-un-mat,
whom I had tied
to my ankles,
and threw her
into the boat
of her servants.

After that
I sailed on
heading
in the direction of
my own stronghold.
I finally
headed toward
my own harbor
and came ashore.
After that
the servants
went running about
this way and that
to unload the boat.
In the meanwhile
I came back
into the stronghold
and threw myself down
on my bed.

I was overcome
with feelings of rage.

    ''The evil deeds
    of the evil woman,
    the contemptible woman,
    have been
    altogether
    too excessive!''

Thinking this to myself,
I was overcome
with feelings of rage,
and this was the way
I continued to live
on and on
uneventfully.
During this while,
I carved on scabbards
and carved on treasures,
with my eyes focused
on a single spot,
and I continued to live
on and on
uneventfully.

II

Doing nothing but needlework,
I remained with my eyes
focused on a single spot,
and this is the way I lived
on and on
uneventfully.

This is what
I thought to myself:

    "I have heard that
    the words of my parents,
    the instructions they left behind
    were that I should marry
    my little elder brother
    Otasam-un-kur,
    and that we were to live together
    as a well-matched couple,
    as a well-matched pair.
    But if I continue
    to do as I am now,
    will he not perhaps
    take a dislike to me?"

Thinking this thought,
this is what
I began to do:
I had seen
a quiver with a sling attached
and a bow wound with cherry bark
which had been hanging
for a very long time
by the window.
Beginning
not long ago,
I began to imitate
a man's clothes
and a man's behavior.
Dressing myself
in men's clothes,
I would toss up

the quiver with the sling attached
onto my back,
and I would grasp
the bow wound with cherry bark
at the center of its handgrip.
Then, using as a staff
a short-hilted spear,
I would take along with me
men servants
six in number,
and we would go hunting in the mountains.
When anyone had caught fish,
I would beat them and take away the fish;
and when anyone had killed a deer,
I would beat them and take away the deer.
From those who were wealthy
I would take away
their hunting swords
together with their deer
as indemnity.
I had continued
to do these things
for a long time.

Then, one season,
I took along with me
men servants
six in number
and went hunting in the mountains.
We went on and on.
When we had come
to a certain place,
ahead of us there was
someone whom I couldn't recognize.

Was he a human,
or was he a god?
Nevertheless,
I approached closer,
and this is what
I sensed:
The force of presence of a chieftain,
the force of presence of a warrior
drove me
backward.
Until this time
I had gone into the mountains
and had seen
any number of chieftains,
but never before
had I seen anyone
who was as awe-inspiring
as this.
I thought to myself:

"Who ever may he be,
what country may he be from,
that he arouses
such intense fear
and apprehension in me?"

Nevertheless,
I did not want
to act as if
I were cowardly,
as if I were weak.
For this reason,
I sent my servants
as messengers,

but he killed
all of them,
all six servants.
Desire to avenge them
sprang up in me.
Therefore,
I went stamping
fiercely toward him.
I stepped up
close by his side.
But even then
I was quite unable
to catch a glimpse
of his human form.
These are the words
that I spoke:

"Are you a human?
What is it that
you may be?
No matter
that I may be
a woman,
I still surpass
the male warriors.
No matter who you may be,
no matter what country you may be from,
you are here
massacring
the chief ones of my kinsmen.
I am one
who loathes
those who conceal
their own identity.

The name
of my native land
is the land of Poi-Soya.
I who am
doing this here
am Poi-Soya-un-mat,
the divine lady.
You have committed
unforgivable indignities
in the mountains
behind my native village,
and this alone
would enrage me.
But you have also
annihilated
my kinsmen.
Nevertheless,
if you have
a native land,
state
your native land.
No matter
that I may be
a woman,
I am a warrior
who slashes down
slow speakers
before they start to speak.
I am a warrior
who slashes down
fast speakers
after they finish speaking.
Come then,
speak up!

Speak quickly!
If you speak slowly,
I will slash you down,
I will kill you
before you start to speak!''

When I said this,
he who had been
thus far entirely
deaf,
sprung up suddenly
from his skinning
and stepped toward me.
However,
his chest
was enveloped
in twisting billows of mist,
and because of that
I was quite unable
to catch a glimpse
of his human form.
From inside the mist,
he took hold of
the hair on my head,
my magnificent locks of hair.
After that,
he knocked me against
the slender fallen tree trunks
and the stout fallen tree trunks
on the mountain slopes,
and my heart grew faint
with the mortal agony of it.
After a while,
little by little,

I could feel him slashing me,
and excruciating pains
gripped my insides.
At this time,
whoever it was,
a human
or a god,
spewed out toward me
harsh words,
biting words.
This is what he said:

    "Evil woman,
    contemptible woman,
    I came into the mountains
    after growing sick of hearing
    about your conduct,
    and now you are acting
    with brazen disrespect
    toward me by the words,
    the evil words,
    you uttered.
    Did you think
    that I have been
    lying in wait
    for you here
    in order to do you a good deed?
    Is this why you dared
    to commit
    such unforgivable
    indignities against me?"

While he said
these words,

I felt him slashing me,
I felt him tearing me,
and excruciating pains
gripped my insides.
After a while,
I lost all consciousness
of what was happening.

After that,
was I dead?
was I asleep?
my mind
was clouded
and dazed.
After a while,
I regained consciousness,
and this was
the state I was in:
Never would I have
thought that such a thing
could have been done to me—
I was tied
with vines
onto the trunk
of a stout
tree growing on the ground.
At that point
I regained
my consciousness.

I was quite unable
to move,
and there were
no signs of life

in me anywhere.
Just then,
my servants
came walking up
underneath me.
They were whispering
to each other,
saying these words:

"This is why
it is better
for women
to stay in the house
and to amuse themselves
with needlework
or with women's work.
But what kind of
behavior of a woman
is this?
The divine lady
does nothing but
imitate
men's occupations
and men's behavior.
Since she has performed
deeds punished by the gods,
she has thus
been punished
so severely."

The servants
whispered these words
to each other
as they cut me loose

from my vines
and let me down.
They spoke these words:

"We also
recall
like a faint dream
only that
we were beaten
with clubs.
After that,
were we asleep?
were we dead?
our minds
were dazed.
After a while,
we awoke
and found that
we also
had remained here
overnight.
However,
we thought
that we probably
were alone.
But all the time,
it turned out,
the divine lady
was here,
tied to
the trunk
of a tree.
This is why
we are now

untying her.''

They spoke these words.
After that,
I came home,
feeling as if
I were dead.
I came down
to my own house,
and after that
I continued
to nurse myself back to health
for a long time.
After some time,
finally
the scabs dropped off
my smaller wounds,
and scabs grew over
my larger wounds,
and I lived on
in this way.

After that,
I did nothing but needlework,
with my eyes focused
on a single point,
and this is the way
I lived
on and on
uneventfully.
As time went on,
my embroidery
had come to the point
of weighing down

the clothing racks in the back
and the clothing racks in the front.

After that,
this is what
I thought to myself:

  ''Though you went
  hunting like a man
  through the mountains,
  a stranger
  from an unknown land
  struck you down
  in this way.
  It would be good
  if you were to travel around
  in order to trade
  your best possessions,
  your best embroidery.''

Thinking this,
I had the servants
take me in the boat.
Loading the boat full
of my best embroidery,
I set sail.
After that
I traveled around,
sailing to
many lands of the *repunkur*,
countless lands of the *repunkur*,
and traveling around
trading.
I traded profitably [and received]

many vessels
and many treasures.

In the meanwhile,
while I was traveling around,
there were some
who became infatuated
with my beauty
and my skill at needlework
and who proposed marriage to me.
This would
make me angry,
and I would fight battles
of revenge,
as I sailed about to
many lands of the *repunkur*,
countless lands of the *repunkur*.
This is the way
I continued to live on.

Then, one season,
I sailed to
the land of Repunshir.
In that place
there lived
the rulers of Repunshir,
two brothers
and one sister.
I came ashore
to their village.
At that time,
the elder one
of the rulers of Repunshir
stated his will

in this way:

   ''The divine lady
   is extremely
   beautiful
   and skilled at needlework,
   and we are infatuated
   with her for this.
   I wish to give
   the divine lady
   in marriage to
   the god whom we are raising,
   our divine nursling,
   my younger brother.''[13]

Since this
made me angry,
I began
to fight battles
of revenge.
I was continuing
to mow down
all around me
many human corpses,
countless human corpses.
Just then,
something happened
which I would never have expected.
All of a sudden,
something came darting
like a spear which is thrown.
Immediately after this,
some sort of being,
I didn't know who,

[13] Here the title *a-reshpa kamui a-reshpa pito* is applied to the younger brother of a chieftain of the *repunkur*.

began to pull mightily
on the hair on my head.
After that
I was beaten violently,
and my heart grew faint
with the mortal agony of it.
After that,
I felt him slashing me,
I felt him tearing me,
and my heart was faint
with the mortal agony of it.
After that,
he continued to beat me,
and I felt him striking me,
I felt him slashing me,
and excruciating pains
gripped my insides.

During this time,
even in my intense pain,
even though I was alarmed
and confused,
I still managed to open
my eyes a mere slit,
and saw that it was
none other than
Otasam-un-kur,
the exalted hero,
my own little brother,
who was beating me.

After that,
he continued to beat me until
I lost all consciousness

of what was happening.
Was I dead?
was I asleep?
my mind
was dazed.
After a while,
I regained consciousness
and looked around.
This was what I saw.

I was tied up
with leather thongs,
both my arms
and my legs.
I was trussed up
like little pebbles.[14]
Otasam-un-kur,
the exalted hero,
had tied
the end of the rope
to his ankles,
and I was
in his ship.
However,
I was quite unable
to move.

After that
we sailed on
in this way:
Whenever he would think
he would grasp in his hand
the boat's scull
and would beat me

---

[14] On Ainu looms for weaving mats, the warp strings are tied up with little pebbles.

using the scull
as a club on me.
Excruciating pains
would grip my insides.
As this was going on,
we continued to sail on.
Now finally
the land of the *yaunkur*
came looming up
toward us
as we sailed on.

After that
we continued
to sail on
until finally
we were sailing
off the shore
of the land of Poi-Soya.
My servants
had been sailing along
in the boat alongside us.
When we sailed
by the shore
of the land of Poi-Soya,
my native land,
Otasam-un-kur,
my little elder brother,
untied me
from his ankles
and threw me
into the boat
of my servants,
into my own boat.

After that
he turned his boat
out to sea
and went sailing
in the direction of
his native land,
the land of Otasam.

My servants
sailed me off
in the opposite direction,
and we came shoreward.
While we were sailing homeward,
I had not
acted at all
as if I were in pain
because I was afraid
that if Otasam-un-kur,
my little elder brother,
were to hear
that I was in pain,
he might punish me
all the more intensely.
However,
now that my servants
were sailing me
and we were on the way home,
I began to utter
many loud moans
one after another
as I was sailing shoreward.
Now finally
we came ashore
at my native landing place.

The servants
brought the boat ashore.
After that
the servants
took me
by my hands
and led me back
to my native stronghold.

After that
I continued to
nurse myself back to health
for a very long time
until, after great efforts,
I finally brought myself
to the point of recovery.
After that,
I continued to live
on and on
uneventfully.
After some time had gone by,
one season,
while I was
doing my needlework,
just then,
there was the sound of someone
coming this way in a hurry.
If it were a woman
it would sound differently.
It seemed to be a man,
for there was the sound of a swordguard
clinking
very loudly.
The clinking continued,

and he seemed to come walking on.
Then, without hesitation,
whoever it was
opened wide
the door hangings.
Before
he came in,
many flashes of light,
countless flashes of light
came streaming in.
Above the flashing lights
a human face
suddenly appeared.
When he entered,
I looked at him
and this is what I saw:
Though Otasam-un-kur
had never before
looked unattractive
or ugly,
he now came in
with his beauty
even more imposing
than before.
He stood
in the vestibule.
This is what he said:

> "Listen well,
> o Poi-Soya-un-mat,
> my younger sister,
> to what I have to say!
> I have been traveling
> in order to trade

with the Japanese,
and I am now sailing
on my way home
from there.
But I have stopped
on the way
because I desired
to leave with you
[some pieces] of silken cloth.
If you will come along with me,
I will give them
to you.''

So he spoke, but
I thought to myself:

"Let me finish
one needle stitch
before I get up.''

Thus, I did not
get up immediately.
Then
fierce rage
flashed forth
on his face.
He came stamping
fiercely toward me.
While he came,
he uttered these words:

"How long,
o evil woman,
o contemptible woman,

are you going to
commit these
unforgivable
indignities against me?''

As he spoke
these words,
he came stamping
fiercely toward me.
He pulled me mightily.
Once again—for when
had he ever
treated me nicely?—
he knocked me against
the upper rafters
and the lower rafters,
and excruciating pains
gripped my insides.
As time went on,
I felt him tearing me
more and more,
and excruciating pains
gripped my insides.
After a while
I lost all consciousness
of what was happening.

Was I dead?
was I asleep?
my mind
was dazed
and clouded.
When I opened
my eyes,

this is what I saw:
I was on the floor,
floating this way
and floating that way
in a pool of blood.
At that point
I regained
consciousness.
However,
I was quite unable
to move.
After that
this is what
I thought to myself:

>   "What evil spirit
>   could have bewitched me,
>   that as a result
>   all my life long
>   I continue
>   to be killed over and over,
>   to be killed again and again
>   in this way?"

Thinking this,
I shed
many sparkling teardrops,
countless sparkling teardrops.
In the meantime
I continued to
nurse myself back to health.
After a while,
with the utmost effort
I finally

brought myself
to the point of recovery.

After that, once again
I continued to do
nothing but needlework,
and this is the way
I lived on.
After I had been
doing my needlework
for not a very long while,
one time again
there was the sound of someone
coming this way in a hurry.
Someone came inside.
I looked at him,
and this is what I saw:
Otasam-un-kur,
my little elder brother,
came inside.
He remained
standing
in the vestibule,
and then he said this:

>   "Listen well,
>   Poi-Soya-un-mat,
>   to what I have to say!
>   You were bewitched
>   by some evil spirit,
>   and as a result
>   all your life long
>   I have been punishing
>   you in this way,

but I have not
been doing this
because I had
any evil intentions.
I have been doing it
because I wanted,
in this way,
to cause your evil conduct
to run its course.
Nevertheless,
I have not
been doing this
because I had
any evil intentions.
This being the case,
please do not
hold a grudge against me,
do not harbor dislike for me!
I have just gone
to trade.
I went
to the land of the Japanese,
and I am now
on my way home
from there,
but I have come
ashore here
because I wanted
to leave with you
[some pieces of] silken cloth
for you to embroider.
Come along with me!''

When he spoke this,

this is what
I thought to myself:

    ''The last time
    when he said this to me
    I took too long
    in getting up,
    and I was
    slain
    as a result!''

Thinking this,
I got up
before he had finished speaking.
I stuck my needle
through my needlework
and put it aside.
After that
I girded myself
with a single sedge stalk.

After that
I followed
close behind
the exalted hero.
I went down
along the path,
the path down to the beach.
I looked out,
and this is what I saw:
A big boat decorated with carvings
was
in the harbor.
A landing plank

had been
thrown up
onto the sandy beach.
The exalted hero
leaped up
onto the plank.
I followed
close behind him
and went
inside the boat.
When I looked around,
this is what I saw:
There were
all sorts of trade goods
filling up
the inside.
The exalted hero
spoke these words:

    "Those pieces of silken cloth over there—
    you may take
    any of them
    that you want."

When he said this,
I thought to myself:

    "Which ones, indeed,
    ought I
    to take?"

While I was
thinking this,
just then,

that big boat
seemed
to move.
Therefore,
I looked around and saw
that that big boat
was being sailed
out to sea
by the servants.
At that time
I let out
a loud shriek.
Just then
I was grabbed by the shoulders
and was held down.
I wondered
who it was
who was holding me down.
I looked back
over my shoulders.
What I saw then
was something
that I never would have expected.
A person I did not recognize,
a total stranger
was holding me by the shoulders.
I screamed out
loud and long.
Then
the one who was holding me
spoke these words:

    "Listen well,
    Poi-Soya-un-mat,

to what I have to say!
I loathe
those who conceal
their own identity.
The name
of my native land
is Moshirpa.
The rulers of Moshirpa
are two brothers,
and they have
two younger sisters.
I am the younger one
of the two brothers.
I set sail
to go trading.
Afterward
I was going home
from trading,
but this is what
I thought to myself:
I have been hearing
all the time
that Poi-Soya-un-mat
is so beautiful
that rumors have
arisen about her among the gods.
Then, beginning not long ago,
this is what
I started to hear:
Even though
Poi-Soya-un-mat,
the divine lady,
has done nothing
to deserve punishment,

she has continued
to be killed over and over,
to be killed again and again
by Otasam-un-kur,
the exalted hero.
When I heard this,
desire to avenge her
sprang up in me.
For this reason,
as I was coming home
from trading,
I decided to pretend
to be Otasam-un-kur,
the exalted hero,
and to go ashore
and bring you with me.
Then I would
take you with me
to the land of Moshirpa,
and we would marry each other.
For what, indeed,
is Otasam-un-kur
punishing you
that he
kills you over and over,
troubling
your youthful heart?
Rather than this,
if you were to marry me,
it would be
exactly as if
you had stepped
inside
an impregnable stronghold.[15]

[15] Literally, a stronghold on a cliff.

Please agree
to my well-meaning request!"

The young boy
spoke these words.
After that
I continued to
scratch at
the face of
the evil wretch
as we sailed on,
but I did not act at all
as if I were angry
at what I had heard.
After that
he instructed me
with many pieces of good advice
as we sailed on.
Then, when we came
to a certain place,
it appeared that
we had come
off the shore of
the place known as
the land of Moshirpa.
They sailed shoreward,
heading toward
the harbor entrance.
They pulled
that big boat
up onto the sandy beach.

After that
the servants

jumped out
and started to unload the cargo,
throwing down
the shorter carrying slings
and racing each other to get
the longer carrying slings.
They worked busily together
to unload the cargo.
In the meantime,
the evil wretch
picked me up
like a baby.
Carrying me,
he went
climbing up
along the path.
As we went along,
I looked out
ahead of me,
and this is
what I saw:
A populous village
stood there.
filling up the entire
lower cliff.
In the center of the village
a divinely made stronghold
could be seen standing
majestically.
I continued to look at this
as we went on.
The evil wretch
made his way
up beside the village,

the village which was
on the lower cliff.
He went inside
the divinely made stronghold
which I had seen
standing
in the center of the village.

He walked along the floor
on the left-hand side of the fireplace
and sat down
at the head of the fireplace.
I looked and saw
a young woman
of amazing beauty.
I did not know
that there could be
such a beautiful young woman.
The brightness of her face
was like the rising sun,
sending out
dazzling rays of light.
Not only was she beautiful.
but in addition to her beauty,
it was amazing
how skillful she was [at needlework].
Many rays of light,
countless rays of light
streamed out
from between the stitches
of her embroidered garments,
her magnificent embroidered robes.
The glittering light sent out
by the young woman,

and the brightness of her embroidered robes
brightened
the inside of the house
like brilliant sunlight.
The woman
was awe-inspiring
for her beauty
and her skill at needlework.

In the meanwhile
the evil wretch
still continued
to hold me like a baby,
to hold me like a child.
Then
the young woman
spoke these words:

> "Listen carefully,
> my little elder brother,
> to what I have to say!
> It would be much better
> for us women among ourselves
> to reach an agreement.
> I will speak to
> the divine lady
> and calm her down.
> My little elder brother,
> please leave
> the divine lady
> in my charge!"

The young woman
spoke these words.

Only then
did the evil wretch
release me.
After that
the young woman
took me by the hand.
At that time
I got up quickly
and threw myself down
in the back corner of the house
on the left-hand side of the fireplace.

After that
I remained lying in bed
all the time.
During this while,
whenever the young woman
would go to bed,
she would always
sleep on top of
my sleeves
on the side away from the fireplace,
and this is the way
we lived
on and on
uneventfully.

Then, during this while,
the village chieftain[16]
sent a message
from the village,
the village which was
on the upper cliff.
This was the message:

"What strange conduct is this?
I detest
the things that you have done,
my evil younger brother.
It is not as if
Otasam-un-kur
were a stranger.[17]
I have heard
it said that
Otasam-un-kur
has been angered
all his life,
his whole life long,
on account of
the evil woman
Poi-Soya-un-mat,
and I have felt
sympathy for him.
But [your conduct]—
if even a stranger
were to do such a thing to me
I would be terribly angry.
For what reason
have you stolen away
Poi-Soya-un-mat
and brought her here?
Rather than this,
act quickly
before
Otasam-un-kur
comes here.
Bring out
your best possessions[18]
and give them up together with

[16] The elder one of the two brothers who are the chieftains of Moshirpa (Moshirpa-un-kur). He lives on the upper cliff, and the younger brother (the one who has stolen away Poi-Soya-un-mat) lives on the lower cliff.

[17] Otasam-un-kur is stated to be a relative of the chieftains of Moshirpa, but their relationship is not specified. Later on, the elder brother calls Otasam-un-kur "my younger brother."

[18] As indemnities to pay for the wrong done.

Poi-Soya-un-mat!''

This message
came down.
Nevertheless,
the evil wretch
whispered
these words
to himself:

"Sooner
or later
if Otasam-un-kur,
the exalted hero,
should come here,
I will make
my amends
with vessels
and with treasures.''

These words
he whispered
to himself,
and this is the way
we lived
on and on.

Then, one day
the outdoor servants
came bustling inside,
and the indoor servants
went bustling outside.
They whispered
these words

to each other:

"A boat bearing
the boat's emblem
of Otasam-un-kur,
the exalted hero,
is coming shoreward!''

These words
the servants
whispered
to each other.
Just then,
there was the sound of someone
coming this way in a hurry.
Without hesitation
he stepped
inside the entrance porch.
He opened wide
the door hangings
and tossed them up
over his shoulders.
A human face
suddenly appeared
over the vestibule.
He was scarcely able
to remain standing
in the vestibule.
His eyes
stood there
beside each other
like little stars.
He came stamping
fiercely along

the left-hand side of the fireplace.
From up very high
there was a clanking sound
as he drew his sword.
He darted
a fierce sword thrust at me.
When he did this,
the young woman
seized me
and held me,
while uttering
these words:

>"It was the fault of
>my evil elder brother,
>it was he
>who did evil,
>and it would [not] be bad for the land
>if he were slain.
>But the divine lady
>was brought here
>by my evil elder brother,
>and ever since she came here
>I have watched over her,
>and my evil elder brother
>has not even
>come near her.
>Do not do this—
>do not slay her,
>do not kill
>the divine lady!"

Thus spoke
the young woman.

The young woman,
holding me,
went flying up
to the smokehole.
The young woman
went dashing
behind the grassy downs,
the upper grassy downs by the beach,
and she hid me there.

After that,
after we had left
fierce fighting
broke out on all sides.
As I listened
to the sounds of fighting,
on the pathway
in front of the stronghold,
the divinely built stronghold
which I had seen
standing
in the center of the village,
the village which was
on the upper cliff,
someone or other
pronounced an oration,
which rang out loud and clear
like the voice of a cuckoo.
This is what he said:

>"Greetings to you,
>Otasam-un-kur,
>o exalted hero,
>my younger brother!

Listen well
to what I have to say!
Never in the world
would I have expected
my evil younger brother
to do such a deed,
but he became infatuated
with the beauty
of Poi-Soya-un-mat,
stole her away,
and brought her here.
I did not
know anything
about this at all.
My younger brother—
if he
were to be slain,
it would not be
bad for the land,
bad for the country.
You seem
to be about
to kill me,
to slay me
as well.
Do not do this!
I will,
together with my kinsfolk,
make my amends
with vessels,
with treasures!''

This oration
came flowing

from the lips
of whoever it was,
and I remained there
listening to it.
The two of us —
the young woman,
Moshirpa-un-mat, and I—
remained there
hiding.

III

All her life long,
Poi-Soya-un-mat,
the evil maiden,
had exalted herself
and behaved with
outrageous arrogance,
and this alone
continued to
arouse my anger.
But all the time
I was unaware that
the younger of the brothers
ruling Moshirpa
had conceived a lewd passion,
a lascivious passion for
Poi-Soya-un-mat.
I became angry
[when I learned of] that.
Then on one occasion,
I decided that
I wanted to go to visit
the younger of the brothers

ruling Moshirpa.
At that time
my foster sister
spoke these words:

"Look here,
o god whom I have raised,
o my divine nursling,
listen well to
what I have to say!
The chieftains of Moshirpa,
the two brothers
and two sisters,
are by no means
strangers to us,[19]
and it is hardly possible
that they should
become infatuated
with Poi-Soya-un-mat
for her beauty
and her skill at needlework,
that they should ever
conceive a lewd passion,
a lascivious passion
for Poi-Soya-un-mat.
Nevertheless,
one who is a chieftain,
one who is a warrior
ought to walk
in peaceful ways.
O god whom I have raised,
o my divine nursling
do not hold a grudge,
do not harbor dislike for them!"

My foster sister
spoke these words.
After that
I stood up.
I attired
myself in
magnificent robes,
majestic robes.
My metal buckled belt
I wrapped around my waist
in a single wrapping.
I placed on my head
my delicately fashioned helmet.
My god-given sword
I thrust down into its sheath
as far as the swordguard.

After that
I strode
toward the door
and stepped
outside.
I walked
down
along the road,
the road going down to the beach.
I came down
by the beach.
I brought down
a small boat
and cast it out
on the sea.

Just then,

---

[19] "They are our relatives." We are never told how they are related.

as I was doing this,
my foster sister
also came down.
She leaped
into the boat,
and I jumped into the boat.
After that
my foster sister
grasped in her hands
the pretty oar
and rowed the boat.
This is how she rowed:
It was incredible
for what reason
my foster sister
was rowing the boat
so very powerfully!
The little boat
glided along
over the waves.

After that
we sailed along
over the sea.
Then a very populous land,
which surely was
the land of Moshirpa,
came into view.
A populous village
could be seen spread out
filling up the entire area
on top of the lower cliff.
In the center of the village
a divinely built stronghold

could be seen standing
majestically.
A populous village
could be seen spread out
filling up the entire area
on top of the upper cliff.
In the center of the village
a divinely built stronghold
could be seen standing
majestically.
It was amazing
how they could possibly
have so many people,
so many kinsfolk.
As I looked at this,
we came shoreward.
We came ashore,
and the little boat
darted up
onto the sandy beach.

After that
I jumped
out of the boat
and went onto the land.
I went stamping
fiercely along
toward the village,
the village which was
on the lower cliff.
As I went on,
in the center of the village
the divinely built stronghold
could be seen standing

majestically.
Without hesitation
I stepped
inside the stockade.
The entire area inside the stockade
was filled by
a big house
which stood there
majestically.

I headed toward
the entrance door.
I pulled
the door hangings
right up to the threads
and sent them flying
like a cast javelin.
I dashed
half-way
into the vestibule.
I was scarcely able
to remain standing
in the vestibule.
I cast my glance out
in front of me.
When I looked,
this is what I saw:
One who seemed to be
the younger of the brothers
ruling Moshirpa
was sitting
at the head of the fireplace.
He was awe-inspiring
in his beauty.

In the back corner of the house
on the left-hand side of the fireplace
Poi-Soya-un-mat,
the evil woman,
was lying in bed.
In front of her,
a young woman
who seemed to be
Moshirpa-un-mat
was sitting.
She was awe-inspiring
in her beauty
and her skill at needlework.

I went stamping
fiercely toward
Poi-Soya-un-mat,
the evil woman.
There was a flash of light
under my arms,[20]
and like an arching rainbow
my fierce sword sweep
darted down
over
Poi-Soya-un-mat.
Though my thrust was swift,
the young woman
Moshirpa-un-mat
seized her
away from the tip of my blade
and held her.
She dashed up
onto the ceiling beams.
I swung at her and missed

[20] I unsheathed my sword with a sudden flash of light.

on the ceiling beams.
She dashed up
onto the rafters.
I swung at her and missed
on the rafters.
It was incredible
how very quick
in fleeing was
the young woman
Moshirpa-un-mat.
She went flying up
to the smokehole.

After that
I whirled around
and darted
a fierce sword thrust
at Moshirpa-un-kur.
When I did this,
just as Moshirpa-un-kur
was getting up,
I sliced him
into several pieces.
His life-spirit[21]
was heard flying up
with a loud roaring.

After that
no enemies to slay
still remained.
Then
I threw into a tumult
the settlement of the common people.[22]
Within the settlement

some fled holding
their children by the hand,
and some holding their women by the hand.
Throngs of fleeing people
surged along one after the other.
After that,
fierce shrieks of terror
followed in my wake.

As this was going on,
from the stronghold,
the divinely built stronghold
which I had seen
standing
in the center of the village,
the village which was
on the upper cliff,
someone—I couldn't tell
exactly who it was—
brought out indemnities.[23]
He was doing a war dance[24]
beside the indemnities.
While he danced,
his voice rang out loud and clear
like the voice of a cuckoo.
He pronounced an oration,
in which he uttered
these words:

"Greetings to you,
Otasam-un-kur,
my younger brother!
Listen well to
what I have to say!

[21] *Inotu orke*, the soul or spirit, especially that which departs from the body at death. Also called *kamui inotu* ("divine life-spirit"). The word *inotu* is derived from the old Japanese word for "life" from which the contemporary Japanese word *inochi* is also derived. Departing life-spirits would fly off with an audible rumbling. Those spirits destined to be restored to life would become "living spirits" and would rumble off toward the east. The "utterly dead" spirits would rumble off toward the west.

[22] *Usekur kotan*. The ordinary rank-and-file members of the community who did not belong to the chiefly stratum were known as *usekur* or *wenkur*.

[23] Treasures brought out and lined up as payment for the wrong done.

[24] *Horipi*, a stamping dance performed during battle.

I am
by no means
a stranger to you.
But on account of
the evil deeds
of my evil younger brother,
the miserable wretch,
Otasam-un-kur,
my younger brother
has become angry.
By no means
do I disapprove of it.
The evil woman
Poi-Soya-un-mat
has exalted herself
and behaved with
outrageous arrogance,
and has committed
unforgivable indignities
against the exalted hero,
Otasam-un-kur.
This alone would
arouse my anger,
but now my evil younger brother
has conceived a lewd passion,
a lascivious passion for
Poi-Soya-un-mat,
and he is now
being punished
in this way for it.
Although I told
my evil younger brother
to give back
Poi-Soya-un-mat

together with
his best possessions,
he continued
to do nothing about it.
In the meantime,
the exalted hero
Otasam-un-kur
has come here.
Since his deeds were evil,
I do not regret it
in the least
if he is slain,
if he is killed.
I wish to
make amends
with vessels,
with treasures,
and this is why
I have brought out
these indemnities.
O exalted hero
Otasam-un-kur,
please accept
my well-meaning request!"

The oration pronounced
by this person, whoever he was,
came ringing out loud and clear
like the voice of a cuckoo.
While I was listening
to his voice,
I had fought to a point
half-way through the village,
the village which was

on the lower cliff.
Just then,
all of a sudden,
someone grabbed me by the shoulders
from behind.
I wondered
what was the matter
and looked back
over my shoulder.
Then I saw
that it was
my foster sister
who had grabbed me by the shoulders
and was holding me.
While she did this,
she uttered these words:

"O god whom I have raised,
o my divine nursling,
look at what
you are doing,
in spite of
what I told you!
One who is a chieftain,
one who is a warrior
ought to walk
in peaceful ways.
But the younger brother
of the chieftains of Moshirpa
followed after
the evil ways,
the evil heart
of the evil woman.
Since his deeds were evil,

he has now
been slain
as a result,
but on the other hand
the common people
could not
possibly
have known anything about it.
Now here
the corpses
of the common people
are being strewn about
on account of
the evil ways
of the evil woman
Poi-Soya-un-mat.
Calm yourself,
I pray you,
o god whom I have raised,
o my divine nursling!"

Saying these words,
my foster sister
grabbed me by the shoulders
and held me—it was she
whom I had felt doing this.
Only at this point
did I come
to my senses.

After that
Moshirpa-un-kur
loaded his indemnities
onto my boat.

After that
I cast
the little boat
out onto the face of the sea.
After that,
I still continued
to be overcome
with feelings of anger,
as my foster sister
bent the pretty oar
this way in the water
and that way in the water.
We continued to sail
heading
in the direction
of our native land.
Then we arrived home
at our native stronghold.

After that,
I would be overcome
with feelings of anger
whenever I would think
of how the evil woman,
Poi-Soya-un-mat,
had committed
unforgivable
indignities against me,
and this is the way
I lived on.
I did nothing but
carve on scabbards,
carve on treasures,
with my eyes focused
on a single spot,
and this is the way
I lived
on and on
uneventfully.
As time went on,
this is what
I thought to myself:

Long ago,
when I was traveling
about trading,
I once went
trading
to the place of
Retarpira-un-kur.[25]
When I was there,
Retarpira-un-kur
had a younger sister,
who was an ugly woman,
an unattractive woman.
So exceedingly
angry was I
at Poi-Soya-un-mat
that I had asked for the hand
of Retarpira-un-mat,
the ugly woman,
and had then come home.
For this reason,
since I was
so exceedingly
angry at
Poi-Soya-un-mat,
I decided that

---

[25] The inhabitant, or chieftain, of Retarpira ("White Cliff"). His younger sister is called Retarpira-un-mat.

I wanted to go to woo
the younger sister
of Retarpira-un-kur,
even though she was
an ugly woman,
an unattractive woman.

For this reason,
I made my preparations
to go there.
In the meantime,
I heard
these rumors:

Moshirpa-un-mat
was traveling about
together with
Poi-Soya-un-mat.
They were staying
at the homes of servants,[26]
at the homes of low-ranking persons.[27]

I kept hearing
these rumors.
Wishing to go
to the place of
Retarpira-un-kur,
I went outside.
Then my younger sister
spoke these words:

"I would be worried about
my little elder brother
if he were to go

all alone.
I will go along
together with
my little elder brother."

Saying this,
she wrapped a carrying sling
around a little woman's bag
and tossed it up
onto her back.
She followed closely
behind me.
We stepped
outside.

After that
we walked
down
along the road,
the road down to the beach.
We came down
by the beach.
After that,
I put out
the big boat decorated with carvings
onto the face of the sea.

After that
the two of us—
my younger sister and I—
went sailing along
heading
toward the land,
the land of Retarpira.

---

[26] *Usshiu,* "servant," "slave."
[27] *Wenkur,* "low-ranking person," "poor person." Sometimes used synonymously with *usekur,* "commoner." The two women are not given lodging in the homes of the chieftains but are forced to lodge with the lower strata of society.

When we had come
to a certain place,
we went sailing along
next to a cliff,
a cliff jutting up above the water.
As we went by,
this is what I heard:
The eddying waters around the oar
bubbled noisily
and churned noisily,
and this is what
I seemed to hear them say:

  "How pitiful it is
  for Otasam-un-kur,
  the exalted hero,
  that his luck[28]
  should always
  be withdrawn!"

These words
I seemed to hear
in the eddying waters around the oar
as they bubbled noisily
and churned noisily.
After that
the god ruling
the cliff
said these things:

  "What strange words are these?
  I detest
  the lies spoken
  by the eddying waters around the oar.

Otasam-un-kur,
the exalted hero,
has luck
stronger
than anyone's.
The eddying waters around the oar
are lying!"

The god ruling
the cliff
said this.
This is what
I thought to myself:

  "Which god,
  I wonder,
  is telling the truth?"

Thinking this,
I sailed on.
After that
I sailed on
and came to
the land of Retarpira.
I brought the ship ashore
in the harbor.
After that
I went
to the place of
Retarpira-un-kur.
The two of us—
my younger sister and I—
both went inside.
I sat down

---

[28] *Sermak orke*, supernatural protection. Any type of being or object which hovers behind a person and provides protection is known as *sermak* (the word literally means "behind").

at the guest's place on the left-hand side of the
   fireplace.
When I looked, I saw that
wine had been prepared,
and a drinking feast
was just about to begin.
Retarpira-un-kur
was an acquaintance
of mine.
He rejoiced to see me
and said these words:

   "So exceedingly
   lonely was I that
   I decided
   to brew
   a little wine
   to amuse myself.
   That is why
   I was just
   brewing
   a little wine
   when Otasam-un-kur,
   the exalted hero,
   arrived!"

Saying these words,
he rejoiced
to see me.
A big wine-tub,
filled brimful
with wine,
was standing
on the floor at the head of the fireplace.

At that time
Retarpira-un-kur
got up and,
leading me by the hand
with much ceremony,
seated me
at the big wine-tub.
Retarpira-un-kur
sat down facing me.

After that
the guests at the noble drinking feast
were all seated in order,
from the head of the festal mats
to the foot of the festal mats.
The elder one
of the younger sisters
of Retarpira-un-kur[29]
wound her way about
among the guests
to pour the wine to them.
At that time
the froth on the wine
churned noisily
and bubbled noisily,
and this is what
I thought I heard it say:

   "How pitiful it is
   for Otasam-un-kur,
   the exalted hero,
   that his luck
   should be withdrawn
   always!"

[29] He had two younger sisters; the one whom the hero Otasam-un-kur intended to marry was not at the drinking feast.

These words
I seemed to hear
in the froth on the wine
as it churned noisily
and bubbled noisily.
At that time
the god ruling
the area below the rafters
spoke these words:

"What strange words are these?
I detest
the lies spoken by
the froth on the wine.
Otasam-un-kur,
the exalted hero,
has luck
stronger
than anyone's.
The froth on the wine
is lying!"

These words
I heard
spoken by
the god ruling
the area below the rafters.
This is what
I thought to myself:

"Which god,
I wonder,
is lying?
Which god,

I wonder,
is telling the truth?"

I thought this
as I drank at the feast.
As time went on,
the drinking feast
was half-way over,
and I stepped outside
because I wanted
to relieve myself.
When I stepped outside
to relieve myself
and was standing there,
I looked and saw that
on the right-hand side of the stronghold
a pretty little house[30]
was standing
majestically.
The pretty little house
stood there,
its walls bound
firmly in place,
and its roof darting
up gracefully.
My heart
was drawn
toward it.
Therefore,
I walked up
outside the house.
I stepped
inside the entrance porch.
Just then,

[30] A house where an unmarried daughter was living alone. This is the house of the youngest sister of Retarpira-un-kur, whom the hero intends to marry.

inside the house
these words were spoken:

"O Retarpira-un-mat,
o divine lady,
listen well
to what I have to say!
I loathe
those who conceal
their own identity.
The name
of my homeland
is Kunnepet.[31]
There are two brothers
who are chieftains of Kunnepet,[32]
and there is
one younger sister.
I am
the elder brother.
As I was listening
to distant rumors,
I heard that
you were to be married
to Otasam-un-kur,
the exalted hero.
Though I heard
these rumors,
I was infatuated
with you
on account of
the many rumors,
the countless rumors
which had risen up
about your excessive

beauty
and your skill at needlework.
This is what
I really did:
I pretended to be
Otasam-un-kur,
the exalted hero,
and I have been
coming to your place
until now
telling you
that I am
Otasam-un-kur.
I have been
lying to you
until now.
But now
it seems as if
Otasam-un-kur,
the exalted hero,
has finally
come here
to woo you.
For this reason,
I thought that,
if I did not come here
tonight
I would lose you.
This is why
I have come.
I ask you to
agree to
my well-meaning request.
If you agree,

[31] "Black River"
[32] Kunnepet-un-kur

I will steal you away
tonight
and will take you
to my native land,
to my stronghold.
Since the *repunkur*
are a very numerous people,
even if Otasam-un-kur
were to come
in pursuit of you,
he would not
require more than
a single sword stroke [to kill].
If you marry me,
we will live together
as a well-matched couple,
as a well-suited pair.''

When he said this,
Retarpira-un-mat,
as if something evil
had been uttered,
poured out
many words of abuse,
countless words of abuse.
She spoke these words:

    ''What strange words are these
    spoken by a stranger
    from an unknown land?
    Your words
    are evil words,
    and you have behaved
    disrespectfully

behind my betrothed's back,
in my betrothed's absence!
I was
keeping myself unsullied,
keeping myself unblemished
for Otasam-un-kur,
the exalted hero,
in his absence,
And to think
that all the time,
you, evil wretch,
were deceiving me
vilely and basely
until now,
and that you
lay with me like dogs,
you did wicked things with me!''

As the evil woman
was speaking
these words,
I opened the door.
I was overcome
with feelings of anger,
and this is what I thought:

    ''It was, to begin with,
    on account of
    the evil deeds of
    Poi-Soya-un-mat
    that I asked for the hand
    of Retarpira-un-mat,
    even though she is
    an ugly woman,

an unattractive woman.
O why is it
that these evil women
are constantly
committing
such unforgivable
indignities against me?''

Thinking this,
I was overcome
with feelings of anger.
I suddenly burst inside.
When I looked around, I saw
on the right-hand side of the fireplace
a silken chamber[33]
standing there
majestically.
At that time
I went stamping
fiercely along
in the direction of
the silken chamber.
I grasped in my hands
the top of the chamber,
the silken chamber,
and pulled it mightily.
I threw it out
into the vestibule.
After it was gone,
I pulled mightily
at the hair growing on the head
of the evil woman
and of Kunnepet-un-kur.
After that

I knocked them against
the upper ceiling beams
and the lower ceiling beams,
and at the ends of my arms
there were thudding noises
and cracking noises.

After a while
the woman,
Retarpira-un-mat,
I tied to
one of the poles
on the right-hand side of the fireplace.
Kunnepet-un-kur
I tied to
one of the poles
on the left-hand side of the fireplace.
After that
I tied up
the door
and the windows
with leather thongs.
After that
I set fire to
the upper thatch layers
and the lower thatch layers [on the ceiling]
of that little house.
That little house
went up in flames
with a deafening roar.

In the meantime,
under the sacred window
I unfastened

[33] *Sarampe tumpu*, a chamber partitioned off with silken curtains. No doubt something like a bed with a silken canopy around it is meant.

my belt
and threw myself down
under the window.
I buried my head
in the collar of a robe,
a metal robe,[34]
a robe adorned with bells,
and I buried my feet
in the hem of the robe.
Just then,
that little house
was going up in flames
with a deafening roar.
At that time,
Retarpira-un-mat
shrieked out a loud wailing.
As she shrieked,
she cried out
these words:

"O my elder brother,
listen to
what I have to say!
All the time
Kunnepet-un-kur,
the evil wretch,
has been deceiving me
vilely and basely.
Until now
he told me
that he was
Otasam-un-kur,
the exalted hero,
and he lay with me like dogs,

and did wicked things with me!
It is only natural,
since I did
deeds punished by the gods,
that I should
be found out.
But since
my actions were evil,
my deeds were evil,
it will not be
bad for the land,
bad for the country
should I die.
But Otasam-un-kur,
the exalted hero,
seems to be
about to commit
suicide!
O please
save his life!"

These words
Retarpira-un-mat
cried out
as she shrieked.
Now by this time
the robe adorned with bells,
the metal robe
had grown hot.
I could feel it sink
down into my body,
and excruciating pains
gripped my insides.

---

[34] *Kane kosonte*, literally "metal robe." Usually "metal robe" means simply "magnificent robe," but here it seems to be some sort of metallic garment.

During this time
I could hear
my younger sister
running
around the house
screaming out
"Brother dear!"
This is the last thing
I recall
as if a faint dream.
After that,
was I dead?
was I asleep?
my mind
was clouded
and dazed.

IV

My elder brother
Kunnepet-un-kur
raised me,
and we lived
together with
our younger brother.
After a certain time,
this is how
my elder brother
began to behave:
He would go out
and would be gone,
and he would not return
for much too long a time.
Then after a while

he would come back.
He continued to do this
as we lived on.
Then one season,
he stepped
outside
and after that
he was gone.

One day,
tidings of calamity
could be heard coming,
echoing resonantly,
moving in the direction
of the beach.
After a while
it sounded as if it had come
as far as the boat landing.
Therefore,
I went out to find out
where the tidings had come from.
It was a servant
bearing a message.
This is what he said:

    "Greetings,
    Kunnepet-un-mat,
    o divine lady,
    it is to you
    that I have come
    to bear the tidings.
    This is the message
    that I bear:
    Kunnepet-un-kur

pretended to be
Otasam-un-kur,
the exalted hero,
and lay like dogs with
Retarpira-un-mat.
As a result
of this,
Otasam-un-kur,
the exalted hero,
set fire to the house
and burned up
all three of them together—
himself as well as
Kunnepet-un-kur
and Retarpira-un-mat.
Otasam-un-kur,
the exalted hero,
has died
by his own hand,
and his death has been
an evil one.
If Kunnepet-un-kur
and Retarpira-un-mat
were to die,
it would not be
bad for the land,
bad for the country.
But if Otasam-un-kur,
the exalted hero
were to die,
it would be
bad for the land,
bad for the country.
It was because

of the evil ways
of Kunnepet-un-kur
that Otasam-un-kur
died an evil death
by his own hand.
For this reason,
Kunnepet-un-mat,
o divine lady,
if you are unable
to restore
Otasam-un-kur
to life,
a war of annihilation,
a war of extirpation
will be launched against
the land of Kunnepet.
These are the tidings
that I have come
to bring!''

Thus spoke
the servant.
After that
I turned around
and went back.
I went inside
the stronghold.
I ran to the back of the house.
I brought out
my woman's treasure bag.
I thrust my hand
down to the bottom of the bag.
I brought out
a silken hood,[35]

---

[35] A shamaness's hood.

and arranged my hair
up high with it.
I put into the front of my robes
a little shamaness's wand.[36]
After that
I fastened the little robes
of my younger brother
under his girdle.
I spoke to him,
saying these words:

"Once a man
has grown this old,
tidings of battle
will surely
come to him.
Otasam-un-kur,
the exalted hero,
has died
an evil death,
they say,
because of the evil deeds
of our evil elder brother.
I have no idea
what I am to do
to restore him to life
as I have been bidden.
This being the case,
o god whom I have raised,
o my younger brother,
one who is a man
must act bravely!
He must never
act fearfully

or act weakly!"

With these words
I heartened
the spirits of
my younger brother.
After that
I held him
by his little hand
and set out.
I came ashore at
the land of Retarpira.

It was amazing
how many kinsmen,
how many relatives
had Retarpira-un-kur.
The crowds of people
were so thick that
the ground under the people
looked black.

Just east of the stronghold,
the stronghold of
Retarpira-un-kur,
was a spirit fence,
and the charred bones
of what must have been
Otasam-un-kur,
the exalted hero,
were there
on the spirit fence.
After that,
beginning from

---

[36] *Tusu pon repni.* The shamaness's wand (*tusu repni*) was probably derived from a drumstick, although drums were not used in Hokkaido.

a distance away,
I began to imitate
a man's speech
and a man's behavior.
I was holding
my younger brother
by his little hand,
and my little brother's
forehead
was shaking and quivering [with fear].
In this way
I made my way
through the thick of
the large crowds.
I went on
and came up
to the spirit fence.
On the charred bones
of Otasam-un-kur,
the exalted hero,
faintly, very faintly,
one could make out
the outlines of his corpse.[37]

Then
I sat down
by the side of
the charred bones
of Otasam-un-kur,
the exalted hero.
After that
I took out
my little shamaness's wand.
I twisted my voice

into subtle melodies of a song
deep within my throat.
I blew
many mighty puffs of breath,
countless mighty puffs of breath
onto what was
nothing but charred bones.
With a magnificent fan[38]
I fanned
onto what was
nothing but charred bones.
Both night
and day
went by, and
little by little
on those charred bones,
the charred bones of
Otasam-un-kur,
the exalted hero,
the flesh
went growing back,
flesh formed itself again.

As I continued my work,
I had by now
restored him
to his previous form,
to his old form.
By this time
he looked like
a man who had died yesterday.
I continued my work,
and now finally
he looked like

[37] The translation of this passage is uncertain. Apparently it means that the bones still bore some resemblance to a human corpse.
[38] *Kane awanki*, literally "metal fan."

a man who had died today.
After that
I blew
many mighty puffs of breath,
countless mighty puffs of breath,
while fanning constantly
with my magnificent fan.
After a while
now finally
from time to time
there were heart beats
in his chest.
After a while,
after great efforts,
the exalted hero
finally opened his eyes
right at my face.
However,
he continued to revive
and die many times.
Then, after great efforts,
I finally
brought him to the point
of coming back to life,
of reviving.
He sat up
amidst the spirit fence.

After that
I went off
a short distance away
and stood there,
holding the hand
of my younger brother.

V

I recalled
like a faint dream
that I had died.
After that,
was I dead?
was I asleep?
my mind
was clouded
and dazed.
After a while
it seemed to me
that I was in the midst
of some sort of voices,
some sort of noises,
and just then
I tried
to rouse myself,
but I couldn't manage it.
After a while,
at the cost of great efforts,
I finally opened my eyes.
There was then
a woman
of unheard-of beauty,
a young woman
I had never seen before.
The brightness of her face
was like the rising sun,
sending out
dazzling rays of light.
Was there ever
such a [majestic] young woman?

I opened my eyes upon her.
Nevertheless,
I continued to revive
and die many times.
Then, after great efforts,
she finally brought me to the point
of coming back to life,
of reviving.
She had restored me
to my previous form,
to my old form.
After that
I stood up
amidst the spirit fence.
When I looked around,
it seemed
as if
I had been dead
for a short time.
A whole crowd
of my kinsfolk
had come
to help me.
My elder sister
had come
leading them.
At that place
the only one
who had not come
was Poi-Soya-un-mat,
the evil woman.

The young woman
Kunnepet-un-mat

was a short distance away.
She was holding by the hand
a little child
of an amazing appearance—
he was awe-inspiring
in his beauty.
The young woman
Kunnepet-un-mat
was shedding
many sparkling teardrops,
countless sparkling teardrops.
At that time
this is what
I thought to myself:

> "For what reason
> should I leave alive
> the offspring of our murderers,
> the offspring of our enemies?"

Thinking this,
I darted
a fierce sword thrust
at the little child.
His mangled corpse
came dropping down.

At that time,
Retarpira-un-kur
gave me
as indemnities
half of his vessels,
half of his treasures.

After that
my elder sister
took by the hand
Kunnepet-un-mat.
Together with
my younger sister,
and my kinsmen,
they sailed me homeward.
After that
we came shoreward
and landed on the shore
at our boat landing.
My kinsmen
carried
into the stronghold
the vessels
and the treasures
that I had received as indemnities.

After that
I came back
to my stronghold
and remained there.
I stayed
on the seat,
the magnificent seat.
After that
I did nothing but
carve on scabbards,
carve on treasures,
with my eyes focused
on a single spot,
and this is the way
I lived

on and on
uneventfully.

After a while
my elder sister
spoke these words:

"On account of
the evil ways of
Poi-Soya-un-mat,
until now
we have not
even brewed wine,
and the spirit fence,
the ancestral spirit fence
is in a state of decay.
This is an indignity
toward the gods
and toward the ancestors.
Let us brew wine,
so that the god I have raised,
my divine nursling
may raise up high
the ancestral spirit fence!"

My elder sister
spoke
these words
and commanded
the servants
to brew wine.
After that
the servants
went running about

this way and that
to brew the wine.
When two or three days
had gone by,
the wine was now
finally ready,
and the odor of the wine
hovered about
inside the house.

After that
those who were straining the wine
darted their wicker baskets
together this way and that,
and those who were whittling *inau*
plied their whittling knives
together this way and that.
After a while,
now the preparations
were finally completed
for holding the drinking feast,
for holding the banquet.

Then we sent messages
to all our relatives nearby
and all our relatives far away.
The invited guests
were shown inside.
Around the fireplace
I addressed my greetings
to my elder brothers,[39]
and I intoned lengthy
words of salutation.
After that

I seated
Iyochi-un-kur[40]
in back of
the big wine-tub.
After that
the guests at the noble drinking feast
were all seated in order,
from the head of the festal mats
to the foot of the festal mats.

After that
we held the feast.
I was amazed
at how very
softened became the spirits
of my elder brothers
as they drank the wine.
The drinking continued
until finally
the excellent wine feast
wore on to an end.

When the drinking feast
had come to an end,
my elder brothers
came up
beside the fire.
After that
my elder brothers
spoke these words:

"Let everyone
select a wife for himself,
and a husband for herself!"

[39] My male relatives older than myself.
[40] Iyochi (Yoichi in Japanese) is a place in the province of Shiribeshi. The rulers of Iyochi are said to be allies and relatives of the rulers of Shinutapka.

Those who were to marry husbands
performed the woman's greeting[41] to them,
and those who were to marry wives
made gestures of salutation to them.
Iyochi-un-kur
made salutations
in order to marry
my younger sister.
Sanput-un-kur
made salutations
in order to marry
my elder sister.

After that
Iyochi-un-kur
went away with
my younger sister.
Sanput-un-kur
went away with
my elder sister.
After they had gone
I remained
together with
Kunnepet-un-mat.
She cooked
the meals for me.

I reflected carefully,
turning over various things
in my mind.

This is what I thought:

    ''It was all on account of
    the evil deeds,
    the evil conduct
    of Poi-Soya-un-mat,
    the evil woman.
    Why on earth
    should I ever have chosen
    precisely
    an enemy offspring,
    a woman of the enemy race,
    to cook my meals
    for me?''

Although
I thought this,
it was thanks to her,
Kunnepet-un-mat,
that my life had been spared,
and I allowed her to cook for me
and took her as my wife.
Two children, three children
were born between us,
we lead
a superb married life,
a magnificent married life,
and this is the way
we live on.

---

[41] The complicated ritual salutations performed by women were called *raimik*. They involved elaborate gestures made with the hands and stroking of the woman's own hair.

33. The Epic of Kotan Utunnai

This is a full-length *yukar* epic recorded in writing by John Batchelor, the English missionary, at some time before 1889. Batchelor does not mention the name of the reciter, but the dialect is apparently that of the Saru Ainu. The epic was sung without a burden. The epic was delivered to the Asiatic Society of Japan on December 4, 1889. The original text and Batchelor's English prose translation were published in April, 1890, in vol. 18, part 1 of the *Transactions of the Asiatic Society of Japan*. Batchelor's translation is rather like a prose paraphrase, and some troublesome details have been omitted or re-phrased. The present translation was made from the Ainu original, although Batchelor's translation was taken into consideration.

In this epic, the hero Poiyaunpe is raised by a *repunkur* woman in a little-frequented place called Kotan Utunnai in the land of the *repunkur*. After the foster sister has told him the story of his origins, Poiyaunpe rushes off into battle. The main interest of the story lies in the hero's battles against a whole series of enemies: (1) the Pestilence Deities (*Pa-kor-kamui*); (2) the six warriors of Kanepet, six warriors of Shirarpet, and Etu-rachichi, and the twelve "younger sisters" of the warriors of Kanepet and Shirarpet; (3) Shipish-un-kur (The younger sister of Shipish-un-kur casts her lot in with the hero and becomes his wife at the conclusion of the epic.); (4) the man and woman living at Terke-santa, Hopuni-santa; (5) the inhabitants of the land of Chirin-nai; (6) the *kuruise*, a horde of fabulous insect-like monsters; (7) the "bad weather demon" (*shiri wen nitne*) and his younger sister.

After the battles are over, the hero and the young woman of Shipish, Shipish-un-mat, go to the hero's native stronghold, Shinutapka, and are reunited with the hero's relatives there. They all celebrate a drinking feast, and the main characters marry each other.

This epic is of great importance because of the early date when it was recorded in writing. The texts written down by Kindaichi mostly date from the period after 1913, and most of Kubodera's texts were written down during

the 1930s. Thus, this epic was written down several decades earlier than the
texts collected by Kindaichi and Kubodera and may be expected to reflect
the diction and concepts of the Ainu epic reciters of an older generation.

I was raised
by an elder sister,
and we lived
on and on.
This is how
she raised me:
she raised me
in a little grass hut,
and we lived on.

During this time
sounds of some gods fighting
could be heard rumbling
throughout the land.
Many gods dying,
countless gods dying
continued to rumble
uninterruptedly.

Now finally
I grew somewhat older,
and these sounds
began to make themselves heard:
atop our grass hut
spirits of the *yaunkur*[1]
from time to time
would come rumbling.
Going out to meet them,

my own companion spirits
would send forth their rumblings
atop the grass hut.
Gods of the same family,
they would prolong
their rumblings together.
What could be the reason for this,
I wondered.
So
I spoke
these words:

> "My elder sister,
> you who have
> raised me well,
> tell me, I pray,
> the story!"
> thus did I speak.

She appeared
to be awe-stricken
to an extreme.
Her forehead
quaked with fear.
Many sparkling teardrops
did she shed.
After a while
this is what she said:

---

[1] The hero is being raised among an enemy people, and his first clue of his own identity is the affinity of his "companion spirits" (*ituren kamui*) with the "spirits of the *yaunkur*" (*yaunkur kamui*).

"I would have told you
after you were a little older.
Then,
even if you killed me,
my heart would have been content
even after death.
Nevertheless,
since you wish to hear it,
I will tell you,
but it would be dangerous
for a mere boy
to act rashly
when hearing a story.
Do not act rashly!
This is the story
I have to tell you.

"Long ago
your father
was resting
between battles.
He was the one
who held sway over the upper
and the lower regions
of Shinutapka
by the river Tumisanpet.
He decided to go trading.
The godlike lady [your mother]
bore her baby on her back
and Kamui-otopush[2]
went along with his father.
They set out on their journey.
When they had come
to the land of Karapto[3]

they were lured shoreward
with *inau*[4]
and came ashore.
Night and day
they were pressed to drink
poisoned drink.
After a while
the drunken man [your father]
speaking under the wine's influence
said such things:
He proposed to buy
together with his kinsfolk
the principal treasure
of the land of Karapto.
Because of this
fighting broke out.[5]
After that
it spread
to the surrounding lands.
The name
of our native land
is the land of Chiwashpet.[6]
Since it is a land
abounding in many warriors,
your father
was slain.

"At that time
I took
your father's
garments
along with his helmet.
I took you
from your mother's

---

2 Kamui-otopush is the name of one of the hero's elder brothers. When the parents departed on their trading expedition, they left the eldest brother (Yai-pirka-kur) and the elder sister (Shinutapka-un-mat) in the stronghold of Shinutapka, taking with them the second son (Kamui-otopush) and the baby hero (Poiyaunpe). Kamui-otopush means "He-has-divine-hair." See note 23, selection 31.

3 Karapto is the island of Sakhalin.

4 The *inau* were set up as signs of peaceful intention to beckon the travelers ashore.

5 Substantially the same account is given in "Repunnot-un-kur," p. 273–74.

6 Literally "Rapids River," evidently a place somewhere in Sakhalin. This is the native land of the elder sister, who is referred to later on as Chiwashpet-un-mat ("woman of Chiwashpet").

back and
tied up tightly
my baby-carrying cords.
After that
I wielded my sword
all around
your mother,
but
your mother,
having spent
her whole life
in doing nothing but fighting,
was killed
in the midst of the battle.
Since then
Kamui-otopush
all alone
has been fighting
his whole life.

"In the meantime
I made off with you.
This land
is a place
never frequented
either by humans
or by gods, and so
it is called
Kotan Utunnai
Moshir Utunnai,
and it is here
that I have raised you
and we have lived.

"Kamui-otopush
all by himself
has to this very day
been fighting
against the demons.[7]
Since you said
that you wanted to hear it,
I have told you, but
do not act rashly!"
Thus did she speak.

I came very near
to killing her but
I barely managed
to calm myself.
I spoke these words:

   "My elder sister,
   you who have
   raised me well,
   bring out
   my father's
   garments
   and give them to me!"
   Thus did I speak.

Then, no sooner
had I spoken,
she ran to the back of the house.
She untied
the fastening cords
of a woman's treasure bag.
From inside the treasure bag
she brought out

---

[7] The Ainu word is *nitne kamui*. The enemies against whom Kamui-otopush is fighting are the "people of the sea" (*repun-kur*), but here they are referred to as "demons." Here and elsewhere one can see clearly the process by which human enemies were gradually transformed in the epic imagination into supernatural beings ("demons," "evil deities").

a god-given sword,
six robes,
magnificent robes,
together with
a metal buckled belt
and a little metal helmet.
She held them out to me.

Overjoyed,
I took off
my own little robe.
I attired
myself in
the six robes,
the magnificent robes.
The metal buckled belt
in a single wrapping
I wrapped around my waist.
The god-given sword
I thrust under my belt.
The dangling cords
of the little metal helmet
I tied up tightly.

Now
I was hardly able
even to stand
at the head of the fireplace.[8]
I limbered
my shoulders
with warlike motions,
with the motions of battle.
On the right-hand side of the fireplace
and on the left-hand side of the fireplace

I strode up and down,
stamping my feet again and again.
As I continued to do this
I headed up toward
the smokehole
of our grass hut.
Over
our grass hut
my companion spirits
sent forth their rumblings.
After that
I went flying up
at the head of a mighty wind.

My elder sister
shrieked wildly.
While screaming
she uttered words,
saying these things:

> "It is no good
> for a mere boy
> to act rashly
> in battle.
> Let me take you home
> to your native land
> Shinutapka.
> After that
> you may go anywhere
> and fight
> in any land,
> in any country you wish."
> Thus did she speak.

---

[8] The hero is suddenly imbued with a warlike spirit and begins to limber up for battle immediately.

Nevertheless,
I continued
to go on somewhere
blown by the mighty wind until
a beautiful country
came rising up
high toward me.

I landed
on the country's shore and
looked and saw this:
the nearby mountains
were rising
up high.
A pretty little river,
seeming to be
a river with a short course,
had its head soaring up high
and its mouth flowing down deep.
Midway along the river's course
was something which must have been
the abode of
some deity, for
black mists
like overhanging clouds
were hanging over
the pretty little river
midway along its course.
Behind them
red mists
like overhanging clouds
were hanging over
the river's course.
Behind them

blue-green mists[9]
were hanging over
the river's course.

My elder sister
shrieked wildly.
While screaming
she uttered words,
saying these things:

  "This is not
  the land of
  any ordinary gods!
  It is nothing but
  the abode of
  the chief of
  the Pestilence Deities![10]
  From this place
  we ought to turn back at once
  and go toward
  some other country.
  Do not, by any means,
  act with disrespect
  toward the deities!"
Thus did she speak.

Nevertheless,
I turned
a deaf ear to her
and went on.

I plunged head first
into the midst of the mists,
the black mists, and

---

[9] The Ainu language has names for only four colors: white, black, red, and *shiunin*. *Shiunin* is the catch-all term for all other colors, including blue, yellow, and green. The mists are black, red, and "blue-green" (*shiunin*), as are the rocks found under the mists and the robes worn by the Pestilence Deities.

[10] *Pa-kor-kamui*, the deities who cause such diseases as smallpox and cholera. The hero has come blundering into their country.

looked and saw this:
the black mists
were hanging
over six rocks,
six black rocks.
This was what
they were doing.

When I walked
onto the rocks,
the black rocks,
as if from nowhere
a fierce sword thrust
came flying at me.
My elder sister—
a fierce sword thrust
came flying at her too.

I was unwilling
to die outright.
Amid the sword blows
I jumped to one side
with a desperate leap,
and those sword blows
struck harmlessly
on my body.
It turned out
that they were
empty blows.

My elder sister
once again
shrieked wildly.
While screaming

she uttered words,
saying these things:

   "This is by no means
   an omen
   foreshadowing
   any trifling consequences.[11]
   Let us turn back at once
   from this place!"
   Thus did she speak.

Nevertheless,
I went straight on.
I plunged head first
into the midst of the mists,
the red mists.
I looked and saw this:
six rocks,
six red rocks,
were piled on each other.
When I walked
onto the rocks,
a fierce sword thrust
which made the one before
seem like child's play
came flying at me.
Nevertheless,
I did not
dodge the blade.
The blow
being an empty one
went sliding off
my body.

[11] That is, "what has just happened foreshadows something terrible which is about to happen." The language abounds in such negative constructions.

Behind this,
blue-green mists
were hanging
over six rocks,
six blue-green rocks.
This was what
they were doing.
From over these rocks too,
from over the blue-green rocks,
a fierce sword thrust
came flying at me.
Nevertheless,
I did not
dodge the blade.
It was an empty blow
and struck harmlessly
on my body.

Behind this
I went on and came to
a mighty mountain.
A stony path
could be seen clearly
coming down
from the mountain.
At the foot of the path
was a metal well
with a metal ladle
on the well.

Down the path
came
mounds of mist,
altogether six of them.

The one who came
first of all
was clothed all
from head to toe
in black robes.
Behind him
was one clothed all
in red robes,
and behind that one
came down
one clothed all
in blue-green robes.
After them
came women,
altogether three of them.
Counting the women,
altogether six of them
came down.

The one who came first
repeatedly made
worshipful gestures with his hands.
While making these salutations,
he uttered words,
saying these things:

>   "Greetings,
>   young Ainu brother![12]
>   Listen well
>   to what I have to say.
>   It is not at all
>   as if we
>   were ones
>   engaged in

[12] *Ainu akpo*, "dear human (Ainu) younger brother," a term of respectful address to a younger man.

warfare.
We are
weighty deities,
Pestilence Deities,
and we are
dwelling here
in this country.
Kamui-otopush
has done nothing but fighting
his whole life.
We felt sorry for him.
So we have supported him
with our protection,
and because of this
he has had
exceedingly
good fortunes
in battle, and now,
of all places in the wide world,
here you have come
to our country!
We would be most unworthy
to receive you
were you to come
to our abode.
That is why
we tried out our swords
against you in that way
on the rocks,
on the black rocks,
the red rocks,
and the blue-green rocks.
We thought that,
if you were human,

you would turn back after that,
but you still come on!
At any rate,
turn back,
I pray you!
We will support you
with our protection
in battle,
in every battle,
and you will have
exceedingly
good fortunes.
Turn back,
I pray you!"

While saying this,
he repeatedly made
worshipful gestures with his hands.
In reply
I pointed
one finger at him.
While doing so,
I uttered words,
saying these things:

> "If the weighty deities
> slay me,
> my heart will be content
> after death.
> Come on
> and slay me!"
> Thus did I speak.

However,

the chieftains[13]
spoke in hushed voices:

"We are by no means
persons
engaged in
warfare.
Turn back,
we pray you!"
Thus did they speak.

This merely served
to rouse me all the more
to a furious rage.
Thus
I darted
a fierce sword thrust
toward the three chieftains,
all of them at once.
Being gods,
they fluttered
on top of my blade
like a bright breeze.
The three young women[14]
were fighting together
with Chiwashpet-un-mat,
my elder sister, and
many metal sword blows
resounded with clanks.

During this time
I darted
countless sword thrusts toward
the three chieftains.

As this went on
they finally
unsheathed their swords.
They countered me
blow for blow.
They darted
countless sword thrusts toward me.
I bent
my utmost efforts
to prevent them from seeing me
in my human form.
I pranced
on top of their blades
as if upon a bridge.
With my left hand
clenched in a fist
like a bunch of grappling hooks,
I grabbed at them
again and again until
by and by
I grasped in my hand
the locks of magnificent hair
of the god wearing
the blue-green robes.
I knocked him against
the large rocks
and the small rocks
with loud cracking noises.
As I continued to do this,
I wounded him mortally[15] and
dragged him behind me
like a dead fish.

After that

---

[13] *Utarpa*, a term applied to a chieftain or a warrior. Here and below the Pestilence Deities are depicted sometimes as humans and sometimes as gods.

[14] That is, the three goddesses

[15] The word is *oan-raike*, which usually means "to kill utterly." In this epic the word is apparently used to mean "to wound mortally." We learn below that his life-spirit has not yet left his body.

the chieftains
continued to swing
their fierce sword strokes
up and down, right and left.
At this time
the mortally wounded man[16]
I swung up high
and I swung down low
as a shield.
They turned their blows aside
before me.
By and by
that chieftain
whom I held in my arms
I sliced
into several bits.
His life-spirit
was heard flying up
with a loud roaring.
Becoming a living spirit,
he went rumbling off
toward the peaks
of his native mountains.

In the meantime
the life-spirit
of the lady wearing
the blue-green robes
was heard flying up
with a loud roaring.

Once again
I twisted in my hand
the locks of magnificent hair

of the chieftain wearing
the red robes.
I knocked him against
the large rocks
and the small rocks
with loud cracking noises.
I swung him up high
and I swung him down low
as a shield.
The chieftain wearing
the black robes
wielded his sword
around me,
but
I held up high
the mortally wounded man
as a shield.
For this reason
he turned his blows aside
before me.
As this continued
by and by
the chieftain wearing
the red robes
who was in my arms
I sliced
into several bits.
His divine life-spirit
could be heard going off
with a loud roaring.
Becoming a living spirit,
he rumbled off
toward the peaks
of his native mountains.

---

[16] *Oan-rai ainu,* "utterly dead man." This is the god (wearing blue-green robes) whom the hero has just mortally wounded.

After that
the god wearing
the black robes
and I
flashed our swords
back and forth at each other.
By and by,
thanks to a stroke of luck,
he was hit
by my sword blade.
I sliced him
into several bits.
His life-spirit
was heard flying up
with a loud roaring.
The lady wearing
the black robes,
the lady wearing
the red robes—
both together
their life-spirits
were heard flying up
with a loud roaring.
All of them
becoming living spirits
went rumbling away
toward the peaks
of their native mountains.

Chiwashpet-un-mat,
without so much as
even a scratch,
dropped down
by my side.

After that
a plateau where spruce trees were growing
stretched out.
The top of the forest
was a metal forest.
The metal forest
stretched out
into the lower forest
and the middle forest.[17]
This certainly was
what was known as
the land having two names,
Ukamu-nitai
Kane-nitai.[18]
The wind was striking
that forest,
making it tinkle.
It seemed
as if this were not
the homeland
of any inconsequential deities.[19]

I went on until
quite suddenly
there was a whiff
of a fire.
Wondering at this,
I ducked
down low
underneath the forest,
the thick forest.
I looked and saw that
there was
a big bonfire,

[17] The diction is confused at this point. The passage means that the upper, middle, and lower portions of the forest had trees of metal. One would expect the word *kane* ("metal") here to be merely a modifier meaning "magnificent" or "beautiful." However, we are told explicitly that these metal trees had leaves which jingled together with a metallic tinkling or clanking.

[18] The first name, Ukamu-nitai, means "Forests Overlapping Each Other," and Kane-nitai means "Metal Forest."

[19] Another negative construction typical of the epic. It should be understood in the opposite sense: "This was certainly the homeland of some most weighty (important) deities."

a fire which had just
been kindled hurriedly.

On one side of the fire
were six armored men
wearing stone armor
and six women
who were all
ugly in appearance.
The six armored men
wearing stone armor
were sitting side by side.
The six women
were sitting next to them.

On the other side of the fire
six armored chieftains
wearing metal armor
were sitting side by side
with their hands on their laps.
Six women
were sitting next to them.

At the head of the fire
was someone—could it
possibly be a human?—
who looked like
a small mountain
with arms growing out of it
and legs growing out of it.
His naked skin
was mangy.
His sword big as a boat's scull
he had strapped to his side

with leather thongs.
His face
was like
a cliff after a landslide.
His nose
was like
a steep mountain spur.
Though he was
a stranger to me,
he was surely the one
who was called
Etu-rachichi[20]—
the evil monster[21]
was seated
at the head of the fire.

During this time—
what ever
could this be?—
the earth where I stood
was lightly
shaken slowly
to and fro, and
the metal branches
of the metal spruce forest
could be heard scraping
against each other
with a loud clanking.
After this continued for a while,
I looked and saw this:
Never in the world
did I expect
to see such a thing.[22]
A mortally wounded man[23]

---

[20] "Nose Dangles" or "Dangling Nose," name of a *repunkur* warrior who often appears in the *yukar* epics. Here he is identified as being a native of the land of Pon-moshir. In some versions his name is Eton-rachichi, which would mean "Snot Dangles" or "Dangling Snot." Probably Eton-rachichi is the older form of the name.

[21] *Wen ainu nitne*, literally "evil human demon." The word *nitne kamui* ("demon") was applied above to the *repunkur*, note 7, selection 33.

[22] A typical epic expression. A less literal translation would be: "I beheld a sight which I had never expected to see."

[23] This is Kamui-otopush, the hero's elder brother. He is not dead, for later on he writhes in his ropes. Finally he is completely restored to life.

was tied to
the top of a spruce,
a large spruce.
The mortally wounded man
had his head
hanging back.
Over his face
many glittering lights
were flashing on and off.
Even though
he was a stranger to me,
he was surely
Kamui-otopush,
my elder brother.
From time to time
he would writhe about
in his ropes, and
this was what
was causing the earth
to shake gently
to and fro.

At that time
my elder sister
Chiwashpet-un-mat
spoke these words:

"My younger brother,
listen well
to what I have to say!
Were we to take
a badly wounded man,
we would be hampered
during the fighting.

In such a case,
we would feel uneasy
during the fighting.
Let me
make off with his body.
Then you
must fight
all alone."
Thus did she speak.

The six chieftains
wearing metal armor
on one side of the fire
all in unison
spoke these words:

"We are
people of Kanepet,[24]
six brothers
and six sisters.
This day
when we came along
hunting in the mountains,
Kamui-otopush,
badly wounded,
having finished his battles,
was heading toward
his native land.
When we saw him,
we might well
have killed him,
have slain him, but
were we to kill him
without the knowledge of

---

[24] Metal River. The natives of Metal River wear metal armor, and the natives of Stone River wear stone armor.

our uncle,
the ruler of
distant Shipish,[25]
we thought
that we might
be blamed for it, so
we tied him to
a large spruce,
and after a while
the six chieftains,
the natives of Shirarpet,[26]
came along
together with their sisters,
and we remained with them.
Just then [you also came along]
are you
a human
or a god?
All together
let us take
the goodly body[27]
of Kamui-otopush
as a present to
Shipish-un-kur.
If we do so,
he will surely
praise us joyfully."
Thus did they speak.

The person who was sitting
at the head of the fire
spoke out,
his voice rumbling out
from deep in his throat.

The sense of his speech,
translated
into the Ainu language,[28]
was this:

    "My native land
    is called by the name of
    the land of Pon-moshir.[29]
    I am
    Etu-rachichi,
    the ruler of Pon-moshir.
    All together,
    let us take
    Kamui-otopush
    as a present to
    Shipish-un-kur.
    If we do so,
    he will surely
    praise us joyfully."
    Thus did he speak.

In the meantime,
my elder sister
had rushed to
the top of the spruce.
There was a clanking sound
as she sliced away the ropes
from the body of
Kamui-otopush.
The band of
evil monsters
all turned around
at exactly the same moment.

---

[25] An unidentified place name, evidently meaning "Great Beach." The ruler of Shipish (Shipish-un-kur) is evidently the paramount chief of the people of Kanepet.

[26] Stone River.

[27] *Pirka kewe*, "nice body," "beautiful body," probably in the sense of a "goodly prey." The corpse of an enemy was regarded as a desirable trophy.

[28] *Ainu itak* means either "human speech" or "the Ainu language." Etu-rachichi is a foreigner (a *repunkur*) speaking a foreign language.

[29] Pon-moshir means "little country" or "little island." Etu-rachichi calls himself Pon-moshir-un-kur, "ruler of Pon-moshir" or "native of Pon-moshir."

At that time
I bent
my utmost efforts
to prevent them from seeing me
in my human form.
Like a bright breeze
I darted
a fierce sword thrust
toward all the band
of evil monsters
by the bonfire.
No sooner had I done this,
the three men
and the three women
on one side of the fire,
six of them in all,
were slashed with a single stroke,
and there was the sound of slicing flesh
at the tip of my blade.
The three chieftains
wearing metal armor
on the other side of the fire
were slashed with a single stroke,
and there was the sound of slicing flesh
at the tip of my blade.
With the back stroke
I darted
a fierce sword thrust
toward Etu-rachichi,
the evil monster.
Then
he who was anything but small
fluttered
like a bright breeze

on top of my blade.
While doing so,
he covered his nose in amazement.
As he did so,
he uttered words,
saying these things:

"Just a moment ago
I thought that he
was a mortally wounded man
who had been tied
to the top of a spruce, but
now here he is
massacring
our kinsmen!
Even though
we were to fight him
with sword fighting,
it seems unlikely
that we would be able
to kill him.
Come then,
let us take him
to the chasm,
the battle chasm,
of Shipish-un-kur.
Then we will be able
to kill him
in the chasm."

While saying these words,
he seemed to be jumping about.
On the mountain slopes
we flashed our swords

back and forth at each other.
We went on and on until
we had come to a certain place, then
my elder sister
could be heard coming this way
with a loud roaring.
She dropped down
by my side.
While she did so,
she uttered words,
saying these things:

"I made off with the body
of your elder brother
Kamui-otopush
and took him
to your native land,
to Shinutapka.
When I arrived there
I found that
the master of the stronghold,
your eldest brother
and your eldest sister
were there.
Into their hands
I delivered
Kamui-otopush, and
we brought him to the point
of being revived,
of being restored to life.
After that
I returned here."
Thus did she speak.

In the midst of this,
the six women
set upon
my elder sister.
They flashed their swords
back and forth at each other.
How could
the evil women
ever be able to
fight so bravely!
One after another
my elder sister
would dart
countless sword thrusts at them,
but
at times
the six women
all at once
would whirl their swords
around their bodies
[darting out] countless sword thrusts.
In a separate place
the women waged their separate battle,
roaming off toward
the distant mountains.

The six men
and Etu-rachichi
all wielded their swords
at exactly the same moment.
At times
they would dart
countless sword thrusts at me.
Time after time

they came very close,
they almost succeeded
in bringing me down
but
I bent
my utmost efforts
to prevent them from seeing me
in my human form.
On top of their blades
like a bright breeze
atop their blades
I fluttered.

As I continued to do this,
a pretty little river
flowing down
came clearly into view.
It seemed to be
a river with a long course, for
the river's bottom soared
up high among
the nearby mountains,[30]
and the river's head sank
down low among
the distant mountains.
Midway along the river's course
there was
a divinely made ravine.
This was surely
the battle chasm
they had been speaking of.
At the ravine's bottom
many sharp stone spears
and many sharp stone swords

were jutting up there.
Over the blades
poisonous water
was trickling down.
The odor of the poison
made my heart
feel sick.

The band of chieftains
all together
chased me farther and farther
toward the ravine.
Time after time
they came very close
to slaying me in
the battle chasm.
Nevertheless,
I fluttered
on top of their blades.
While doing so,
I uttered words,
saying these things:

"O gods of the ravine,
gods of the chasm,
listen well
to what I have to say!
If I were the only one
to die,
you would not have enough
blood wine
to drink.
Cast in your lot
on my side,

---

[30] A curious archaic expression. The river's bottom (in the literal sense, its "rear end," its "rump,") rises up high near the river mouth; here there are no deeply cut ravines. Further upstream, the river's "head" sinks down deep in deeply cut canyons among the faraway mountains. The river is spoken of almost animistically, as if it had a "head" and a "bottom." There was another similar expression above on p. 371.

I pray you!
Since it is the *repunkur*
who are many in numbers,
you will never
have an end to your feast
of blood wine!''
Thus did I speak.

Now it was my turn
to turn the tables on
the band of chieftains.
With my mighty sword sweeps
I drove them
toward the ravine.
As I continued to do this,
the oldest one of
the warriors wearing the stone armor
fell to
the ravine's bottom.
He landed
on the blades,
the blades in the chasm.
He went flying about
exactly like chunks of stew meat.
His life-spirit
was heard flying up
with a loud roaring.

Once again,
the biggest one of
the warriors wearing the metal armor
fell down
into the ravine.
He landed

on the blades in the chasm.
He went flying about
exactly like chunks of stew meat.
At frequent intervals
I would kill one of them,
I would kill two of them.
Of those who died in the ravine,
there were none at all,
not a single one,
who were living dead.[31]
Becoming utterly dead spirits,
they sank down
rumbling toward
the west of the land.
I continued to do this until
I had killed all
six of the chieftains.

After this was over,
Etu-rachichi,
the native of Pon-moshir,
alone was left.
After that
the man alone
wielded his sword.
Time after time
he came very close,
he almost succeeded
in bringing me down.
I countered him
blow for blow.
I continued to swing
my fierce sword sweeps
up and down, right and left.

---

[31] *Shiknu raipe*, "living dead," that is the dead who survive after death. They are destined to be restored to life again. See note 21, selection 32.

But
at times
like a bright breeze
he would flutter
on top of the blade
over my fierce sword sweeps.
For this reason
I was unable
to get at him.

After this had continued
for some time,
he who was anything but small
stripped off his clothes.
He put aside
his trusty sword.
He said these words:

"Come now!
Chieftains
do not fight
only a single battle.
Let us have
a contest of strength!"

As he said this,
he lunged toward me.
I bent
my utmost efforts
to prevent him from
getting the best of me.
I laid down
my trusty sword
behind me and

I lunged toward him.
We wrestled together.
Etu-rachichi
brought together
his big hands
around my middle, and
my heart
grew faint with agony.
Nevertheless,
I slipped through
his hands
like trickling water.

After that
we wrestled together
on the surface of the ground.
At times
he came very close
to hurling me down
into the ravine, but
a breeze blowing up
from the ravine's bottom
would blow me up high.
As this went on,
I finally managed
to throw
Etu-rachichi
to the ravine's bottom.
He landed on
the blades in the chasm.
Atop the blades
of the sharp stone spears
and the sharp stone swords
he went flying about

exactly like chunks of stew meat.
His life-spirit
was heard flying up
with a loud roaring.
After it was over,
everything grew quiet all around.

At that time
I thought to myself:

"Who ever may be
this person called
Shipish-un-kur,
whose name was mentioned
to frighten me
in battle?
Were I to return to
my native stronghold
without seeing him,
I would be regarded
as a coward."

Thinking this,
as I went down
along the river,
that little river,
my companion spirits
sent out rumblings
over me.
Therefore,
I spoke to them,
saying these words:

"My companion spirits,

quiet your rumblings
for me!
I want to catch
at least a glimpse of
Shipish-un-kur's
abode.
After having done so,
I may well be slain there,
but at any rate
I wish to compare
my valor with
Shipish-un-kur!"

When I had spoken these words,
my companion spirits
went rumbling off toward
the distant mountains.
After they were gone,
everything grew quiet all around.

I flew up
at the head of
a cloudless breeze,
a faint divine wind.
I went down until
by now
the sounds of waves on the beach
came closer and closer.
The pretty little river
swirled down
emptying its rapids
out into the sea.
A populous village
stood crowding

the river bank.
Over the populous village
hung smoke
floating slowly
over the village
like a low mist.
In the middle of the village
a divinely made lone peak
could be seen standing,
soaring up majestically.
The path up to it
went winding around
in many bends.
The divinely made lone peak
had billows of mist
wrapped around it.
On top of the peak
was a divinely built stockade,
which appeared to be
a stockade built long ago, for
the older posts
like black clouds
were bending
up backward toward
the heavens, and
the newly erected posts
like white clouds
rose up
high toward
the heavens.
On top of the stockade
the noble companion spirits
hovered with billows of clouds
wrapped around them.

The fearful deities,
the fearful spirits
were sending out their rumblings
on top of the stockade.
Their rumblings trailed
out long and far.

I stepped
inside the stockade.
I made my way up
beside the house,
the large house.
I peered through
the window hangings.
I looked and saw
someone who surely was
Shipish-un-kur,
the one who had been mentioned.
I had expected
that he would be
a grown man, but
he was quite young,
and only that same year
had faint whiskers
begun to darken
his chin.
He was awe-inspiring
because of his clothing
and because of his swords.
He sat
by the fireside
with his legs crossed.

On his right

there sat
a young woman.
Although I had thought
that my elder sister,
Chiwashpet-un-mat,
could alone be
so beautiful,
here was one
whose beauty
was awe-inspiring!
Beyond that,
she was apparently a wizardess[32] also, for
the facial features of wizardry,
the appearance of a shamaness[33]
could be seen clearly
on her countenance.
The master of the house
was worried
about something, for
on his face were seen
many woeful expressions.
After they had sat there for a while,
he raised
his eyebrows sharply.
As he did so,
he began to speak,
the words ringing out
sonorously from his throat.
He spoke these words:

   "My younger sister,
   ever since childhood
   you have dabbled
   in shamanism.

Come now, shamanize!
I wonder
why it is that
these forebodings
of approaching danger
are hanging over me
today.
Come, shamanize!
I want to hear
the prophecy!"
Thus did he speak.

Just then,
the young woman
tied her hair up high
with a shamaness's headband.
She took in her hand
a shamaness's wand.
A song
came twisting subtly
from deep in her throat.
The prophecy
came flowing forth
from her lips.
These were her words:

   "Suddenly
   over the chasm,
   the chasm at
   the headwaters of the river,
   of our native river,
   fierce fighting
   breaks out.
   The people of Kanepet,

---

[32] *Nupurpe*, "wizardess," synonymous with *tusu-kur*, "shamaness." The word *nupur* means "magic powers," "wizardry,"
or "shamanism." In the epics, the practitioners of shamanism are almost always female.
[33] *Tusu ipottum*, a shamaness's countenance.

the people of Shirarpet,
and Etu-rachichi
all of them together
are tangling their swords,
their trusty swords,
in confused battle with
the sword of the *yaunkur*.
From time to time
they appear together.
I lose them
in many clots of gore.
But now again
from time to time,
in the east
all of them together
are tangling their swords
in confused battle.
This goes on until
by and by
the swords of the *repunkur*
all at once
are broken off
next to the swordguards.
I lose them
in the west.
My vision is unclouded—
the sword of the *yaunkur*
is shining bright
in the east.
Just then,
down the river,
our native river,
a little *kesorap*[34]
is fluttering through

the heavens,
or so I thought.
But now
it disappears,
I don't know where.
I strengthen the power
of my shamanizing until
the little *kesorap*
is transformed
into raindrops and
is slipping
through the layers of earth.
As this goes on,
look!
once again
he is changed
into a little *kesorap* and
is going downstream
along the river,
our native river.
Suddenly
fierce fighting
bursts forth
in our native land.
In a single swoop,
the settlements of the common folk
are completely
ravaged.
After that
the sword of the *yaunkur*
and my elder brother's
trusty sword
are tangled
in confused battle.

[34] The *kesorap* ("speckled feathers") is a fabulous bird appearing in Ainu myths and legends (See also introduction to selection 12). It is apparently based on native ideas obtained from peacock feathers. The *kesorap* here represents the hero Poiyaunpe.

I lose them
in many clots of gore.
At times
my vision is clear
and unclouded again.
In the east
there are swords tangled
in confused battle.
This continues until—
o what dreadful
thing is this?—
my elder brother's
trusty sword
is broken off
next to the swordguard.
I lose it
in many clots of gore.
The sword of the *yaunkur*,
it seems to me,
is shining bright
in the east.
This is all,
the vision vanishes
from before my eyes.
O what terrible things
have I
been prophesying?"
Thus did she speak.

Fierce rage
flashed forth
on the face of
the master of the house.
In his rage,

he uttered words,
saying these things:

"What strange words are these?
I detest
my wretched younger sister's
evil words!
I am one
who disdains
to fight with humans.
I am worthy only of
warfare with the gods.
I have heard
that the cursed *repunkur* folk
have banded together
against Poiyaunpe[35]
all his young life.
Nevertheless,
since I am one
who rules
in peace,
even if he comes
some time,
I intend
to greet him
in peace
and with kindness.
Even though these prophecies
may be of divine origin,
what you have said,
my wretched younger sister,
has disheartened me
exceedingly!"
Thus did he speak.

[35] The name of the *yukar* hero, meaning "little *yaunkur*" or "young *yaunkur*." (*poi* = *pon*, "little," "young"; *yaunpe* = *yaunkur*)

Then
tears came streaming
down the face of
the young woman.
While she wept,
she uttered words,
saying these things:

   "What strange words are these?
   I detest
   the words spoken by
   my elder brother!
   For what reason,
   my elder brother,
   do you think
   that I would make
   false prophecies?
   Why is it
   that you say this?"
   Thus did she speak.

Just then
I went gliding through
the window hangings.
I darted up
onto the rafters.
Back and forth
I went striding along
stamping my feet mightily
on the rafters.
As I did so,
the upper beams of
that big house
shook up and down.

The roof beams
were jumping about
on top of the posts
with a loud creaking.
The rows of noble treasures[36]
in the northeast corner of
the noble house
seemed frightened,
seemed startled;
the insignificant deities
sent forth
prolonged rumblings together.
Wondering
what was the matter,
the master of the house
turned around
first this way
and then that.
However,
the young woman
remained there
without even
raising her eyes slightly.

Just then
I dropped down
from the rafters
onto the floor.
I twisted in my hand
the master of the house's
locks of magnificent hair.
I turned his head around
first this way
and then that.

---

[36] *Inuma*. The rows of household heirlooms or treasures lining the north wall of the house consisted chiefly of lacquered tubs and boxes of Japanese manufacture. They were considered to be deities of insignificant degree, as is apparent below.

While I did this,
I uttered words,
saying these things:

>"Well now,
>Shipish-un-kur,
>you warrior,
>what was it you said?
>Say it again!
>I want to hear it!
>Why, o why was it that
>Kamui-otopush
>in all his beauty
>was taken prisoner
>and tied to
>the top of a spruce,
>a little spruce tree?
>To avenge this,
>I fought against
>the people of Kanepet,
>the people of Shirarpet,
>and the ruler of Pon-moshir,
>Etu-rachichi.
>In the course of the fighting
>they mentioned
>the valor of
>Shipish-un-kur
>to frighten me, and
>this is why I have come.
>Even though you greet me
>in peace
>and with kindness,
>I will not listen.
>Let us test

each other's valor.
Should we both perish,
our hearts
will be content
even after death.
Come,
do your worst against me!"

While speaking these words,
I seized,
I grasped in my hands
the young woman
who was on the right
of the mighty warrior.
I jumped up with her
to the smokehole.
At this
the young woman
shrieked wildly,
her bosom
heaving.
These were her words.

>"My elder brother,
>you said that
>I had made
>false prophecies.
>Well then, which one of them
>was false?
>A stranger
>from an unknown land
>is carrying me off
>a prisoner.
>Hurry to my rescue!"

When she said this,
the master of the house
drew his sword
with a flash over his arms.
Though I strove mightily,
ahead of me
he swang
scores of sword blows
up and down, right and left
at the smokehole.
I was hard pressed by his sword play.
Turning back again,
I darted
down
to the window.
But when I had done so,
ahead of me
scores of sword blows
came raining down
by the window.

After that
we flew back and forth
like birds.
Under the ceiling
I flew about fleeing
like a bird with hands.

Fierce anger
flared out
on the face of
the mighty warrior.
In his anger,
he poured forth

a stream of curses.
These were his words:

"My wretched younger sister,
since you
disheartened me
exceedingly
with your prophecies,
I shall slay
you first!"

As he spoke these words,
he darted
many sword thrusts
toward both his sister
and me together.
I held her aloft
as a shield
to receive the blows,
but he still
did not turn
aside his blows.
While this was going on,
the young woman
terrified
clung for dear life
to the tops of my hands
and the palms of my hands.
At the same time,
she kicked
from the back
and kicked
from the front
at the mighty warrior's

noble face.
In the meantime
the young woman
addressed herself to me
with confidential speech,
saying these words:

"Although there was
nothing at all
about your coming
that I did not know,
it is also true
that I did
try to dishearten
my elder brother
with my prophecies.
Let me down!
I want to come
to your assistance,
even though I may be of no more help
than an old worn-out mat
which merely gets in the way."
Thus did she speak.

For this reason
I let go of her.
She went crawling
along the floor
on all fours.
Then she sprang up.
She drew out a dagger
from the front of her robes.
She darted
fierce stabs

at her elder brother.
While doing this,
she uttered words,
saying these things:

"O wretched brother of mine,
you have always
doubted
my prophecies.
And this is why
you seem to want
to slay me also
together with
the mighty warrior.
If this is so,
I will go to the aid of
the mighty warrior.
Come, my wretched elder brother,
do your worst
against us!"

As she said these words,
she darted
countless stabs
at the mighty one [her brother].
After a while,
bands of commoners,
armies of armored men,
began to jostle together
trying to enter the house
through the windows
and through the doorways.
After that
I went stamping fiercely

back and forth
by the doorways,
and went stamping fiercely
by the windows.
The throngs of warriors
jostled together
swarming
all over the floor.
The two of us,
the young woman and I,
bestirred ourselves,
shaking our chests,
in slashing at them.

In the meantime,
the companion spirits of the others
and my companion spirits
united their rumblings
as if they were a single spirit.
They sent forth their rumblings
on top of the stockade.
As the rumbling continued,
a mighty divine wind
came blowing down.
Through the doorways
and through the windows
the wind came rushing inside,
and wild confusion broke out
all over the floor.
The flames of the fire,
the fire burning in the hearth,
were whipped up by the divine wind.
After a while
the house

burst into flames.
Just before
it collapsed,
we all went
rushing outside.

There were separate
armies bringing up the rear,
while the companies of spearsmen
came advancing
toward me.
The companies of swordsmen—
nothing but their sword sweeps
could be seen flashing.

After this,
on purpose I did it,
the throngs of warriors
I chased back with my sword
and drove them
into the arms of
the young woman.
Droves of them
jostled together.
Even then,
she did not
retreat
a single step.
She still bestirred herself
shaking her chest
in slashing at them.

Just then,
there was seen

far away
over a distant land
a bank of thick clouds
arising.
It came darting
as swiftly as an arrow.
Above it
a weighty god
was sending forth rumblings.
Some chieftain
dropped down
by my side.
I looked and saw
that it was
Kamui-otopush,
my elder brother.
He saluted me with his sword.
I saluted him with my sword.
After that
the numbers that I slew
and the numbers that
the young woman slew
were but few in comparison with
Kamui-otopush—
nothing but his sword sweeps
could be seen flashing.
Wherever he passed
the corpses mowed down like grass
lay stretched out in the distance.

At that time,
Shipish-un-kur,
the mighty warrior,
poured forth

a stream of curses:

"How detestable
that my wretched younger sister,
hoping to gain profit for herself,
should lust after
this enemy offspring.
This is why
she is wielding
her sword against
our own kinsfolk.
You will surely
receive your punishment
in the midst of the battle,
in this very battle.
Mark my words well!"
Thus did he speak.

Just then
the young woman
suddenly
began to shriek wildly.
As she screamed,
she uttered words,
saying these things:

"O mighty warrior,
listen well
to what I have to say!
Your elder sister,
Chiwashpet-un-mat,
is fighting battles
which have spread over
many surrounding lands.

Your elder sister
has now made her way as far as
a distant
land called
Chirinnai,[37]
but now
she has gone to
the homeland of the
tumunchi demons,[38] and
it appears as if
she may be slain,
she may be killed.
If you
delay,
you will never
see
your elder sister again.
As for this battle,
this fighting here,
we can leave
Kamui-otopush
alone
to deal with it.
Let us go to the aid of
your elder sister.''

While speaking these words,
she drew herself up into
the heavens.
At this time
I sheathed
my sword and
went flying up
right behind

the young woman.
This was the way
we went along:
at times
she would leave me far behind
as much as one bowshot
or more than one bowshot.
As she did so,
she would turn
back toward me
and would say these things:

> ''Are you
> a mighty man or not?
> How is it that
> you are bested
> by me
> in traveling!
> Make greater haste!''

Whenever she said this,
I would strive mightily, and
I would leave her
far behind
as much as one bowshot
or more than one bowshot.

When we had come
to a certain place,
there was a populous village
stretching down to the water's edge.
The head of the village
could be seen only faintly.
In the middle of the village

---

[37] "Trickling Stream"
[38] *Tumunchi kamui*. The word *tumunchi* means "war," but *tumunchi kamui* appears to mean simply "demon" or "fiend"
without any particular connection with warfare.

a large stronghold
could be seen standing
majestically.
It was a stronghold with a lid.[39]
From time to time
the stronghold's lid
would go swinging up
toward the clouds
in the lower skies.
Turning around again,
the stronghold's lid
would then close up
with a clank.
This is what it was doing.

Just then
the young woman
spoke these words:

    "The name
    of this land
    is called
    Terke-santa,
    Hopuni-santa,[40]
    Let us have
    a little fun!
    Remain waiting
    for me!"

While speaking these words,
she went down
onto the smokehole,
and I went down
by her side.

I looked and saw
an amazing sight.
An awe-inspiring person
because of his noble swords
and because of his armor
was sitting
cross-legged
at the master's place
by the fireside.
On his right
there was a woman—
could there ever be
a woman so beautiful?–
one utterly awe-inspiring
for her beauty,
for her comeliness.
The brightness of her face
was like the rising sun.
It radiated
dazzling light.

Just then
Shipish-un-mat
seized
the young woman
and grasped her in her hands.
She darted out with her
through the smokehole.
At that time
the young woman
shrieked wildly,
her breast
heaving.
Her words were these:

[39] *Puta un chashi*, a fortification with a cover on it. The cover rises and falls. This type of stronghold is often mentioned in the epics, but it is uncertain what sort of building is meant by it. Perhaps there is some connection with the name of the place, Terke-santa, Hopuni-santa ("Jumping Santa," "Flying Santa").

[40] "Jumping Santa," "Flying Santa." Santa is the Ainu name for Manchuria or the area around the Amur estuary. The ethnic group called Santan by the Japanese may be the Goldi or the Ol'cha, groups that speak closely related languages of the Tunguso-Manchurian group.

"A stranger from an unknown country
is carrying me off
a prisoner!
My elder brother,
hurry to my rescue!"
Thus did she speak.

Just then
the shouts uttered by
the master of the house
could be heard resounding.
He came trailing
right after
the young woman.
He darted out
through the smokehole.
Just then
I darted
a fierce sword thrust at him.
I sliced him
into several bits.
His life-spirit
was heard flying up
with a loud roaring.

After that
Shipish-un-mat
dragged
the young woman
along after her,
knocking her against
the large rocks
and the small rocks
with loud cracking noises.

Feelings of sympathy
sprang up in me.
I came very near
to killing
Shipish-un-mat
as we went on until
by and by
Shipish-un-mat
sliced
into several bits
the young woman
she was holding in her arms.
Her life-spirit
was heard flying up
with a loud roaring.

After that
we went on until [we reached]
a place which seemed to be
the land of Chirinnai
which had been mentioned before.
Battle mists
were hanging
over the land.
In the meantime
at frequent intervals
many gods dying
countless gods dying
could be heard rumbling together
with loud crashes.
The companion spirits
of my elder sister,
Chiwashpet-un-mat,
were emitting

many mournful rumblings
which went crashing down low
over the surface of the ground.

I rushed
to her rescue.
When I reached her,
I looked and saw
my elder sister,
who had been
such an imposing woman.
Only her chest
was still attached
to her robes.
Only her backbone
had they been unable to get at.
Her entrails
were hanging out.
By now
she would swing her sword once or twice,
and in the intervals
she would faint
and then regain consciousness.
Even during this time
she continued to strive
at slashing at the foe.
But
when I
dropped down
by her side,
as soon as she caught sight of me,
tears welled up
in her eyes.
As she wept.

she uttered words,
saying these things:

"O god whom I have raised,
listen well
to what I have to say!
Since I am
a wretched woman,
it would not be
bad for the land,
bad for the country
if I were to die.
But you,
if you were to die,
it would be bad for the land.[41]
Strive on fiercely,
fight on valiantly!
If you carry on
after I am gone,
my heart
will be content."
Thus did she speak.

After that
I wielded my sword
all around her.
Just as before,
the numbers that I slew,
the numbers that I killed
were but few
in comparison with the swordfighting of
Shipish-un-mat.
Wherever she passed,
the corpses mowed down like grass

[41] A patriotic expression frequently encountered in the epics in such situations. The speaker's concern for the welfare of the homeland (the land of the *yaunkur*) is emphasized. The hero alone is capable of defending the homeland, and his death would be a disaster for the country.

lay stretched out in the distance.
So many human corpses
were lying spread out
over the ground that
my legs
would get tangled up in them.

In the meantime
my elder sister
fell down
headlong on the ground.
A whole shower of spears
came plunging down
toward her.
I pulled her out
from under them
and held her in my grip.
I sliced her
into several bits
as I held her in my arms.
I swung her up
toward the heavens.
While doing this,
I uttered words,
saying these things:

    "O gods worshiped by
    my father,
    Chiwashpet-un-mat
    has raised me
    well.
    Even though she is
    enemy offspring,
    restore her to life

    for me, I pray!"

While I spoke these words,
I swung her up
right into the sky.
From my hands,
becoming a new spirit,
becoming a living spirit,
she went rumbling off
toward the top of the land,
the land of the *yaunkur*.

After that,
the two of us,
Shipish-un-mat
and I fought on until
finally
the land of Chirinnai
had been ravaged
completely.

Then
tears came streaming
down the face of
Shipish-un-mat.
As she wept,
she uttered words,
saying these things:

    "The land of Chirinnai
    is now a land
    with no human warriors
    of any importance
    left in it.

Nevertheless,
to the west of
the land of Chirinnai
the storm demon,
the bad weather demon
dwells
together with his younger sister.
Besides that,
a numerous race of
kuruise demons
dwells
to the west of
the land of Chirinnai.
If the *kuruise*
make war on us,
as they are likely to do,
their war
will be worse than
two or three human battles.
It is uncertain
whether
the two of us
will be able
to survive.
After the war of the *kuruise*
is finished,
the storm demon,
the bad weather demon
will make war on us.
The woman demon
will attack me
separately.
The man
will come against you.

Since you are a man,
you will succeed
in killing
the bad weather demon.
Since I am a woman,
the younger sister of
the bad weather demon
will attack me.
Even though I am
only a dabbler in shamanism,
it seems likely
that I will succeed
in slaying her.
If you fight
only halfheartedly,
the fiend
will slay me
before your eyes,
and this will not
suit you in the least.''
Thus did she speak.

Just then,
to the west of
the land of Chirinnai
a black mist
arose.
Before long,
that mist
descended
right over us.
It felt
exactly as if
I was being thrust into

a black abyss.
After that
bird-like creatures
could be heard flying
all around me
with whirring, whistling sounds.
At the same time
shallow gashes
and deep gashes
were gouged on my body.
Excruciating pains
shot through my inwards.
There was something
gleaming brightly
at the tip of my sword.
I couldn't tell
when it was daytime
and when it was nighttime.
I went raging around everywhere
within the mist,
the black mist.

This continued until
I reached a point where
only my chest
was still attached
to my robes.
Only my backbone
had they been unable to get at.
I would faint
sometimes during the fighting.[42]

I continued in this way until
the black mist

disappeared in
the skies.
There was good weather
everywhere.
I had no idea at all
what sort of creatures
I had been fighting.
Just then,
Shipish-un-mat
blew puffs of breath
on my body.
No sooner had she done so,
my large wounds
and my small wounds
mended themselves together
and were healed.
Shipish-un-mat
blew puffs of breath
on her own body.
No sooner had she done so,
her large wounds
and her small wounds
mended themselves together.
The robes I wore
made my old ones
seem insignificant
in comparison.

Then once again
to the west of the land,
the land of Chirinnai,
a mist of storm clouds,
a bad weather mist
rose up.

[42] Or, I fainted during some fighting.

The clouds spread out
over the face of the land,
over the face of the sea.
Bad weather
came dropping down.

Just then
a creature came this way—
could it be a human?
His naked skin
was mangy.
His face
was like
a cliff after a landslide.
He looked like
a small mountain
with arms growing out of it
and legs growing out of it.
He wore in his belt
a sword big as a boat's scull.
Close behind him
came
a woman wearing
leather armor
made from the leather of land animals
and the leather of sea animals
sewn together.
She advanced
toward
Shipish-un-mat,
grasping in her hand
a red knife.
It clinked musically
next to her face.

Shipish-un-mat
darted
fierce sword strokes at her,
and she darted
countless stabs,
many stabs at her.
In the meantime
the naked man
darted
fierce sword strokes at me.
I was unwilling
to die outright.
Therefore,
I dodged here and there
like a bright breeze
between the sweeps
of the chieftain's blade.
In return
I also darted
fierce sword strokes at him,
but
none of them
struck home.
Even though I struck
a number of good blows
and a number of bad blows,
wherever my blade would strike
it would bounce
right off.
I didn't know
how I could ever
get at him.

Then by and by,

I looked and
discovered
the place where the cords
of his armor were fastened together.
I took
careful aim.
Finally
I held my sword
in my hands
like a good spear.
I stabbed mightily.
Thanks to a stroke of luck,
it was like a spear blow against something soft,
and there was the sound of ripping flesh
at the tip of my spear.

The naked man,
whom I had thought all along
to be a human being,
went sprawling out flat
over the face of the sea.
It turned out, after all,
to be merely armor.
Some sort of creature
came springing out
from inside the armor.
Although I had
expected that
it would be a grown man,
it was
a mere child,
a young boy.
It was incredible
how the bad weather demon

could ever be
so beautiful.
He had a single cloth
wrapped around him.
A god-given sword
was thrust under his belt.
He uttered words,
saying these things:

    "It is astounding,
    Poiyaunpe—
    is it possible that
    you are a human?
    The gods,
    even the most ferocious gods,
    have never been able
    to destroy
    my armor,
    but now
    you have destroyed it.
    Be that as it may,
    well-matched chieftains
    ought to fight each other
    without armor,
    and even should both of them perish,
    the fame of it
    will rise up
    from the head of the country
    to the foot of the country.
    Now let us test
    each other's valor!"

As he said these words,
he drew his sword

with a flash over his arms.
He darted
fierce sword strokes at me.
But
like a bright breeze
I fluttered
between his thrusts.
Then in return
I darted
fierce sword strokes at him.
We flashed our swords
back and forth together.
This continued until
by and by,
thanks to a stroke of luck,
I managed to slash him,
and there was the sound of slicing flesh
at the tip of my sword.
His slices
dropped down
over the surface of the sea.
His life-spirit
was heard flying up
with a loud roaring.
After that was over,
everything grew quiet all around.

In their own separate battle
Shipish-un-mat
and the bad weather demon's
younger sister
were flashing their swords
back and forth together.
She struck

a number of good blows
and a number of bad blows
on the leather armor,
but wherever her blade would strike
it would bounce
right off.
Undeterred,
Shipish-un-mat
continued to strike
good blows and bad blows.
Then quite suddenly
fierce sprays of blood
went spurting up
from her body.

I went up
by her side and
examined
the leather armor
carefully all over.
After a while
I discovered
the place where the cords
of her armor were fastened together.
I held my sword
in my hands
like a good spear.
I aimed the spear
at the armor's cords.
Thanks to a stroke of luck,
it was like a spear blow against something soft,
and there was the sound of ripping flesh
at the tip of my spear.

The leather armor
went sprawling out flat
over the surface of the sea,
and a young woman
came springing out
from inside the armor.
Although I had thought
that Shipish-un-mat
could alone be
so beautiful,
the bad weather demon's
younger sister,
being a deity,
surpassed her
in her divine beauty.

At that time,
she covered her nose
and covered her mouth in amazement
and spoke these words:

> "Is it possible,
> Poiyaunpe,
> that you are a human?
> Even the gods
> have never been able
> to destroy
> my armor,
> but now
> you have destroyed it.
> Without their armor
> the gods
> are soft, and so
> you will probably

succeed in slaying me.
Even so, should I die
by your sword,
my heart
will be content
after death.
Do not, on any account,
let Shipish-un-mat
slash me!"
Thus did she speak.

No sooner had she said this,
Shipish-un-mat
poured forth
a stream of curses.
These were her words.

> "What strange words are these?
> I detest
> the words spoken by
> the wretched maiden!
> Women also
> ought to test
> each other's valor
> without armor.
> Then, even should both of them perish,
> the fame of it
> will rise up
> after death.
> Even while you had
> this godly form,
> you still wore
> leather armor
> made from the leather of sea animals

and the leather of land animals
sewn together,
so that I wasn't able
even to slash you.
On the other hand,
you were able to slash me,
and now it is my turn
to return the blows.
For what reason
are you now saying
that you don't want
me to slash you?
What is this you say?''

As she said these words,
she darted
fierce sword strokes
at the bad weather demoness.
Just as she was getting up,
she sliced her
into several bits.
After that
her life-spirit
was heard flying up
with a loud roaring.
Just before
she died utterly,
she became a living spirit
and was heard going off
toward the east
with a loud roaring.

At that time
the young woman,

Shipish-un-mat,
spoke these words:

    ''After we left,
    Kamui-otopush
    and Shipish-un-kur
    continued to fight until
    Shipish-un-kur
    was quite defeated.
    As usually happens
    when a brave warrior
    is slain,
    he became an utterly dead spirit
    and went away to
    the land of the gods.

    ''Now then,
    since I am
    an enemy offspring,
    if you will kill me
    right now
    with your own hands,
    my heart
    will be content
    even after death.
    On the other hand,
    if you take
    pity on me,
    you may
    take me with you
    to your native land.

    ''Another thing is this.
    It is no good

to exceed
one's powers
in warfare.
Let us go
to your native land
and rest
between battles.
Please agree
to my request!''
Thus did she speak.

After that
we headed
in the direction of
my native country.
We made our way
along the shores
of many countries of the *repunkur*.
After some time,
the land which is called
Tumisanpet
Shinutapkashi
rose up high
toward us.
The house which had been
my father's
long ago
stood there
majestically.
We dropped down
at the head of
the path leading down to the beach.
Then I called out again and again
with soft cries

and loud cries.
While I called,
I uttered words,
saying these things:

> "Kamui-otopush
> and Chiwashpet-un-mat—
> have they arrived
> or have they not?
> If they have
> not arrived,
> I will go
> right away
> to the land of the *repunkur*
> once again."

When I said this,
a herald
called out soft cries
and loud cries.
In his cries
he uttered words,
saying these things:

> "Kamui-otopush
> has finished his battles
> and has returned.
> Chiwashpet-un-mat,
> she also,
> has been restored to life
> by the gods,
> has returned,
> and is here."
He said these words.

After that
I went to
my father's stronghold.
When I went inside,
it was indeed true:
Kamui-otopush,
my elder brother,
had finished his battles
and was there.
Chiwashpet-un-mat,
who had apparently been
restored to life by the gods,
looked even more beautiful
than before.
It was indeed true:
my eldest brother
and my eldest sister
were there.
We waved swords
at each other in salutation
up to the point of slashing each other,
even going beyond slashing each other.

After that
we lived on until
one day
my eldest brother
Yai-pirka-kur
spoke these words:

> "I have not been
> a good eldest brother.
> Yet please agree
> to my request!

Chiwashpet-un-mat
took pity on
our younger brother,
and thanks to her
his life was saved.
During the battles,
the young woman
of Shipish
came to the assistance of
our younger brother,
and thanks to her
his life was saved.
We are
grateful.
Come now,
let Kamui-otopush,
my younger brother,
marry Chiwashpet-un-mat.
They will be a well-matched couple."
Thus did he speak.

Then once again
he turned
toward me and
spoke these words:

> "O god whom we have raised,
> listen well
> to what I have to say!
> The young woman
> Shipish-un-mat
> has endured
> painful trials
> by your side

in battle.
Marry her.
Then all your lives,
in every battle
you will protect
and guard each other.
Give your assent,
I pray!''
Thus did he speak.

Then once again,
one day
he spoke these words:

"Until this day
my younger brothers
have been leading lives of hardship,
doing nothing but fighting wars.
This is why
we have gone on
without even
brewing wine.
Now let us brew
a little wine,
invite
our nearby relatives
and distant relatives,
and have a feast!''

When he spoke these words,
Kamui-otopush,
my elder brother,
agreed.
His heart was

suddenly relieved.
Going to the storehouse,
with his own hands
he rolled out
six baskets.
He brewed wine
in six wine-tubs.
When two or three days
had gone by,
the odor of the wine
began to hover everywhere
inside the house.
Now when
the wine was ready,
messages of invitation
were sent out.
As the guests,
Shishiripet-un-kur[43]
together with his younger sister, and
Iyochi-un-kur
together with his younger sister
were invited.
They arrived, and
the circle was closed.

My elder brothers
exchanged greetings.
After they were finished,
the peerless feast
got under way.
We continued to feast
all night long
without sleeping.
After it was over,

[43] Shishiripet is an unidentified name. Batchelor says that the Shishiripet river is the Ishikari river.

Iyochi-un-kur
spoke these words:

   "Come now,
   listen well
   to the well-meaning request
   which I have to utter!
   We have been
   living together
   with only our younger sisters
   and up till now
   we have not
   taken wives.
   Therefore,
   let me give
   Iyochi-un-mat,
   my younger sister,
   to your eldest brother.
   In exchange,
   I want to marry
   Shinutapka-un-mat."
   Thus did he speak.

Then

my eldest brother
agreed.

After that
my eldest sister
wrapped a carrying cord
around a large woman's bag.
She went together
with Iyochi-un-kur
to his village.
Iyochi-un-mat
was given in marriage to
my eldest brother, and
we lived on and on
uneventfully.
Kamui-otopush
married
Chiwashpet-un-mat.
The young woman,
Shipish-un-mat,
was given to me in marriage,
and we lived on and on
uneventfully
and peacefully.

Index